INTERNATIONAL ENCYCLOPAEDIA OF ISLAM

Vol.-5

Judicial System in Islam

INTERNATIONAL ENCYCLOPAEDIA OF ISLAM

Vol.-5

Judicial System in Islam

Editor

A.H. Qasmi

ISHA BOOKS

DELHI-110 033

International Encyclopaedia of Islam
(*Religion*)

ISBN: 81-8205-320-X (Set)

ISBN: 81-8205-325-0

Published in 2006 in India by
Isha Books, D-43, Prithviraj Road,
Adarsh Nagar, Delhi-110 033

Printed at : Rajdhani Printers, Delhi.

Contents

Preface

Man is a social creature. It is the society where he learns how to live in this vast cosmos. Apart from society, people are divided into different castes, cultures and creeds. All these factors go in developing a man's personality. Of all the factors, mentioned above, religion is most important.

There exist about more than two thousand religions in the world today. A religion is regarded as a sacred institution, which governs a man's life here and hereafter and teaches him how to lead a happy and prosperous life.

What's unique to Islam is its endowment to humanity from the divine creator or the Almighty. It is not a set of principles and dogmas scribed by a scholar or thinker. It was sent on the earth circa fifteen hundred years ago, but its principles and preachings hold good even today. Besides showing humanity a straight way to the eternal success, it also has a say in various other walks of human life, such as economy, politics, human rights, social relations, judiciary, marriage and so on and so forth.

Another distinguished feature of Islam is that apart from being the latest religion, it is also the last one. That is to say, whatever is there in Islam, it is valid upto to the doomsday. Now, there will not come any other religion till the Day of Judgement. Therefore, it is the most powerful and as well as the most human-nature-friendly.

Given the present global scenario, there was being felt a dire need to bring out such a mini-encyclopaedia of Islam which may cater to the maximum needs of man in the least possible sheet of paper.

The present series is an humble attempt in the same direction. It comprises ten volumes which cover all the major disciplines of human life like, Prayer, marriage, justice, human rights, social justice and so on.

We are sure that the endeavour would prove to be a capsule of treasure of knowledge about Islam, prepared perfectly. Nevertheless, considering the adage 'to err is human', we would be obliged if the readers suggest some improvements for further editions.

Editor

1

Concept of Judiciary

No man is sufficient unto himself and if he tries to be so, he succeeds only in destroying himself. Islam regards the self-adequacy in human conduct as a source of all evil. This means that his social existence is necessary. It makes him aware of the competition, his own claims on persons and the properties of others and the perpetual necessity of adjustment between them. However, when per necessity men get together, the problem of adjustment of rights and liabilities immediately arises. The men swell into tribes, states and nations and their problems multiply. They become ever more pressing and complex because of the violence men use in the love of wealth *(Surah Adiyat* 100/8) and their contentiousness. *(Surah Israel* 17/100). There are very few men possessed of balanced good sense who restrain themselves and prohibit others from mischief on the earth. The wrong-doers, however, pursue the enjoyment of good things of life which were given to them and persist in sin too. *(Surah Hood* 11/116). Such nations are then destroyed as stated in *Surah Israel* (17/16).

- The philosophers tell us that man is the only true subject and object of justice. That apparently deprives the animals of their due. The mere fact, that the wronged animal is incapable of asserting its own claim to right, should not be taken for granted that it has no right to be treated justly. Even they react when treated unfairly. It is also known by experience that there is not a mere predatory violence and certainly not unrestricted warfare of one against the other. Some where, within it, is a process of allocation and some rules of the game for the coexistence of even brutes and savages. There is some decree determining as to what is lion's share and what is the jackal's.

- We find thus inbuilt, in all living beings, a mechanism which compels them to revolt against injustice. The revolt may result in physically stopping the perpetrator, if he is weak, or in mere resenting or disapproving of it, otherwise. History bears testimony that no wrong is resented more than injustice, though it may be suffered sometimes willingly, for the sake of higher good. Justice, thus is part of every living being's consciousness, by intuition. It ripens in man by experience and anxious cultivation. It has been rightly said that justice is a reflection of the Divine. God Almighty, says in *Surah Al-Tariq* (86/4) that He is the Protector of all living beings and He taught some rules to the animals as well. The difference is that all that is in the universe, follows faithfully His laws except man who is given volition and power to think and decide. He is also given a code of guidance and made answerable here and in the Hereafter. He can thus be just and loyal or disobedient and transgressor as he wills. In *Surah Al-Momin* (40/40) is stated that:

"He that works evil will not be requited but by the like thereof: and he that works a righteous deed, whether man or woman—and is a believer-such will enter the Garden (of Bliss): therein will they have abundance without measure."

- But what is that which restrains the mighty from doing

injustice? It could either be the same virtue as mentioned above or because of fear. A French Philosopher La Rochefoucauld says that 'love of justice is, in most men, merely the fear of suffering it'. Thrasymachus says in the *'Republic'* that 'those who denounce injustice, do so, not because they are afraid of doing it, but of suffering it'. It has also been happening generally that some people may evolve concepts, as they suit them, in the name of something good and high, to sound it attractive and acceptable to all, though they themselves may know that the same is just a misrepresentation or farce.

- It has been remarked by C. K. Allen that Abominable injustices have been done in the name of justice, even as terrible oppressions have been done in the name of liberty, because, when men sink to the lowest, they clutch for excuse at the highest'. Quran, however, abhors such a treacherous conduct or a misinterpretation as it says in *Surah Al-Imran* (3/78) :

"There is among them a section who distort the Book with their tongues, (As they read) you would think it is a part of the Book, but it is no part of the Book: and they say, 'That is from Allah', but it is not from Allah; It is they who tell a lie against Allah, and (well) they know it!"

And in *Surah Baqara* it is quoted that (2/79) :

"Then woe to those who write the Book with their own hands and then say: This is from Allah, to traffic with it for a miserable price! Woe to them for what their hands do write, and the gain they make thereby."

- It is said that the tones of the society are many and it is the function of justice to blend them. In the situation, the need of justice and that too in its pure, true and effective form is necessary. The term 'justice' as we know and understand, may be equated to the concept of *'Adl'*, *'Qist'*, or *'Mizan'* as used in Quran. These terms are antonyms of *'Zulm'* or 'injustice'. According to Imam Raghib Isphahani, *'Adl'* means. In the view of Syed Sharif, it is the mean of excess and less Abul Baqa Hanafi says it is the antonym of *'Zulm'*. It means that the grievance of a person be redressed and his rights restored to him. Allama Aini says that *'Adl'* is the duty to obey such commands which are entitled to obedience and the injustice be totally eliminated. The justice, as a common man understands, means 'getting a square and fair deal', 'equality before the law and 'sticking to the rules'.

- Justice may be analysed and classified into many different forms, like judicial, constitutional, administrative, social, economic, distributive, natural, positive, universal, political, cumulative, recognitive, national, international and parental, etc. This wealth of terminology and this spectrum of so many hues, does at least suggest that there is scarcely any relationship of life into which the question of justice does not enter. In our dealings, with our fellow-men, our superiors and subordinates, our families and relations, our friends and neighbours, in our conduct under the laws which govern us, in our commitments to others and perpetually in our inmost consciences, we can never escape this mentor. The difference between Islam and other systems is that while Islam enjoins on man to do all sorts of justice and the government or the society may compel its performance, the other systems draw a line in between and the government or the society cannot go beyond some of those, to require performance.
- It is our belief and history bears testimony to it, that Islam offers and dispenses the very required concept of justice. Islàm is a religion made up in essentials of a revelation and represents the actual expression of the

Divine Will. It embodies eternal truths and is, therefore, good and valid for all times to come. Its doctrines are given in Quran and *Hadith.* Some of the matters are expressly provided for. As regards others we have to rely on the principles or concept as can be gathered from Quran and *Hadith* and chart our course on the basis of *Ijtihad, Ijma, Qiyas,* etc. at every given time or age, to suit the needs of a given society. The norms and precepts which are expressly provided are rigid and immutable possessing absolute and eternal validity. They are not susceptible to change or modification. As regards the norms and concepts which are expressed in terms of general principles, they can admit of varying interpretations and varying applications according to the circumstances of the time. We do also follow the interpretations made by our predecessors, if the circumstances have not changed.

- Islam means unreserved and unconditional obedience of, and compliance with, the directives of God Almighty, their propagation, establishment of an organization for the purpose, and for securing peace and prosperity for the people. Quran says in *Surah Baqara* (2/177) :

"It is not righteousness that ye turn your faces towards East or West; but it is righteousness—to believe in Allah and the Last Day, and the Angles, and the Book, and the Messengers; to spend of your substance, out of love for Him, for your kin, for orphans, for the needy, for the wayfarer, for those who ask, and for the ransom of slaves; to be steadfast in prayer, and practise regular charity; to fulfil the contracts which ye have made; and to be firm and patient, in pain (or suffering) and adversity, and throughout all periods of panic. Such are the people of truth, the Godfearing."

As also in *Surah Nisa* (4/1 25) :

"Who can be better in religion than one who submits

his whole self to Allah, does good, and follows the way of Ibrahim the true in faith? For Allah did take Ibrahim for a friend."

- Islam also combines temporal and spiritual affairs into one indivisible whole and does not permit a division as done in Christianity or other religions. The *Din* of Islam is a way of life and Quran is the Code to follow. This has been given to man only, as he only, out of the Universe, is likely to go astray. It is stated in *Surah Nisa* (4/27) that:

"Allah doth wish to turn to you, but the wish of those who follow their lusts is that ye should turn away (from Him),—far, far away."

In *Surah Nahl* (16/4, 49) the Quran says :

He has created man from a sperm-drop; and behold this same (man) becomes an open disputer!

And to Allah doth obeisance all that is in the heavens and on earth, whether moving (living) creatures or the angels; for none are arrogant (before their Lord)."

In *Surah Hajj* (22/18) :

"Seest thou not that to Allah bow down in worship all things that are in the heavens and on earth,—the trees, the animals, and a great number among mankind? But a great number are (also) such as are fit for punishment :"

and in *Surah Yasin* (36/77) it is said :

"Doth not man see that it is We who created him from sperm? Yet behold he (stands forth) as an open adversary".

- The concept of justice in Islam is thus all pervading and has to be manifested in every sphere of human life. God Almighty warns mankind in *Surah Asr*

(103/2, 3) that he is in loss except those who have faith, live clean and pure lives and know how to wait in patience and constancy. It is also in the scheme of things that he is not to be left without guidance as provided in *Surah Qiyamat* (75/36) :

"Does man think that he will be left uncontrolled?"

- God created heavens and earth, sent down rain from the skies for growing fruit and crops for food and other necessities, made sun and moon, night and day and all that is on the earth subject to him *(Surah Ibrahim* 14/ 32–34, *Surah Nahl* 16/10–16, *Surah Hajj* 22/65 and *Surah Luqman* 31 /20) so as to provide for every need of man. He created man to do homage to God, to obey and adore his Creator, to praise Him and to serve Him and His servants. He then placed him in the centre of the universe so that he may have authority over it and administer it. It is an obligation of man as an administrator on the earth that in case the mankind be to coexist peacefully, he must preserve a measure of balance by enforcing some regulative principles. According to Kant such a regulation should be 'the idea which proceeds from the condition under which each man's power of action can exist in harmony with the power of action of others, in accordance with a universal law of freedom. The man has thus been told that the universe has been designed and balanced in such a way that a little deviation or imbalance may cause the whole system to crash and so he is required likewise to create a balance in his affairs and dealings with others in order to succeed.
- The Quran in verses 1 to 9 of Chapter *Al-Rahman* says:

"Allah is most Gracious. It is He Who taught the Quran. He has created man. He has taught him speech. The sun and the moon follow exactly computed courses. Both herbs and trees bow in adoration to Him. He has raised high the vault of Heaven with its clouds and stars and He has set up the balance of justice in order that you may not transgress it. So establish right with justice and fall not short of the balance."

We may also refer to *Surah Al-Hijr* (15/19) which is as under :

"And the earth We have spread out (like a carpet); set thereon mountains firm and immovable; and produced therein all kinds of things in due balance."

In *Surah Baqara* (2/188) it is ordained :

"And do not eat up your property among yourselves for vanities, nor use it as bait for the judges, with intent that ye may eat up wrongfully and knowingly a little of (other) people's property." 14. The most important scheme of things in Islam unlike other legal system is that one who acts is burdened with a duty and an obligation to honour and convey to others their rights. It imposes a duty on every man, including the head of the State and its functionaries, not to violate the rights of others and to convey to them their due. Further, it is the bounden duty of the State to protect and preserve the life, liberty and property of its citizens in the light of Quranic injunctions and principles, provide them with their essential basic needs and an equal opportunity in life with others. The Holy Prophet even directed a son to provide maintenance to his father in the light of *Surah Israel* (17/23) in two different cases. Dower of wife is recoverable through Courts under *Surah Nisa* (4/24). The Western philosophy speaks of rights and powers more than the duties and the obligations. The state functionaries in that system enjoy powers and wield authority but have no responsibility to see and ensure that the rights of the citizens are duly protected or honoured. In Islam, on the other hand, we are reminded again and again to maintain balance as that is the very basis of stability and durability of a social order.

- God Almighty also assures mankind that if it obeys His dictates, it shall have no fear, grief or worry *(Surrah Baqara* 2/21, 38, 11 2 and 262) :

O ye people! Adore your Guardian - Lord, who created you and those who came before you, that ye may have the chance to learn righteousness;

We said: 'Get ye down all from here; and if, as is sure, there comes to you Guidance from Me', whosoever follows My guidance, on them shall be no fear, nor shall they grieve.

Nay,—Whoever submits his whole self to Allah and is a doer of good, —he will get his reward with his Lord; on such shall be no fear, nor shall they grieve.

Those who spend their substance in the cause of Allah, and follow not up their gifts with reminders of their generosity or with injury,—for them their reward is with their Lord; on them shall be no fear, nor shall be no fear, nor shall they grieve."

This Book is complete in all respects with regard to all matters and furnishes all the required details as stated in *Surah Nahl* (16/89), *Surah Bani Israil* (17/9), *Surah Rum* (30/58) and *Surah Sumar* (39/27).

- As said above, the command of God to do justice, is directed to the individuals as well as to the functionaries of the State and if everyone follows it faithfully there will be no disputes and insignificant litigation in Courts. It will be appreciated that Courts are the institutions where an aggrieved person complains against an injustice done to him either by a fellow man or a functionary of the State. Thus if justice is done in all directions and at all levels, we do not need Courts. There will be no waste of time and money and no worries on this account at all, inasmuch as that it will give rise to an ideal social order. It is for this reason that the command in Quran, to do justice, is addressed to all human beings. I may refer here to a few verses in:

Surah Shura (42/15) :

"I am commanded to judge justly between you in accordance with the Book which Allah has sent down and in which I believe."

Surah Al-Aaraf (7/'29) : Say, My Lord has commanded justice. *Surah Maida* 5/9 :

"O ye who believe! stand out firmly for Allah, as witnesses to fair dealing, and let not the hatred of others to you make you swerve to wrong and depart from justice. Be just: that is next to piety: and fear Allah, for Allah is well-acquainted with all that ye do."

Surah Nahl 16/90 :

"Allah commands justice, the doing of good, and liberality to kith and kin, and He forbids all shameful deeds, and injustice and rebellion: He instructs you that ye may receive admonition."

Surah Nisa 4/58 :

"Allah doth command you to render back your Trusts to those to whom they are due; and when ye judge between man and man, that ye judge with justice: Verily how excellent is the teaching which He giveth you! For Allah is He Who heareth and a seeth all things."

In *Surah Sad* (38/26) Hadrat Daud was directed :

"O David! We did indeed make thee a vicegerent on earth: so judge thou between men in truth (and justice): nor follow thou the lusts (of thy heart), for they will mislead thee from the Path of Allah: for those who wander astray from the Path of Allah, is a Penalty Grievous, for that they forget the Day of Account."

In *Surah Nisa* (4/105) it is said :

"We have sent down to thee the Book in truth, that thou mightiest judge between men, as guided by Allah: so be not (used) as an advocate by those who betray their trust;"

God Almighty directed the Holy Prophet in *Surah Al-Anam* (6/114) :

"Says shall I seek for judge other than Allah when it is he who sent unto you the Book explained in detail."

In *Surah Maida* (5/45) it is ordained :

"If thou judge, judge in equity between them, for Allah loves those who judge in equity."

It is ordained that the judge must give full weight to the facts and circumstances of the case in accordance with his capacity, capability and lights and does justice even if a near relative is concerned. (6/152).

It is said in *Surah Maida* (5/47) as under :

"Therefore, fear not men but fear Me and sell not My signs for miserable pittance. If any do fail to judge by the light Allah has revealed they are unbelievers.

5/48: And if fail to judge by the light of what Allah has revealed, they are wrong-doers.

5/50: Let the people of the Gospel judge by what Allah hath revealed therein. If any do fail to judge by (the light) of what Allah hath revealed, they are (no better than) those who rebel."

- Thus God Almighty ordains expressly at the pain of penalty and the society finds it necessary to maintain equilibrium in human affairs so that justice must be done to all. It is, however, not optional. It is the duty of the State that man honours the rights of his fellow-man and the State functionaries discharge the trust reposed in them. In case of an omission or negligence to do, it is provided to compel obedience and performance. Reference be made to *Surah Hadid (57/25)*:

Guardian Angels

It is important to note that despite the fact, that the *Sunnah* of the Guardian-Angels (82/11) are beyond suspicion and God Almighty also knows the truth of the matter *(see* 2/77, 4/42, *Hajj* 22/1 7, *Al-Imran* 3/119), the person who was killed (81/8-9), the earth on which offence was committed, (99/4) the tongue, hands, feet (24/24) and even the Prophets and other witnesses (39/69) shall be called to depose if any objection is raised on doubt expressed. Such is the right of defence in Islam. Can anyone quote a better procedure anywhere? Such being the right of defence no-one can offer anything less in scope in an Islamic system, for no-one can amend or change the Quran. *See* 5/89, *Yunus* 10/59. It will be appreciated that even the Prophet has not been allowed to bring about change in the express provisions as laid down in *Surah Yunus* (10/15) and *Al tahrim* (56/1). Also refer to the case of Shahid Afzal (PLD 1977, Lahore. 117).

Here it is worth to mention that 'bias in a judge which makes even an order correct, on facts and in law, as void, has no place in the Islamic Concept of Justice. In Islam, a judge is expected to do justice in all circumstances and if he severs from that path for any reason whatever, he is not a fit person to act as a judge. It is, therefore, the correctness of the order which is to be looked into and not the interest of the Judge. This is the view of the Federal Court also.

This may be compared with the Western concept where even decision of a Lord Chancellor was set aside on the ground that he held some shares in a company which was one of the parties before him in a case. *See* Dimes *v.* Grand Junction Canal Company Proprietors (1852) 3 HLC 759). The poor judge died of that shock later. This concept is based on a principle that justice should not only be done but should manifestly be seen to have been done. If this be the justification for striking down an order then perhaps in all those cases where government or other powerful and influential persons are pitched against weak, poor and uninfluential persons there will be no possibility of any justice, whatever. If the reason be of frailty of human-beings then why cannot a judge fall for greater temptations such as bribe, offer of higher position, etc. Even fear may prevent him from doing justice. Again there are hundreds of laws in force in many countries where one is a judge in his own cause. Can the courts strike down those decisions or have they done it on that score? Thus Islam looks for a better man as a judge. His attributes and qualifications are also given in the letter of Hadrat Ali.

The Quran aims at building a better social order and teaches individuals to develop very high integrity so that no person can conceive even for a moment that a judge who undertakes to decide a matter will go astray for any reason whatever. I refer here to a case which came up before Hadrat Umar. Hadrat Umar issued an order against acceptance of gift by anyone holding office since it is a type of bribe. Hadrat Umar prohibited taking or acceptance of gifts by office holders. The Quran thus ordains judges to decide against themselves, their parents, relations, friends, etc.; *(Nisa* 4/135) if the situation so requires, and not to decide against an enemy just only for that reason *(Maidah* 5/8).

Here, we can also mention that some of the legal principles that we generally follow in deciding cases are given in the Quran. Their origin is not to be credited to the modern system of law and justice :

(i) Judge with justice (4/58).

(ii) Apply your mind anxiously (1 7/35).

(iii) One is innocent unless proved guilty (24/12-13).

(iv) No offence without men's rea (33/5 and 6/54).

(v) No offence can be created retrospectively (44/22, 8/38, 5/96 and 2/275).

(vi) There is no offence if an act is done under compulsion (16/106).

(vii) The punishment should be commensurate with the offence and not more (2/194, 10/27, 22/60, 40/40, 42/40 and 16/126).

(viii) Self defence is no offence (42/41).

(ix) An abetter is also guilty (16/25).

(x) No-one can be held responsible for offences of others (42/15 and 39/7).

(xi) Writing is necessary for contracts except if it is unavoidable (2/282).

(xii) Agreement is binding but not so if the other side has broken it (8/56 and 9/4).

(xiii) The aggrieved is entitled to compensation (17/33).

(xiv) No more burden will be placed on one than he can bear (2/286).

(xv) Decide according to the evidence produced (4/105).

You will find 100 such principles, as embodied in *Mejellah*, in PLD 1966, Journal 50.

No-one is considered above law in Islam and so no-one can claim legal immunity. It is in direct conflict with the British notion that the "king can do no wrong" or the Western concept that the head of State or certain other functionaries are neither answerable to anyone nor can they be sued or prose cited. A legacy of this concept has been finding a place in our Constitutions. Article 248 of the 1973 Constitution may be quoted for reference. It is as under :

> Formerly, all witnesses appeared together. Qadi Shuraih made an important change that they should appear separately. Evidence could be oral, documentary, direct or circumstantial. Oral evidence could be direct or hearsay. The latter was permissible to prove paternity, death and reliable character. It had to come from competent witnesses. An adulterer, a person noted for dishonesty, bad character, drunk and a known liar were not considered reliable witnesses. Evidence of a slave in favour of his master was not admissible. Arbitration was allowed but either party could retract before award was given. Award when made became conclusive and could be referred to Qadi for execution.

The emphasis was on reformation and not imposition of sentences for crimes. Forgiveness was preferred to penalty. The Quran, Traditions of the Holy Prophet and, in their absence, personal judgement, were to be resorted to. *Ijma* and *Qias* were added to later by *Khulfa-i-Rashidin.* Hadrat Umar created a new precedent by accepting the evidence of an expert in a defamatory suit filed by Zibriqan bin Badr against a poet Hutaya. The verse which was the cause of dispute was vague and therefore it was decided on the opinion of another poet Hassan bin Sabit. No court fee had to be paid for seeking justice.

It seems appropriate in this respect to reproduce a letter written by Hadrat Umar to Abu Musa Ashari about Qadi's functions :

> "After the praise to God the Administration of Justice

is a duty. The Court must observe equality between the parties so that the weaker party may expect justice and the stronger may not expect concession. The burden of proof is on the plaintiff and the defendant may be put on oath, but let this not defeat the ends of justice and law. If you have decided a case, then after due care and thinking you may revise your decision. If you are doubtful in a point which is mentioned in the Quran and *Hadith* then think over it again and again and then apply *'Qiyas'* (a process of deduction). When a party wants to tender evidence then fix a time limit and if he proves his case then decide accordingly. All Muslims are fit to be witnesses except those who have received the prescribed punishment (flogging) for *Hadd* (fornication, adultery) and those who have tendered false evidence."

The system of judicial administration remained more or less the same even under the Umayyads. It is, however, unfortunate that special care was taken in appointing to office only persons who owned loyalty to the executive head and belonged either to the same family or shared in status as clients. The Qadis were appointed and dismissed publicly. During this period the judges were given executive powers like appointment of guardians of infants, administration of *waqf* properties, execution of punishments and looking after testamentary dispositions.

There were no regular Courts of Appeals but usually the Khalifah himself performed the duties of a High Court of Appeal. During the rule of Khalifah Al-Mamoon, a *Nazir-fil-Mazalim* or Board for Inspection of Grievances was established. It was presided over by Khalifah himself. It included the Chief Qadi, the Chief Wazir and one or two Secretaries of state and jurists or *Muftis* as members to correct miscarriage of justice. There was no set procedure as we know it today. The Board could apply the principles of equity to secure the ends of justice. Its powers were similar to the constitutional jurisdiction of the High Court.

During the rule of Abbasides science of jurisprudence flourished, traditions of Holy Prophet were collected and commentaries on the Quran were written. The four great schools of *Sunni* Law were established in this period. Administration of justice commenced on definite lines which had close resemblance to the modern systems. If the case was settled or terminated by a decision, a written judgement had to follow. The Qadi also had the right to pass an *ex-parte* decree. He could review his own judgement. The Abbasides developed a procedure for consulting specialists in the *Shariah* Law through '*Muftis*' and jurists who also assisted the litigants with written opinions or '*Fatwas*'.

Muhtasibs or Ombudsmen were also appointed during the Abbasid period. They were responsible for the enforcement of moral duties and obligations in accordance with the Quranic injunctions. The *Muhtasib* had the power to act *suo-moto* and enforce obedience by striking fear of the Hereafter. He was concerned with observance of prayers, fastings and other religious acts, non payments of debts without excuse, failure to fulfil official obligations, nuisances, right of way, easements, etc. The *Muhtasib* exercised control over attorneys and *vakils* so that they did not tamper with the administration of justice.

I propose now to wind up my address by pointed reference to the difficult task which lies ahead of all of us, to achieve the avowed objective of shaping ourselves as true Muslims, as best as one can, and adopt and practice the Islamic System of doing justice. The enormity of the task is indisputable but it is not impossible to achieve. It entails care and caution so that we reduce to the minimum the chances of trial and error.

Let me quote in the end a Latin—American saying :

"It is better to know where to go, but know not how to go, then know how to go but know not where to go."

Thus what is important is the destination. In so far as we Muslims are concerned God Almighty has given us our destination precisely and also the way to reach it. So my friends you are the lucky ones, the chosen ones and the blessed ones. If we stick to the faith and righteousness and obey the commands of *Rabb-e-Zuljalal,* of the Holy Prophet, and of those provided by a body of resolute men of faith and firmness, we are, *'Insha-Allah',* bound to succeed.

Justice in Islam

Islam presents a well articulated and coherent model of justice. The Islamic view of justice includes an understanding of how society can maintain a balance in its network of social relationships and how it can prepare individuals to accept and adopt the Quranic mandate reflecting the Will of Almighty Allah. This view of justice can be completely vindicated by empirical methods.

The Concept of Justice in Islam is contained in the principle: "to each his due". The just state of affairs in Islam is that in which each individual has exactly those benefits and liabilities which are due to him by virtue of his personal characteristics and circumstances. Common examples are the claim that justice means giving each man what he deserves and it also means equality.

The definition of justice in Islam has two important corollaries. First, it implies that where two men are equal in the relevant respects (so that their dues are the same) they should be treated the same way. Islam endorses the principle "Treat Equals Equally'. It is also supported by another fundamental principle "Render To Each His Due". An inference can be drawn from these two statements that the amount of benefit a person enjoys or the amount of burden he suffers should be proportional to the quantity of the relevant attribute which he possesses.

A possible distributive principle of Islam is that everyone should retain what he currently possesses. Resources have to be distributed in such a way that the greatest total amount of happiness is produced. The distribution of resources is recommended as a means to an aggregate goal, not as an end in itself.

Natural Urge

Justice as Virtue : Justice is regarded as a virtue in an Islamic social setting. There is usually a natural urge to perform acts of justice, as there is for acts of benevolence, such as helping a man who is in pain. Justice is vital to Muslim society. It is founded partly on the concept of *Ummah's* interest. Justice and the interests of *Ummah* are interdependent.

Justice in Islam serves the general happiness, conforms to the laws of life and gives each individual what he deserves. An adherence to distribution according to capability is guaranteed to produce maximum happiness. Islam endorsed the view that men should have rights in proportion to their merit.

The domain of justice in Islam can be sub-divided into two spheres of legal justice and social justice. Legal justice includes *"Tazeer"* which concerns the punishment of wrong-doing and the compensation of injury. It stipulates the conditions under which punishment may be inflicted and adjusts the scale of punishment to fit the nature of different crimes. In the sphere of civil law, the legal justice regulates the amount of restitution which must be made for injuries. Both the sections of legal justice lay down procedures of a fair trial and also rights of appeal. Social justice concerns the distribution of benefits, material and otherwise, and liabilities throughout the Muslim society as it results from social, economic, religious and political institutions. It deals with such matters as regulation of wages, administration of profits, protection of individual rights, allocation of food, clothing and shelter, and provision of education, health and welfare benefits.

The concept of justice in Islam tends to preserve the existing order of rights and possessions and restores it when any breach has been made. It consists in the recognition and protection of legal rights and also comprises principles for maintaining these rights according to the Quranic standard. The concept emphasises, in all segments of political life of Islamic society, the notion contained in the maxim "To each according to his or her rights".

Rights generally derive from publicly acknowledged rules, established practices, past transactions, current behaviour and individual qualities. Rights are also concerned with the citizens' expectations from the state and with ensuring that they are not disappointed. Men ought to be rewarded according to their deserts. A man's deserts may be measured by the accomplishments, his productive efforts, his capacities and capabilities. Thus Islam presents a healthy amalgam of three principles "To each according to his rights; To each according to his deserts; To each according to his needs". Each of the three principles embodies an important reason why Islam works out their synthesis.

The three principles whose synthesis is produced by Islam demand that a person's share of goods to which he is entitled by virtue of someone rule and by virtue of its affiliation to the other two principles should be made available to him. This availability should be a factor contributing to the maximum possible happiness. Given certain empirical assumptions, maximum possible happiness can be produced by recognising the claims of rights, deserts and needs.

Granted that it would be useful for Muslims to adhere to this synthesis; more happiness will be produced if desert is generally rewarded. The expectation of reward in the case of private citizens and of promotion in the case of public servants encourages people to acquire useful skills and perform deserving actions.

A more specific conception of justice within the Islamic framework expresses itself in the requirement that each person is to have an equal right to the most extensive basic liberty compatible with a similar liberty for others. Social and economic inequalities are to be minimised. They must provide great benefit to the least privileged. All public officers and positions have to be laid open to all under conditions of fair equality of opportunity. The principle of fair equality of opportunity demands that positions and offices should be assigned on the basis of ability and skill rather than on the basis of birth and influence. It covers such issues as freedom of conscience and the rights of citizens to participate in the affairs of Government.

It can safely be maintained that justice in Islam is not mostly procedural as it is in Roman Law. Islam provides reasonable criteria for judging whether a given allocation of financial resources to persons or institutions is just or unjust. Such an allocation can, however, be just if it has arisen through the operation of fair procedures. Islam visualises an institutional framework within which these criteria can be applied.

There is to be a competitive market economy, a "transfer branch" of government to guarantee a basic social minimum, another branch to prevent the formation of monopolies, and so on. The Quranic law will then provide a guideline as to how wealth and other goods should be distributed to persons. Once institutions are established on the Islamic model, individuals participating in these institutions will form certain expectations about how they are to be treated, and these in turn will give rise to entitlements.

Islam does not endorse the socialistic conception that the position of the under-privileged should be materially improved by expropriating wealthy landowners without just compensation. The expectations of the landless and of the land-owners have to be kept in proper balance. The objective of land reforms in Islam is not to deprive the land-owners of their landed property and to make them the under-privileged members of society.

Islam accepts in full the common-sense precepts of justice, such as the precept "to each according to his contribution" or the precept "to each according to his effort". Someone who makes a larger than average contribution is creating more value for the Muslim society, and it is, therefore, worth paying him a larger wage. Rewards and incentives are essential to encourage the Muslims to acquire skills, work harder, and take on unpleasant work. Islam provided justifications for the payment of exceptionally high rewards to people with scarce but useful talents. Surely all of those currently receiving high rewards must deserve them.

Islamic social system does not discard the belief that every man must have the opportunity to climb the social ladder and to achieve the highest rewards that the society has to offer. Islam does not impose barriers of a legal, social or economic type that could prevent a citizen from gaining rewards. Anything that a man may justly claim he must earn by exercising his capacities in a socially useful way, in which case the institutions of property, contract and exchange will ensure that he gets a fair return.

The Islamic society makes service to the community the dominant motive in work. The social well-being is eventually broken down into individual benefits and the chief constituent of individuals' well-being is the satisfaction of needs. Thus the better-off can show their own rewards to be just by meeting the just claims to their services made by those in need.

The cardinal feature of Islamic society is that the Muslims characteristically evaluate the social distribution of benefits by reference to Quranic standards of distribution. The general criteria of social justice can only be implemented by establishing Quranic doctrines and principles, and thus by conferring certain positive rights upon individuals. Once a right has been established, it gains its own intrinsic value because individuals come to govern their actions by reference to Quranic standards.

In an Islamic social setting, the traditional network of social relationships produces a commitment to values such as generosity. The society is concerned with the protection of human rights as well as with the relief of the needy.

The Islamic view of justice incorporates a number of distinguished characteristics. For example, each man can choose the kind of occupation he will adopt, instead of being assigned to it by birth or authoritative command. He works for the rewards which he can gain, not under compulsion or for fear of sanctions. He competes freely with other individuals for these rewards. He is free to make contracts with others as he wishes. There is no inherited social status: a man's place is determined by his actions, by the agreements he makes, and the rewards they bring him.

There are no rigid institutions which constrain people to act in ways they would not otherwise do, whether by compulsion or by the sanctity of custom; every institution is created and sustained by the free agreement of the individuals who wish to use it to gain certain specific ends. Efforts of the people are combined, in an Islamic society, for mutual advantage. Occupations are determined by the principle of efficiency. The social institutions are erected on the basis of free contract. Contracts are not simply expressions of mutual self-interest. They are subject to the moral control of society which determines the forms of contracts that are permissible.

The economic system is composed of independent producers who group themselves into associations for mutual advantage. Within the association, independence is preserved and competition of a nondestructive type is continued and rewards are proportional to merit. There are no status barriers between men. Thus justice is not a constraint on individuals seeking their private ends. It becomes instead an expression of their independence, of their individuality and of the religious milieu.

In an Islamic society any expenditure of talent and energy which is socially useful must be recompensed at the appropriate rate, which is agreed on in advance. Rewards gained in the open society are just, because to gain them a man must have contributed sufficiently to the welfare of society. Every individual should receive a fair recompense for his labour, and this is given quantitative expression in the principle that he shall be rewarded according to his competence and capabilities. Justice is satisfied when each gets out of the undertaking an equivalent of what he has put in.

The Islamic Concept of Justice can be rationally defended. The defence consists partly in showing that the conception corresponds to Allah's Will, partly in showing that it represents the rational choice of individuals placed in a real situation in which they are cognisant of their personal qualities and of their place in society. The whole enterprise of delineating a conception of justice on the basis of rational choices abstracted from Holy Quran is well taken, because these abstracts have the prerequisites for making a sound conception of justice. It follows from this thesis that Muslims hold conception of justice as part of specific Islamic views of society, and that they acquire these views through their experience of knowing, assimilating and following the Quran.

Salient Features

Justice, as an abstract quality, is difficult to define. To say that it enables distinction to be made between right and wrong does not simplify the matter because opinion on rights and wrongs vary widely. To say that every human being is equipped with a sense of justice is of little help, since the thought of each individual is limited by the conscious knowledge he possesses. It is clearly a quality attaching to actions, and therefore to living things that are capable of action. The effect of an action could be particular in a certain aspect, such as the Courts deal with, on a large scale, as between human beings. Despite the scope of the judicial function, within a community, being ever on the increase, it yet does not, in my opinion, represent the widest stretch of the meaning of the word 'justice'. That, perhaps, is to be found in the relationships of all living things to everything in their natural environment. With the exception of man, all other things have limitations upon the extent of their activity, which are designed to operate for promotion of a balanced life for all, so that the Will of the Almighty should be fulfilled by the continual betterment of His Creation.

The agency of man, to whom has been entrusted control of everything else in nature, is an element of the greatest importance in that fulfilment. If, in exercising that control, he is to carry out the Divine purpose, he must have appreciation of the exactness of the adjustments that nature, in its justice, has provided for the governance of relations between living beings and inanimate things in creation. Lately, evidence has been gathered which shows the enormous damage done to the environment by the naked pursuit of advantage and profit to themselves, by groups of human beings, notably in Western countries. They had interfered with the economy of nature, without understanding of the linkages between and the justice operating through all its creatures, animate and inanimate, until the detriment to themselves started them in the face. They had done injustice to their environment and punishment had followed.

A definition of the quality of justice has been attempted in the great work of Shah Waliullah, entitled *Hujjatullah al-Baligha*. *Adalat* is there specified as one of four faculties, by the fostering and development of which, perfection in human happiness may be attained. *Adalat* is that quality in a member of a society which enables him, without effort and with perfect naturalness to act always so as to strengthen the bonds of union in the society. The ideal is that of a healthy body, made of perfectly co-related parts operating in unison, free from internal obstruction.

The just man has the special capacity, by his actions in everyday life, of assisting towards the end that all the members of the society live together, in their separate walks, as limit of a single corporate, integrated body. Such a person furthers the intention of Allah, in respect of all human communities, that their affairs should be conducted in the best possible way, to ensure continuous improvement. Being imbued with a feeling of total involvement in the activities of the people, in the manner of a head of a family, being sensitive to their innermost feelings and thoughts, cognizant as their settled technique in the implementation of their desires, he is competent to guide their energies into beneficial channels. Possessing the basic virtue of gentleness in thought and action, and free from harshness and hatred, his adaptation to the human environment is such that all his action's are in just proportion to the occasions. Such a person, with this special quality, is, in Shah Waliullah's opinion, well suited to control the affairs of a State. Among those affairs, not the least in importance is the function of the judiciary, for the dispensation of justice in the wide area of conflict of interest between citizens and the ruling authorities.

Among the many distinctions to which the religion of Islam can lay claim, one that in the context of human affairs can claim the highest importance is that its acceptance and establishment proceeded concurrently with the establishment of the Islamic State, under the inspired leadership of the Apostle of Allah, the Holy Prophet Muhammad (peace be upon him). In the first thirteen years after he received the call to Prophethood, he received the bulk of the revelations vouchsafed to him by the Almighty, while being tested and tempered through a fierce fire of determined and seemingly invincible opposition by his own people in the holy city of Mecca. Under Divine guidance, he then moved to the city of Medina, and immediately the number of his followers multiplied to the extent that it fell to him to lay down the Constitution of his State, and to provide it with the full apparatus of a Government. That he did so in the light bestowed upon him by Allah is apparent from the fact that a great proportion of the Divine injunctions relating to human affairs is to be found in the four *Surhas,* Nos. 2 to 5, which were revealed at Medina. Under direct guidance from the Almighty, the Holy Prophet conducted all the central affairs of the new State, laid down principles of government and organization, established institutions, directed foreign affairs, conducted negotiations and concluded treaties, sent out embassis carried the war with his Meccan opponents to a successful conclusion. He at the same time, in direct touch with all his followers, accessible at all times to each of them, and he judged every case himself.

The record of the revelations he received is contained in the Holy Quran; the record of his actions as reported by his personal Companions or other reliable persons who had received it from the Companions is in the *Sunnah.* It is from these two Scriptures that the governing principles of justice in Islam are derived. Over and above the detailed and particular principles, there is to be read the direction of Allah, contained in *Surah* IV, verse 106:

> "We have revealed the Book comprising the Truth, so that you would judge men in the light of Allah."

And it is made plain that the dispensation of justice is to proceed on regulated lines in the injunction to King David, in *Surah* 38, verse 27 :

> "And judge between men on right principle, and do not follow your own inclinations, for they will cause you to stray from the path of Allah."

Decisions were not to be based on whim or caprice, but on

proper canon and justice and equity. A model was thus set up for the Holy Prophet, and his successors, to follow, and indeed they followed it. Equity, which may be described as mitigation of the harsher aspects of justice according to the circumstances, is a basic rule of Islamic Justice.

The Holy Quran is replete with injunctions that are relevant to justice. In *Surah* IV, verse 136 it is said 'Believers! bear aloft the standard of justice', and verse 9 of the *Surah* V proclaims that justice has quality that brings it near to piety and the fear of Allah. Verse 9 of *Surah* V and verse 153 *of Surah* VI warn against allowing ill-will or affection to colour a judgement. In the matter of private retributive justice, there are several directions for the observation of equality and proportion, and each is supplemented by a recommendation to mitigation or forgiveness.

For instance, verse 178 of *Surah* II, says that for murder, the retaliation must be equal, freeman for freeman, slave for slave, woman for woman, but immediately thereafter comes the mitigation in His Mercy, Allah ordains that the next-of-kin has the option to refrain from retaliation on receiving material compensation, which should be agreed in proper manner, and received graciously, that is retaining no rancour. Verse 127 of *Surah* says — 'Believers! if you must take revenge, do it in proportion to the injury suffered and immediately after 'but if you suffer patiently, that is better for the sufferers'. Self-defence is approved in verse 39 of *Surah* 42, where it is said 'the return for an evil deed is a similar deed—but he who forgives has his reward with Allah verse 47 of *Surah* XXIII takes the matter even further, when it says-'Meet evil by repaying it with good and this is repeated in verse 35 of *Surah* XLI, which reads — 'Good and evil are not alike; repay evil with good, and your enemy will become a sincere friend.

The jurisprudence of a particular system of justice is founded on maxims, rules, principles and precedents. These are not to be expected, in precise form, in such a Scripture as the Quran, but there is a great deal to be found which is of directory effect to the spread of justice within the community of Islam, as well as to the dispensation of justice. The entire field is placed under the religious obligation, surrender to the Will of Allah, and answerability on the Last Day. But there are rules of conduct laid down in many matters out of which resort to law most frequently arises, which may be recounted briefly.

Thus, provocation which is a common cause of conflict, is frowned upon in verse 12 of *Surah* XLIV, where the faithful are enjoined against mocking, calling names, fault-finding, spying and the nursing of suspicions. Verse 149 of *Surah* IV says—'Do not use foul language, even if wronged', and in verse 54 of *Surah* XVII, it is said—'Use gracious words to each other, for Satan is alert to create discord among you . Aggressiveness in behaviour is condemned in verse 34 of *Surah* VI and verse 92 of *Surah* XVI, in the words – 'Allah forbids unlawful aggression'. 'Oppression is blameworthy' says verse 42 of *Surah* XXXVII and verse 10 of *Surah* XLIX requires that the aggressor should be humbled. Oath-taking in order to deceive is expressly forbidden in verse 95 of *Surah* XVI which says—'You will thereby abandon firm ground and incur punishment'. Scandal-mongering receives special treatment at many places. Thus, *Surah* 104 declares 'Woe to all backbiters and slanderers', and a biting condemnation is contained in verse 13 of *Surah* XLIX, in the words – 'Avoid backbiting: would you wish to eat the flesh of a dead brother? The spreading of rumours not based on knowledge is declared 'a grave fault' in verse 15 of *Surah* XXIV, of which verse 27 says that calumniators cannot injure any people. Indecency in behaviour, both open and hidden, is forbidden by Allah in verse 34 of *Surah* VI, and a painful punishment in both the lives is declared for those who spread immorality. Privacy of homes is safeguarded by injunctions in verses 28 to 30 of *Surah* XXIV, where entry only with permission and after greeting the inmates is enjoined. Careless behaviour in this regard could be a source of grave trouble. Correct and respectful behaviour between the sexes is particularly prescribed in verses 31 and 32 of the same *Surah:* men are to lower their gaze on meeting women, and women must do likewise when meeting men, and at the same time, should cover themselves up.

Extravagance being contrary to just behaviour, a bad example to others, and a way towards sinful acts, is specially mentioned in verse 188 of *Surah* II, where it is said – 'Eat not up your property in vanity' and in verse 27 of *Surah* XVII, squanderers are characterised as 'brothers of the devils'. Drinking and gambling are condemned in verses 90 and 91 of *Surah* V, as 'Satan's handiwork out of which enmity and hatred grow' and as such make you 'forget prayer'. In both, says verse 21 9 of *Surah* II, is great sin.

For the dispensation of justice, an indispensable requirement is evidence, oral as well as documentary. It is important that evidence should be forthcoming, and verse 283 of *Surah* II gives the direction 'Do not conceal testimony: to do so in sinful', and verse 136 of *Surah* IV says 'Let no low motives keep you from the path of justice'. 'Bear true witness' says verse 9 of *Surah* V, and in verse 64 of *Surah* XXV it is said 'The servants of Allah the Gracious One, do not give false evidence'. Those who stand by their testimony are said, in verse 33 of *Surah* LXX to be 'saved from hell'. To give evidence 'for the sake of Allah' without fear or favour, is enjoined in verse 136 of *Surah* IV, where it is said 'Bear testimony even against yourself, your parents and your kinsfolk'. Documents have value for avoidance of falsity and fraud, and the Holy Quran prescribes the writing of deeds in, at least, five cases, viz. loans, sales, wills, divorces and the freeing of slaves. A debt should be put into writing; the scribe should not refuse to record it; the contents should be dictated by the debtor, and there should be at least two witnesses; persons asked to witness should not refuse. *(Surah* II, verse 282). The same verse requires that sales should also be put into writing and witnessed in the same way, and the scribe and the witnesses should be held free of harm. By verse 2 of *Surah* LXV, it is directed that when a woman is given release from her marriage, a deed should be inscribed, attested by two witnesses. Special provision is made for wills to be in writing, attested by two witnesses from among the relations, by verse 107 of *Surah* V, and the testator may put these witnesses to the oath that they will, when the occasion arises, support the will, and not back out for money or for fear of offending other heirs. It is even laid down that if the attesting witnesses back out, others may be produced, who should be put to the oath that their testimony is true. One sees the great care taken to ensure that truth and justice should prevail. By verse 33 of *Surah* XXIV, it is required that a slave should be given a written release if he asks for it. In certain cases, e.g. the attesting of wills, a standard of competency for being a witness is laid down: they must be 'just men.' Certain persons, e.g. those found guilty of preferring a false charge of unchastity against honourable women are debarred for life from giving evidence (*Surah* XXIV, verse 5). To keep the judiciary free from corruption, the faithful are warned by verse 188 of *Surah* II not to use their money to gain the favour of judges, and so to devour the property of others.

To ensure the orderly devolution of estates, bequests are recommended, in verse 180 of *Surah* II, to be made to parents and near relatives, as a 'safeguard against sin', and those are commended who advise the testator on making a fair distribution. Blood relations are to be preferred above other believers and the refugees, but even to a friend, a bequest may be made (*Surah* XXXIII verse 7). A person approaching death should make special provision for his wife, leaving enough for a year's maintenance, while living in his house (*Surah* II, verse 240). These precautionary admonitions are clearly designed to secure the doing of justice to all entitled persons in the distribution of the estate of a deceased relative, out of which commonly great and lengthy disputes are apt to arise.

To the same purpose, there have been provided clear rules of succession to such estates in *Surah* IV, verses 7, 12, 13 and 177. These are too well-known to require mention by me. They are still in force throughout the Muslim world. The scheme is elaborate and, what is more, unique among known systems of succession. It is so close to the ideal both from the viewpoint of the beneficiaries as well as the health and well-being of the economy that, in India, Hindu Judges of High Courts have applied it to the distribution of estates in regard to which the personal law of the parties was not clear, at the same time observing that the system was both just and beneficial.

Similar comprehensive rules are laid down in the Holy Quran in regard to the regulation of matrimonial affairs, out of which troubles are apt to arise in all societies. These too are very well-known, and there is need to only touch upon them briefly. Women were not to be forced into marriage against their will. The practice of widows being forced to marry a kinsman of the deceased husband, as a matter of inheritance, was forbidden in verse 19 of *Surah* IV.

The consent of the relatives of a slave-girl was made requisite, by verse 34 of *Surah* XXIV, for her marriage to her owner. By the same verse, the man was required to give a portion at marriage to the wife, even if she were a slave, and taking back of what was so given was forbidden by verse 20 of *Surah* IV, unless the women were guilty of flagrant lewdness. In case of disagreements between the spouses, recourse was first to be had to reconciliation (verse 129 of *Surah* IV) but when a total breach was feared, their case was to be referred to two *hukma* (judges or Arbitrators) one from each side. (Verse 34 *of Surah* IV). The care of the Almighty for the good of the parties was indicated by the words in the same verse—'if they are inclined to peace, Allah will bring them to agreement, but if they are bent on separation, verse 131 of *Surah* IV gives the assurance that 'Allah will fulfil the needs of both'. Elaborate rules to govern divorce are contained in *Surah* II. Two golden threads run through the entire code of divorce, namely (1) kindness and consideration for the woman, and (2) avoidance of haste in divorcing. A period of waiting was imposed upon the divorced wife before she could marry again, for the obvious purpose of keeping the lines of pedigree pure. Such women were not to be prevented from marrying again.

Rules are also laid down in the Holy Quran in regard to such matters as trusts, and business relationships. By verse 283 of *Surah* II and verse 58 of *Surah* IV, fulfilment of trusts is enjoined, and *Surah* 70 imports the religious obligation when it says that paradise is assured to those who are faithful to their trusts and convenants. Honesty in trade is enjoined by the injunction 'Weigh and measure full and fair' contained in verse 153 of *Surah* VI and verse 36 of *Surah* XVII, and *Surah* 83 condemns traders who demand full measure from others but give less themselves. Observance of contracts is made obligatory in verse 2, *Surah* V and verse 35 of *Surah* XVII, and again the religious sanction is brought in by the words 'you must account for them'. There are severe injunctions against usury, by which money is doubled and quadrupled; some practice it under the cover of trade; it is a thing of the Devil and Allah puts a blight on it. (verse 275 of *Surah* II and verse 130 of *Surah* III).

Orphans being easy victims for their guardians, the Holy Quran makes special provision in many places to ensure proper treatment for them, and proper care of their property during their minority. *Surah* 93 condemns ill-treatment and contemptuous behaviour and *Surah* 89 forbids harshness, towards orphans. The best course, says *Surah* II, verse 220, is to improve their lot, and bring them up as brothers. Deal fairly with orphans' property, says verse 153 of *Surah* VI, and verse 35 of *Surah* says. Do not touch orphans' property, except for a proper purpose. Verse 2 of *Surah* IV gives a comprehensive direction—Look after orphans till they reach marriageable age, then give them their property, and have the transaction witnessed. During their minority, be careful in spending their money, do not mix their property with your own, and charge your expenses reasonably.

There is much more in the Holy Quran that is relevant to law and justice, but for the present purpose, this account of the directions on certain subjects is sufficient to establish that a comprehensive jurisprudence was given to the faithful of Islam thereby. That the injunctions were to be observed as law appears from following verse, among others - 'When they consult you concerning women, say' Allah has given you decrees and the Scripture that has been recited to you" (Verse 127 of *Surah* IV). In verse 59 of *Surah* IV, there is the overall injunction— 'If you are at variance over any matter, refer it to Allah and His Messenger'. This has throughout been interpreted to mean that the line of decision is to be sought in the Holy Quran, and the word of the Holy Prophet (peace be upon him) spoken in his lifetime and as recorded in the *Ahadith* or *Sunnah* after his death.

We have not dealt with the matter of crimes and punishment that are detailed in the Holy Quran, as these are very well-known. The best known matters seem to be the *Hadd,* i.e. the maximum punishment. What is much less known is that the principle of mitigation in relation to the circumstances has been applied from the very first days of Islam. In Verse 178 of *Surah* II, which is mentioned earlier, where blood-money was declared to be an acceptable alternative to equal retaliation, the words were added 'this mitigation is provided through the mercy of your Lord'. Shah Waliullah, in the *(Hujjatullah Al-Baligha)* points out that the *Hadd* punishments were applied to offences of three kind— (1) those subversive of public order and disturbing to the community, (2) such as, if not prevented early, could be repeated so as to become habitual, and (3) such that the victim could not get redress for himself. For treason and sedition, the most severe punishment was prescribed and mitigation was inadmissible. For theft, the punishment was prescribed in the

Holy Quran, namely, hand-cutting, the offence being one easy to commit, and therefore apt to become both habitual and widespread. The Holy Prophet (peace be upon him) as a law giver is reported to have imposed this punishment only where the value of the stolen property was more than a quarter of a *dirham.* He also laid down the principle that for applying this punishment, the taking must be from actual safe-custody, or under protection, besides being of the requisite value. So, for plucking fruit from a tree or taking animals that were straying in the hills, lesser punishments were given, including a fine of double the value of the thing taken.

Cases of crimes which cannot be requited by the victim are outraging the modesty of respectable women, highway robbery, false imputation of unchastity, and for these the *Hadd* punishments were appropriate. Mitigation was also laid down for slaves, who did not possess full freedom of will; for them punishments were halved. The Holy Prophet (peace be upon him) said – 'if a female slave commits an offence, beat her; if a male slave commits theft, sell him'. Another tradition is to the effect that when a complaint was made against a slave by his owner, that he had committed theft, the Holy Prophet said 'both belong to you; one is merged in the other'. There are traditions also with reference to the *Hadd* punishment for adultery that qualified mitigation was applied, according to the facts. With regard to intoxication through drink, the Holy Prophet strengthened the Quranic injunctions by declaring it to be *Haram.* He ordered the punishment of 40 lashes to a drunken person. Here too, the offence is one easily committed, and apt to become habitual so that full severity in punishment was justified. Later, it was increased to 80 lashes. A very impressive instance of the Holy Prophet's inclination towards mercy is to be found in the tradition that when a man brought before him, as an offender who had incurred a punishment of 100 lashes, proved to be sick and a cripple, he said 'take a branch with a hundred twigs and give him one blow with it'.

During the period when the Holy Prophet (peace be upon him) was the sole Judge of his people, he enlarged the jurisprudence of Islam in several directions. The record of his decisions and dicta is contained in the *Ahadith.* It was he who laid down the rule that in the trial of suits, the onus of producing evidence to support his claim is on the plaintiff; the defendant must take an oath that his case is true. The reason given was that if relief were always given to plaintiffs on evidence alone, unjust results could follow.

Another rule that he laid down is that in cases of doubt, the antecedents of witnesses should be checked. Supplementing the rule of the Quran that one who is proved to have made a false imputation of unchastity against an honourable woman is for ever disqualified as a witness in judicial proceedings, the Holy Prophet disqualified also persons who have committed breach of trust or adultery, as well as those who were enemies of a party. Rules were laid down as to the taking of oaths—the formula of words, the time and the place. The words should bring to mind the total power and the total knowledge of Allah; the time should be after the *Asar* prayer; in Mecca the place was within the precincts of the *Kaaba,* and in Medina, at the mosque of Tayyiba. The Holy Prophet greatly disapproved of litigious persons saying that in the view of Allah these were the most troublesome, but those who avoided contention were praised as magnanimous.

False evidence and false cases were regarded with a very severe eye; they show disrespect to Allah, they disturb the harmony of society and so attract the wrath of Allah, who loves not the troublemaker and desires that social order should be maintained. The Holy Prophet said—'he who makes a false case to get another's property is not of my people; he should find his place in Hell'. A judgement does not make that lawful which is itself unlawful, and the Holy Prophet added great emphasis by saying:

'Remember that I am like one of you. If a clever

litigant, by artful words, convinces me so that I decide a case in his favour, such a litigant will go to Hell.'

In his decisions, the Holy Prophet always upheld the principle of public good. Thus in a case of damage to a garden by a stray camel, he laid down that if it happened in the daytime when the garden-owner should have guarded his property, there was no blame to the camel-owner, but if it happened at night, when the camel-owner should have kept his animal secure, the camel-owner was liable.

The maxim *'al-khiraj biz zaman'*, meaning that the profit from a thing belongs to him who is responsible for its existence, from which is derived the corollary *'al-uzm bil-ghanam'* meaning he who pays for a thing is entitled to the benefit from it, comes from the Holy Prophet himself, and in his time was laid down the salutary principle that all transactions that predated the advent of the Islamic State were to be left as they were, untouched by the new order of things. The rule favouring the person in possession, where the ownership of property is involved, and the evidence is either doubtful or equal on the two sides was applied by the Holy Prophet in a case he decided. With regard to property of which no owner could be found, he laid down that its disposal should be governed by the element of benefit to all Muslims as well as to the thing itself, and secondly, by the element of prior possession; failing these, by the casting of lots. He held that contracts should be enforced to the letter, unless anything agreed makes that *halal* (lawful) which religion declares to be *haram* (unlawful). Where the parties are not agreed as to the terms of a contract, it should be declared void, and in a particular case, the Holy Prophet said—'When seller and buyer are not agreed, and the word of neither can be accepted, if the thing allegedly sold be there, the word of the seller should be accepted, but if the buyer does not agree, the contract should be declared void."

Many cases are recorded in which the Holy Prophet (peace be upon him) laid down canons of justice of general application.

The paternity of the child of a slave-girl being contested, one party claiming that his brother, when dying had said the child was his and should be looked after in his family, and the other declaring it is the child of my father's slave, and was born in my father's house, the Holy Prophet pronounced judgement as follows : 'the child belongs to the owner of the house in which it was born; for the adulterer there is stoning.' He decided that in a built-up area, where trouble had arisen through the paths being encroached upon by builders, the minimum width of the path should be seven cubits; so a public nuisance was removed. In a case where a person had cultivated land belonging to another tribe than his own, without authority, the Holy Prophet decided that the man had no right to the produce, but could ask for payment of his expenses of cultivation. He laid down the principle in a pre-emption case, that the 'right of pre-emption exists only so long as partition has not been effected, so that rights remain joint; when every field has been demarcated, and each owner has his separate way, no right of pre-emption remains'.

These could be found examples in Shah Waliullah's book, to which reference had been made earlier and there is no doubt that many other precedents are recorded in the main books of *Hadith.* What has been said so far is sufficient to show that by the time that it became necessary for the Holy Prophet (peace be upon him) to send Qadis (judges) to the new provinces which had acknowledged Islam and the rule of the Prophet, there was already established, in the Holy Quran and the record of decided cases, a sufficient volume of maxims, rules, principles and precedents to constitute the Islamic Jurisprudence. The procedure of trial of cases through presentation by the parties, supported by evidence in the face of the Court, was well established. A code classifying offences and the *Hadd* punishments therefore, as well as the grounds of mitigation, had already been settled. It is recorded that the Holy Prophet interviewed a person who was to go as Qadi to the new Province of the Yemen; part of the dialogue was as follows :

Q. On what will you base your legal decisions?

A. The Quran.

Q. But if that contains nothing for the purpose?

A. Then upon your tradition and practice.

Q. But if that also fails you?

A. Then I will follow my own opinion.

The Holy Prophet approved these answers. In common with many persons who have read that little dialogue, it seems that the Holy Prophet was only testing the man's faith and allegiance to the Holy Quran, and to himself. Its true significance was brought home to me, in the course of the study that has gone into the present paper. The Holy Prophet (peace be upon him) was making sure that the man realised that he was being sent to operate and propagate the new jurisprudence of Islam, according to right principles and that he knew where those principles were to be found. He was not to dispense justice in the manner of the pre-Islamic period, the *Jahiliyat*, or in the indigenous way of the people who had been recently brought within the authority of Islam. The fact was recognised also that the code, being new, was not complete so as to provide, in detail, for every kind of case, and so the appointee was permitted to use in such cases, his own judgement.

The compilation of the *Ahadith* went on for almost a hundred years, and we may be sure that copies were sent to all the administrators and judges, far and near. Work on the formulation of the *Sham*, the comprehensive code for the guidance of Muslims, continued for the next three hundred years, when it was completed separately, with variations, by the four great *Imams*. It was settled that the laws of the Muslims were to be derived firstly from the Quran, secondly from the *Sunna* of the Holy Prophet, thirdly by assemblies of the learned, known as *Ijma,* and lastly, by *Ijtihad,* meaning ratiocination by individuals. Three of these sources were in operation from the outset, with the approval of the Holy Prophet himself, as we have seen. The fourth, the making of laws by assemblies failed of its purpose, since the assemblies were to be confined to scholars of individual schools, and the results produced lacked universality. But one thing is clear, namely, that from the very inception of Islam, the dispensation of justice has proceeded on regulated lines, on principles formulated in writing, and with the aid of precedents, in the form of judicial decisions that go back to the Holy Prophet himself. The people of Islam can take just pride in the thought that their judicial system was placed from the beginning on lines that in substance are no different from those of the best systems of today. Compared with the other prevalent systems, it was distinguished by a higher degree of humanity towards criminals, even towards prisoners taken in religious wars, and a deeper understanding of the basic needs of human beings living in settled communities. In the common belief, that remains the condition even today.

The progressive elements among the recognised sources of law in Islam are those of *Ijtihad,* the advancement of law through ratiocinative processes, and *Ijma,* which means codification and modernisation of laws through deliberative assemblies. Our poet-philosopher, Iqbal, relates *Ijtihad* to the original thinking of exceptionally gifted persons, a very acceptable view, but it is possible to see that at the level of our superior Courts, the process of *Ijtihad* is applied in every case where under minute examination, the Judges are expected to apply the law to new and unanticipated situations, and even in some cases, to fill gaps in the law. As for *Ijma,* under modern conditions, and in the enlarging fields of human affairs that are outside the strict teaching of the four main schools, it is possible to regard the legislative assemblies of today as being competent to discharge that function in this aspect of modernisation. The task of codification has been frequently attempted by Muslim rulers of the past. Such an attempt was made by the Mughal Emperor, Aurangzeb Alamgir, and the result was the *Fatawa-e-Alamgiri,* which retains importance even today despite its character of a compilation of judicial dicta, often related to particular facts, whose application to new cases gives rise to difficulty. The collection was made about 275 years ago. Another attempt at codification of Islamic laws was made by the Sultan of Turkey, entitled *'Mejelle el-Ahkam-i-Adliya'*. It is much more recent, having been completed and promulgated as the law of the vast territories of the Turkish Empire about a hundred years ago. It was replaced by a new Code in 1926.

An English translation of this valuable source book of Islamic law has been published in Pakistan, by the All Pakistan Legal Decisions of Lahore, and is readily available. When published originally, it was described as 'A Complete Code of Islamic Civil Law', though it excludes the important subject of marriage *(munakiahat)* and is confined to 'dealings between people and their relations with and conduct towards each other' that are included within the comprehensive description of *muamlat.*

The book is prefaced by a collection of a hundred maxims, followed by 1851 Articles, adapted for application by the *Nizam* Courts, as distinguished from the *Shariah* Courts. Although the propositions of law are not set out or worded in the manner of statutes in the English mode, and the translation is cumbrous through being too literal, yet the book has the merit of being arranged in chapters, subject-wise, from contracts of sale and lease, surety and pledge, to torts, pre-emption, judicial guardianship, partition and partnership, limitation, etc. and so is practically usable for reference. It contains elaborate provisions for implementation of the Holy Prophet's injunction 'proof is for the plaintiff; oath for the defendant' besides rules of evidence. The Holy Prophet's direction to examine the credibility of witnesses is carried out in a set of rules on the subject.

This compilation was the work of a Commission of Jurists

appointed by the Sultan for 'the production from the practical part of the *Shar' (Fiqh)* of a beneficial work, so that it shall be sufficient for application to the transactions of people, which happen everyday' in the words of the compilers, who purported to follow 'those opinions of *Hanafi* doctors which are most in harmony with the exigencies of modern life and business' (from the Foreword by Mr. Justice S. A. Rahman of the Supreme Court of Pakistan). The duty of adherence to *Shar'* law in the *Hanafi* school was borne in mind by the compilers, and there is thus assurance of such conformity for those who seek guidance in the paths of Islamic jurisprudence from this book. For that purpose, it can safely be recommended for study by the great number of persons in Muslim countries, who have been encouraged by recent events to hope for the establishment of a genuine *Nizam-e-Mustafa* in Muslim countries.

And it has given me very great pleasure to demonstrate to you that the edifice of justice in Islam was founded and built up to a substantial degree by no other than the Apostle of Allah, Muhammad *Mustafa* (peace be upon him). There can be no greater proof of its excellence and its right to be accepted with total confidence.

The Departure

1. The Concept of Justice in Islam is different from the concept of the remedial justice of the Greeks, the natural justice of the Romans or the formal justice of the Anglo-Saxons. Justice in Islam seeks to attain a higher standard of, what I might call, 'absolute justice' or absolute fairness as suggested by the *'Meezan'* for Balance. The Holy Quran proclaims :

"We sent aforetimes Our Apostles with clear signs and sent down the Book and the Balance, that men may stand forth injustice (25—57)."

2. This verse clearly postulates two essential principles. Firstly, that justice is to be done not only in accordance

with law but also in such a way that it results in complete fairness. Secondly, that the doing of justice is not the concern of the judge alone but the collective responsibility of the community as well. Every member of the community is involved in this process. If an injustice is being committed to a person's knowledge he cannot stand apart as a silent spectator even if he is not personally affected. Allah commands :

"Oh ye who believe! Stand out firmly for justice, as witnesses to Allah, even as against yourselves, or your parents, or your kin, and whether it be against rich or poor; for Allah can best protect both. Follow not the lusts of your hearts; lest ye swerve, and if ye distort justice or decline to do justice, verily Allah is well acquainted with all that ye do." (4–135).

3. This too indicates the degree of fairness demanded in the Islamic system. The *'Meezan'* not only symbolizes this degree of fairness but also refers to the God given faculty by which a person can judge between right and wrong even as against oneself or one's parents or kin. *'Adl'* according to Islamic concepts thus demands a perfect standard of comparison or estimation which cannot be swayed by any other consideration.

4. The Arabic word *Al-Adl* though used in various senses in the Holy Quran nevertheless always imports a moral duty to act with fairness. Justice is, therefore, also a religious duty which has to be performed "as witnesses to God" and the importance that is attached to it is so great that it has been placed next to *Taqwa,* i.e., piety itself. Allah ordains :

"Oh ye who believe stand out firmly for Allah as witnesses to fair dealing, and let not the hatred of others to you make you swerve to wrong and depart from justice. Be just; that is next to Piety." (5–9).

5. It follows from the above that the exercise of *Al-Qada* is a vital principle of religion and the administration of justice is a devotional act—a *Fard- Al-Kifayah*-a collective obligation upon every Muslim. Another consequence which flows from this is that Law and Morality become merged. Whatever is immortal is also illegal, because, no law can sanction that which is prohibited by the Holy Quran or is opposed to the practices and precedents of the Holy Prophet (peace be upon him).
6. Justice being also one of the attributes of Allah has to be done in His name and bearing in mind that He is All-Seeing and All-Knowing from Whom nothing is or can be hidden. The administration of justice is, therefore, not based only upon the overt acts but has to search out the innermost motives of man and then determine what will be just in a given case. The principle that the Devil himself knoweth not the mind of man and as such his (latter's) intention is to be deduced from his words and deeds is not acceptable under the Islamic system. Motive is always relevant and has to be ascertained as far as humanly possible.
7. Islamic justice is not also blind justice. The Holy Quran itself commands:

"Allah commands justice, the doing of good and liberality to kith and kin" (16-90). Justice in its comprehensive sense, as Abdullah Yusuf Ali puts it in the notes of his translation of the Holy Quran under the above verse, "may include all the virtues of cold philosophy" but Islam asks "for something warmer and more human". This 'something warmer' is called 'Ehsan or goodness proper. *'Adl'* simpliciter, according to the Islamic concept is the doing of good for good but *'Ehsan'* is the doing of good even where *'Adl'* does not strictly demand it and there is no question of receiving any reciprocal benefit. Justice, according to the command of Allah has, therefore, also to be tampered with mercy and it is on this principle that an otherwise legal claim may be withheld or a legal obligation not imposed upon considerations of hardships or the best interests of the community as a whole.

8. The principle that Allah is the Fountain-Head of Justice being the Supreme Law-Giver and that Sovereignty vests in Him firmly establishes the Principle of Equality before the Law and the equal application of the law. There is no room under this system for bringing in any concept of 'equal but different'. Islam permits no distinction on the basis of race, caste, colour, creed or birth. All Muslims are equal and no-one how high so ever is above the law. No-one enjoys any immunity and no discrimination is possible in the application of the law. Decisions on the basis of *'Qiyas'* or *'Ijtihad'*, do not constitute a departure from this principle. They are merely analogical deductions derived from the law to meet cases which are not directly covered by the law itself, viz., the Quran and the *Sunnah.*
9. The above principle also indicates that under the Islamic system, Law and Equity are not different concepts. Equity does not, as in the Anglo-Saxon system, come in only to fill the lacuna in the law but, as stated in the Turkish *Mejallah-el-Ahkam-i-Adliya.* "Many legal rights allowed by the Canon Law, such as loans, *hawale,* and inter edict are branches from the origin and the indulgences and reliefs shown by jurists in matters of *'Sher'* law are deduced from this rule". There are no separate Courts of Equity in Islam nor do different principles govern the grant of equitable remedies. *Restitutio in integrum* and specific performance were the rule and not an exception. Damages were allowed only where this had become impossible or would cause

hardship for "hardship *(Meshaqqat)* causes the giving of facility" as pointed out in the *Mejella.*

10. So far as criminal justice is concerned the principle adopted under the Islamic system is preventive rather than punitive. The endeavour is to prevent crimes being committed and not only to punish the offender after the commission of the crime, because, the State considered it to be its duty to protect the person and property of its citizens in the real sense. The concept that punishment of a criminal would deter others from committing crimes was not considered sufficient. The State took upon itself the responsibility of creating conditions in which crime would become almost impossible. To discharge this function the Islamic State had set up a special department called the *"Al-Mazalim"*. The jurisdiction of this department was very wide. It could take all actions necessary for restraining persons from committing transgressions or injustices. It could also enforce all moral and religious obligations. Its powers were both correctional and remedial. An officer under this department called the *Muhtasib* or Public Censor enforced the moral obligations and also the *Huquq-ul-ibad;* whatever is due to men. He thus exercised the correctional power and the *Sahibul-Mazalim,* who was the magistrate, exercised the remedial powers of punishment.

11. Under this system torts and crimes came within the same jurisdiction. The State considered it to be its duty not only to see that the culprit is punished but that the victim is also indemnified. Diya-Blood price-could be realized not only from the culprit but also from his kinsmen and tribe like a collective fine. Where the culprit was not traceable the head of the local police— the *Sahibul Ahdas* or the *Kotwal* (under the Mughal Kings) was held responsible for making good the loss to the victim.

12. Justice was always considered to be an essential duty of the State and had therefore to be administered free. No fee could be charged for it. There was thus no question of any court-fee being charged. For the same reason there is no law of limitation in Islamic Jurisprudence. Mere delay cannot be made an excuse for denying justice. Principles of the British Common Law that the law comes to the aid of those who are vigilant and not dormant or that delay defeats equity have no application under the Islamic System of Administration of Justice.

13. If this is the Concept of Islamic Justice then the next question that arises is whether this kind of justice can be achieved under our existing legal system. If not then what kind of legal system should be evolved for its enforcement. Before we take up the consideration of this question we propose to examine briefly the systems under which this concept was enforced in the early Islamic States which functioned under the *Shariah* Laws.

14. The earliest models for us are, of course, the periods under the Holy Prophet (peace be upon him) and the *Khulafa-e-Rashidin* which formed the republican period of Islam and provide us with what is universally regarded by Muslims as the ideal periods during which the system worked in its purest form.

15. In the first Islamic State formed in Medina by the Holy Prophet (peace be upon him) himself under the Charter of Medina, the Holy Prophet (peace be upon him) was the paramount judicial authority for all Muslims and non-Muslims—and was the final court of appeal. The administration of justice was, however, a matter of common concern, in so far, as all were collectively responsible to see that no one dared to harm or encroach upon the rights of others. Everyone, according to the teachings of the Holy Quran, had to act with absolute

fairness, free from any kind of bias or partiality, fear or favour even though it be against one's own interest or the interest of one's parents, kinsmen or tribesmen. The rule of decision so far as Muslims were concerned was the *Shariah* Law.

16. So far as non-Muslims were concerned they were to be governed by their own laws, customs and traditions except that the custom of revenge and counter revenge was totally banned and no interference on the basis of kinship or tribal affinity was permitted, particularly, in the affairs of administration of justice. They had complete freedom of religion and also administered their common law through their own ecclesiastical courts.

17. In disputes between Muslims the Holy Prophet (peace be upon him) administered justice according to the Holy Book but his decisions also became precedents for the future because his interpretation of the Quranic *Ayats* had of necessity to be most accurate for whenever he was in doubt he received revelations giving him the solution of his doubts. Nevertheless he never hesitated to point out that he decided the disputes brought before him upon the evidence adduced and that he was liable to err like any other human being. Such error, however, on his part was unthinkable and it is for this reason that his decisions treated as *"Ahadith"* which along with the Holy Quran form the main sources of the *Shariah* Law.

18. During this period the judicial power was not delegated in Medina to anybody although the savants of Medina consisting of the senior most companions *(Sahabis)* were sometimes consulted. However, when the territories of the State expanded and Provinces were set up this power was also delegated to the Governors of the Provinces. When Muaz-bin-Jabal was appointed

Governor of Yemen he was asked by the Holy Prophet (peace be upon him) as to how he would decide cases. He is reported to have replied that he would judge by the Quran but if no solution can be formed therein he would seek guidance from the precedents of the Holy Prophet (peace be upon him) but if even that did not provide a solution he would set according to his own *'Qiyas'* or independent judgement. Upon this it is reported by both Abu Daud and Tirmidhi that the Holy Prophet (peace be upon him) praised God and said that he agreed with this procedure. *'Qiyas'* did not, however, mean whim or caprice but had to be based on analogical deductions from Quran and *Hadith.* This was really the basis of what later came to be known as *'Ijtihad'* which was resorted to for meeting new situations not covered by Quran and *Sunnah.*

19. The *"Al-Mazalim"* jurisdiction was introduced by the Holy Prophet (peace be upon him) himself. This was a wide jurisdiction for enforcing both *Huquq-ul-lah* and *Huquq-ul-ibad* i.e., the rights of God and of Man. Under this jurisdiction persons doing each other wrong *(Mutazalimun)* could be compelled to do mutual justice and even litigation could be prevented by deterring the refutation of just claims.

20. During this period the procedure was simple but even in this period the rule had been established that the parties must be present personally during the proceedings, that the burden of proof lay on the party asserting a claim and that the party refuting the claim had to deny it on oath. Only upon such denial the party asserting a claim was called upon to adduce evidence in proof of his claim. If there was no denial on oath this was treated as an admission and a decree was passed on this basis. Possession was treated as *prima facie* proof of title to property. Thus where evidence of

both sides claiming a property was equal the decision went in favour of the party in possession.

21. The rules of evidence were also simple but evidence could be either oral or documentary or even circumstantial. The Holy Quran advises that trans actions should be recorded in writing by a scribe in the presence of two witnesses. On the analogy of this normally two male witnesses were considered necessary for proof of any fact unless the Quran required a larger number of witnesses as in the case of *Zina* where at least four witnesses were required. Where there were only female witnesses the number had to be doubled for two females were equal to one male witness. Adulterers or persons who had once given false evidence or had the reputation of being dishonest were incompetent to give evidence. Similarly, the evidence of a close relation or slave was not admissible in favour of the relation or the master as the case may be.

22. The Holy Prophet (peace be upon him) also laid down two important constitutional principles. The first was that everyone was equal before the law and the second was that no-one enjoyed any immunity. Even the Head of the State could be sued both as a private individual also in respect of his public acts. He established this by his own acts and precepts. Thus he once declared that even if his daughter (Fatima) committed theft he would cut off her hand. Again during the course of his last sermon *(Khutba)* at the *Hajjatul Wida* he publicly offered to the community that if he owed anything to anyone or had done any harm to anyone's life, reputation or property he was present there to answer for it. The audience was amazed but one person came forward to demand a few *'dirhams'* which were immediately paid.

23. After the Holy Prophet the *Khulafa-e-Rashidin* followed the same pattern of administration of justice but to

meet new situations *'Ijtihad'* had often to be resorted to even though disputes were few and the people by and large acted with utmost fairness. Under the first Khalifah, Hadrat Umar was appointed the Qadi of Medina but it is reported that not a single case was brought before him for adjudication. Hadrat Umar, however, on assumption of office as Khalifah brought in certain reforms. The reforms were as follows:

(i) Separation of judicial office from other offices of the State;

(ii) Setting up of a department of police called the *'Ahdas'* under a *'Sahibul-Ahdas;'*

(iii) Setting up of jails and the introduction of the punishments of imprisonment and transportation;

(iv) Introduction of the *'Ifta'* jurisdiction under which the judiciary could also consult *'Muftis'* on complicated questions of *'Fiqh'*; and

(v) Constitution of a *'Majlis-e-Shura'* which apart from advising the Khalifah on matters of State also served as a forum for evolving a consensus on questions of law. This became the *'Ijma'* of the *Ummat* and the *'Shura'* a legislative body to that limited extent.

24. As regards the procedures to be followed they can best be gathered from two *'Firmans'* issued by Hadrat Umar himself. One to Qadi Shuraiah the Qadi appointed at Basra and another to Qadi Abu Musa Al-Ashari appointed at Kufa. The first reads as follows:

"If a case is presented which is treated in the Quran then decide accordingly and do not go against the Quranic injunctions and if such a case is presented which is not treated in the Quran, then follow it in the *Hadith* and decide accordingly, but if a case is presented about which there is no provision in the Quran and *Hadith,* then look for its solution in the

'Ijma-ul-Umma, and follow that decision. However, if such a case is presented about which there is no precedent in the Quran and *Hadith,* and not even decided by anyone before you then you may decide according to your own judgement after due care and caution. I approve of such a course."

The Next is as follows

'The Court must observe equality between the parties so that the weaker party may expect justice and the stronger may not expect concession. The burden of proof is on the plaintiff and the defendant may be put on oath, but let this not defeat the ends of justice and law. If you have decided a case, then after due care and thinking you may revise your decision. If you are doubtful in a point which is mentioned in the Quran and *Hadith* then think over it again and again and then apply *'Qiyas'* (a process of deduction). When a party wants to tender evidence then fix a time limit and if he proves his case then decide accordingly. All Muslims are fit to be witnesses except those who have received the prescribed punishment (flogging) for *'Hadd'* (fornication, adultery) and those who have tendered false evidence."

25. To preserve the independence of the Judges, Hadrat Umar prohibited them from doing any trade or business and gave them an allowance which was considered to be sufficient to meet their needs. Hadrat Ali the fourth Khalifah turned this into a salary which was expected to enable them to live in a manner befitting their position and keep them away from temptation.
26. During this period the Khalifah under his supervisory jurisdiction *(Al-Mazalim)* was the final court of appeal and any citizen could complain to him against any authority, executive or judicial. At first these complaints were made on the occasion of the Hajj which was attended by all officials but later they could be made at any time.

27. So far as the law of evidence is concerned Hadrat Umar and Hadrat Ali both clarified that cases were to be decided not merely on the basis of the number of witnesses, but on the basis of truth as the essential principle of Quranic teaching that justice could only be done on the basis of unimpeachable evidence. It is the quality of the evidence and not its quantity that matters. Hadrat Umar also set a new precedent by admitting evidence of an expert in a defamation suit filed by one Zibriqanbin-Badr against a poet Hutaya. Since the defamatory verse was not clear another poet Hassan bin Sabit was examined as an expert and the case decided according to his opinion.

28. During this period there were no separate criminal courts. The same Courts had jurisdiction over both civil and criminal matters but in criminal matters proceedings were initiated by the *Sahibul-Ahdas,* the Officer-in-charge of the Department of Police *(Ahdas).* The procedure followed was also the same. The rules of evidence were also same for both civil and criminal matters but the principle that the benefit of doubt should go to the accused was strictly adhered to from the earliest stages. The presence of *mens rea* or criminal intent was a necessary condition for the infliction of punishment This is deductible from a *Hadith* which is to the effect that "my community is excused for what it commits under duress, in error or as a result of forget fullness". The principle of self-defence was also duly recognized on the basis of verses 42 and 43 *of Surah 'Al-Shura'*

"42. There is no blame on those who defend themselves after they have been wronged;" and

"43. The blame is only on those who wrong men and transgress in the Earth without justification."

29. In the process of administration of criminal justice the

judge was in fact bound to take into account all such circumstances as were likely to affect his criminality, such as his capacity to do the act (infancy or insanity), the nature of the offence, the circumstances in which committed (duress, mistake, defence or even necessity) the previous history of the offender, the character of the offender, his personal details and other relevant circumstances (Al-Mawardi—*Ahkam-at-Sultaniyah,* pp. 344-350). Indeed the rule followed was that "it is better to discharge an accused by mistake rather than to punish by mistake" (A. A. Qadri-Islamic Jurisprudence, p. 290).

30. With the assassination of Hadrat Ali and Imam Hassan, the republican period of Islam came to an end and a hereditary dynasty was set up by Muawiyyah yet the system of administration of justice set up by the *Khulafa-e-Rashidin* survived in more or less the same form even under the Umayyads with minor organizational changes necessitated by the exigencies of a far-flung empire extending from Persia to Egypt. There was a Chief Qadi at Damascus and Qadis for each of the provinces and under them were subordinate Qadis with limited jurisdictions. Those with such limited jurisdiction were restricted either to the duties or to the territories specified in their *Firmans* of appointment but the others had jurisdiction overall things authorized by law.

31. An important change was, however, made in the reign of Khalifah Al- Mamoon. He set up a *Nazir-ul-Muzalim* or Board for the Inspection of Grievances consisting of the Khalifah, the Chief Qadi, the Chief Wazir, one or two Secretaries of State and Muftis or Jurisconsults. This Board had control over the judiciary and could correct all miscarriages of justice. It was thus the final court of Appeal but the Khalifah still remained the court of ultimate appeal if he had not participated in the proceedings of the Board in that particular matter.

32. In this period the judiciary also came to be burdened with certain other executive duties such as the appointment of guardians of infants, administration of *waqf* properties, looking after testamentary dispositions, supervision of law officers like public notaries and some secretaries. The execution of punishments prescribed by law *(hadd)* was also made their responsibility.

33. The Umayyads did not also have separate criminal courts but the Qadis were vested with the *Mazalim* jurisdiction which extended to correcting all wrongs. It is through this jurisdiction that the judges also came to exercise jurisdiction to review executive acts in somewhat the same manner as is now done under the writ jurisdiction. Since the Khalifah invariably presided over the Board of *Mazalim* it could also check cases of injustice committed by members of the royal family and thereby also acquired some influence over the sovereign himself.

34. This was, however, still the formative period of the Islamic system of administration of justice in a vast empire spread over the best part of then known civilized world but the system flowered into perfection in the Abbaside period (749–1258 A.D.). It is during this period that the science of Islamic jurisprudence attained its golden age. It is in this age that traditions *(Hadith)* were methodically collected and verified, commentaries on the Quran were written, the science of the sources of law developed and the four great schools of *Sunni* Law, *Hanafi, Shafii, Maliki* and *Hanabali* came to be established. The administration of justice also came to be conducted upon a definite system.

A department of Justice known as the "*Darul-Adl,* was set-up with "*Qadi-ul-Qazzat*" as its head. Though appointed by the Khalifah he was independent of executive control. The entire judiciary was under his supervision and control. Each city had its own Qadi. Some big cities had also Naib-Qadis or Deputy Qadis. The *ifta* system for consulting specialists in the *Shariah* through *Muftis* or jurisconsults was further developed. Litigants could also obtain their advice free of charge but later *Muftis* were also permitted to charge a fee and still later to appear before Qadis as *Vakils* under the Islamic Law of agency or mandate by submitting a *Tawakkil Nama* or power-of-attorney. The origin of this practice lay in the fact that Muslim States treated it as their responsibility to provide citizens with legal aid so that no-one should suffer due to ignorance of law. As against this the common law principle is that ignorance of law is no excuse.

35. The Board for the Inspection of Grievances now called the *Dewan- ul-Mazalim* was continued but a modification was introduced by providing that in the absence of the Khalifah it would be presided over by a *Rais* or *Sadar* whose position was higher than that of the *Qadi-ul-Qazzat*. The latter as a Member of the *Dewan* came under the *Rais* and thus the judiciary also came under the *Rais*. Apart from the *Rais* and the Chief Qadi the Principal Secretaries of State *(Wazirs)*, some nominated *Muftis* and the *Hajib* or Chief Door-Keeper were also made Members of this *Dewan*. The last named came in as the person responsible for the protection of the Khalifah against the free access of petitioners. Nevertheless the Khalifah under the Persian influence retained the right to receive complaints and hear appeals as an ultimate court for setting right cases of grave miscarriage of justice.

36. The powers of the *Rais* of the *Dewan-ul-Mazalim* were very wide. He was authorized to apply the Principles of Equity *(Isthasan)* to secure the ends of justice. He

supervised and corrected not only miscarriages of justice by Qadis but also corrected cases of injustice and tyranny committed against the people by Governors of Provinces and other executive officers, e.g., injustices in the levy of taxes, claims of illegal reduction or withholding of pay of government servants. Claims for the restoration of property taken by force, the government of *Auqaf* and the suppression of open civil cases which had not been suppressed due to the weakness of *Muhtasibs* also came within the jurisdiction of this *Dewan*. This is wider than the writ jurisdiction as we now know it and the *Dewan-ul-Mazalim* may well be compared with the Star Chamber of the English Court or the Council of State or the Privy Council.

37. The *Muhtasib* or Public Censor was an officer responsible for the enforcement of moral duties and obligations. His duties were concerned with matters relating not only to *Huquq-ul-lah* but also the *Huquq-ul-ibad* and to both. He could act *suo moto* and his jurisdiction was very wide. He enforced not only the observance of religious duties but also all obligations of the public, individual or collective; such as non-payment of debts without any excuse, rights of way, easements, nuisances and even irrigation rights. He exercised disciplinary control over attorneys and *vakils* and saw to it that they were not encouraged tamper to with the administration of justice in any way.

38. It is in this period that separate criminal courts Were also set up under magistrates—at first called *Sahibul Mazalim* but later *Qadi-us-Shurtah*. The *Shurtah* was a department set up for the investigation of crimes and other breaches of law as also their disposition. Such magistrates supplemented the authority of the Qadis and were responsible for securing compliance with the orders and decrees of Qadis more or less like executing courts.

39. The system of court officials developed in this period was that each court had a *'Katib'* who kept the record of the cases and was thus the Registrar and Court Clerk rolled into one. Under him were *"Awans"* or auxiliaries who maintained order within the court and a Door-Keeper called *"Abwab"* who was the Security Officer responsible for the protection of the Qadi. There was also an official translator or interpreter called the *"Muslim"*. In addition there was a *"Khazin-Diwanul-Hakam"*, who maintained the archives of the court, and can be compared with the modern Record-keeper, and an *"Ammat-ul-Hakam"* who looked after the properties of orphans. He can be said to be the official Trustee of the present times. An another important official whose equivalent does not exist now was *'Muzakki'* who investigated the character of the witnesses and kept a record of the persons who were not competent to give evidence such as those who had been convicted with the *'Hadd'* punishment or were persons who had the reputation of having bad moral character.

40. In the *Nazir-ul-Muzalim* or the *Dewan-ul-Mazalim* there used to be attached in addition to the above officials a panel of judges to carry out research and find solutions of difficult questions of law like the law clerks attached to judges of the Supreme Court in USA or research officers in our own Supreme Court. The judges of this ultimate Court had also secretaries to keep the minutes of their proceedings.

41. This system was perfected by 1176 A.D. when Nuruddin Mahmud, a President of the *Nazir-ul-Mazalim* set up a *'Dar-ul-Adl'* a High Court of Judicature and settled the hierarchy of Courts with the High Court and *Nazir-ul-Mazalim* at the apex as courts of final appeal from the Courts of *Qadi-ul-Qazzats* in the Provinces. The latter heard appeals from other Qadis under their jurisdiction.

42. Such was the final pattern of Courts under the Islamic system of administration of justice which remained more or less unchanged under the Ottomans and also the Mughals in India apart from changes in the nomenclature of officials and in the organizational pattern. The Umayyads in Spain also followed this pattern with the addition of a system of *ad hoc* Courts of *Mazalim* to try very high officials. This was the origin of the system of State-Trials.

43. The Ottomans improved the *'Ifta'* jurisdiction and made it a department of State under the *Sheikh-ul-Islam* with *Mufti-e-Azams* in the Provinces. These alone had the power of advising the Khalifah and the Qadis and of issuing *'fatwahs'*. This had become necessary with the change in the concept of sovereignty. The Turkish Sultans claimed the power of supplementing the *Shariah* by royal *'Firmans'* and, therefore, there had to be an institution for advising the Sultan on the legality of the *Firman,* because, even the Sultan could not make a *Firman* which was repugnant to the Quran and *Sunnah.* Under the Ottoman system the *Sheikh-ul-Islam* became a very important person as he had the power to veto legislation and he often exercised this power very effectively.

44. The Muslim rulers of India up to Sher Shah Suri followed the same pattern and we have records of many instances in which the Qadis or the *Muftis* came into clash with the executive. It is on this principle that Qadi Mughisuddin of Jaunpur incurred the wrath of Sultan Allauddin who did not like ecclesiastical interference in matters of law. He (the Qadi) had told the Sultan that he had no right over the *Bait-ul-Mal.* He could only take what was given as pay to a chief officer and in addition such sum as was needed for meeting legitimate State expenses.

45. The procedure followed in these Courts were as follows. In civil matters all litigants, no matter how high or how low were treated in an impartial and strictly equal manner. The case was started by a *Dawa* (plaint). If this made out a *prima facie* case then both sides were summoned on a particular day and the judge listened to the pleadings of the parties. The plaintiff *(Muddai)* addressed the Court first. Then if the defendant *(Muddah Alaih)* denied the claim on oath the plaintiff was called upon to prove his claim. He was considered to be a person who has no right without proof *(Hujjah)*. The trial was conducted in open court and in the presence of the parties. Where defendant was not available a representative had to be appointed for watching his interest according to the *Hanafi* School. The *Shafii* School, however, permits the passing of an *ex-parte* order without the representative. Witnesses are then examined, the evidence is taken down verbatim by the *Katib*. Cross-examination is made both by the opposite party or his *Vakil* and even by the Court. After conclusion of trial a written judgement *(Ilam)* is delivered giving its reasons and a formal decree *(Hukum)* is drawn up so that the same cause is not again litigated upon. Thus the rule of *Res judicata* was also observed. Copy was supplied to the successful party and also to the losing party, if requested. After judgement the losing party could commence a claim in rebuttal (enter a *caveat)*. If this failed or no such claim was filed then the decree was put into execution.

46. The Court was not permitted to reconsider its judgement except by way of a review on the ground that it was not in conformity with the principles of the *Shariah*. The Court could, however, correct accidental or clerical errors. Judgements could also be revised in appeal by superior Courts right up to the Khalifah upon the principle that complete justice should be done.

47. The law also made it compulsory that for the protection of minors, insane persons or those suffering from any other legal incompetence a legal represe-ntative or *guardian-ad-litem* should be appointed if the person did not have a competent natural guardian. Joinder of parties was also permissible for doing complete justice. The Courts had also the jurisdiction to pass interim orders if considered necessary for protecting the interests of the parties *ad-interim.*

48. Arbitration was encouraged. Indeed every judge was required to attempt to bring about an amicable settlement without taking sides. The arbitrator had to possess the same qualifications as a Qadi and was bound by the same code of conduct *(Adab-al-Qadi)* drawn up for judges. An award when made had to be referred to a Qadi. He confirmed it if he agreed with it and put it into execution in the same way as a decree. This is what we now call making the award a rule of the Court.

49. The *Adab-al-Qadi* was an elaborate document laying down in detail the rules of conduct the judges were required to observe so as to abstain from doing anything which might destroy "the majesty of the Court" as the *Mejelle* puts it. He could not be a judge in his own cause or in the cause of his near relatives. He could not accept presents or invitations from litigants or meet only one of the parties or even speak to one of the parties either by sign or language unknown to the others. He had to avoid doing anything which might even cause suspicion of bias or partisanship. *(Mejelle*-318 and *Minhaj-et-Talibin* – 504).

50. On the criminal side the complaint was required to give a precise account of the offence *(Istighasa)* mentioning whether it was premeditated or voluntary or whether there was any accomplice or not. If the complaint did

not make out a *prima facie* case it was dismissed in *limine.* If such a case was made out then the accused was summoned and the trial was continued after administration of oath to accused. The rest of the procedure was the same as in a civil case. The accused was thus a competent witness.

51. Crimes were divided according to punishments into three categories, namely, (1) those involving *'hadd'* punishment, (2) those involving *'Qissas'*, and (3) those involving *'Tazir'*. The Penal Law of Islam had been worked out most comprehensively. It had a dual function. It provided both for the punishment *(Uqubat)* of the wrong-doer as also for remedying the wrong caused by such violation *(Masiyah).* It thus combined with it the law of torts. It is applied and enforced on all criminals irrespective of their being Muslims or non-Muslims. Muslims committing offences outside the limits of an Islamic State are indictable on their return to the Muslim territory on the basis of the extraterritoriality of the *Shariah* Law. *(Minhaj-e-Talibin* – Books : 47 to 56).

52. We don't have not the time at our disposal to go into the details of the *Usul-e-Fiqah* (jurisprudence) regarding the administration of criminal law but since this branch of Islamic Law has been made the target of attack by Western critics, it is necessary to mention here that most of this criticism is based on ignorance of the concepts of Islamic jurisprudence and what is worse ignorance of their own concepts which prevailed even up to the 18th Century. These critics seem to forget that in their own countries thieves were hanged, robbers were hung from a tree on a highway crossing, perjurers were pilloried, witches were burnt alive and adulterers were branded. Even civil trials were conducted on the basis of oracular predictions, omens,

ordeals, compurgation or battle while the Muslims had long before perfected an adversary system of trial on the basis of evidence by fully observing the principles of natural justice in a humane and civilized manner with such perfection that law, morality, equity and mercy all came into play at one and the same time.

53. Thus even in a case involving the imposition of *'hadd'* which are punishments provided by the Quran and *Sunnah,* the principle based on a *Hadith* was that every effort should be made to avoid the imposition of such punishment. The benefit of every doubt went to the accused. So much so that even if a person had confessed his guilt and sentence had been passed yet he retracted from his confession before the execution of the sentence the *'hadd'* punishment could not be imposed upon him. It could only be imposed upon a mentally capable, careful, strong and legally fitted offender. Thus it cannot be imposed on a pregnant woman, a minor or an instance person or when the act is committed under a mistake of law or fact. Hadrat Umar actually suspended the *'hadd'* punishment for *Sarqa* (theft) during a period of scarcity. Emperor Aurangzeb by a Firman of 1672 directed :

> "If a man has committed theft only once either less than or only up to the amount of *Hisab* then chastise *(Tazir)* him. But if he repeats the offence then after *tazir* keep him in prison till he repents. If he is not cured by *Tazir* and imprisonment, but commits theft again, then sentence him to long-term imprisonment or *siysat* and execution and restore the stolen property to the owner, after legal proof of ownership."

54. So far as evidence is concerned in cases liable to be punished by the imposition of the *'hadd'* strict compliance was required with the requirements of legal proof. Thus four eye-witnesses were necessary to prove

Zina and at least two in other cases. The testimony of females was not admissible in cases of *'Hadd'* and *'Qisas'*. In all other cases female testimony was admissible on the basis of two females for each male witness. Again in cases which did not admit of the possibility of male inspection, e.g. virginity or child birth, female evidence was admissible in the same ratio. Imam Shafii, however, holds that even in such cases there must be at least four female witnesses. Sentence could also be passed on voluntary admissions and confessions. Indeed this was quite frequent as the art of falsehood had not developed to the extent it is found to prevail these days. The plea in confession and avoidance was also recognized. Silence was treated as a plea of not guilty provided it was not contumacious. *(Minhaj-et-Talibin – Book* 66).

55. So far as civil cases were concerned even a simple or isolated testimony *(Ahad)* was sufficient if no other witness was available. Admissions were frequent and the rule of estoppel either by admission or conduct was quite elaborate. Direct evidence was the rule but hearsay was admitted to prove death, paternity, family relationships and general character or reputation. The law of presumptions was also known. Thus there was a presumption against indebtedness, against change or rather the continuance of the state of things proved to exist once and a presumption in favour of possession. *(Mejelle* – 3 and 4).

56. In this background can one really say that the system of administration of justice in Islam was radically different from the system with which we are familiar today or that the Islamic system was archaic or outmoded. We submit not. Our thesis before you is that our system is the one that has been copied by the West and that the defects of the Western system arise from the embellishments sought to be imposed thereon,

particularly, by the codes framed for India by the British which were different even from the laws prevailing in their own country. The impact of Islam though not often recognized by European scholars was so great that it revolutionized their thinking in all branches of law. Our concepts trickled into Europe mainly through Spain where European scholars came to study in the Universities of Cordova, Seville and Granada.

57. We venture, therefore, to say that the present court system in this country is not basically different. Only minor adjustments are necessary. This appears to have been accepted by the establishment of the *Shariat* Benches as parts of the High Courts and Supreme Court. Our Courts are also administering *Shariat* Law on the civil side in many matters under various *Shariat* (Application) Acts. These matters include dower, divorce, marriage, inheritance, wills, gifts, legacies, *waqfs* and trusts.

58. In our opinion, the present courts are quite capable of administering the *Shariat* Law if only a few changes are made. The main change required is to find a way for ending the curse of false evidence. The present procedure for the punishment of perjury is so cumbersome and dilatory that courts do not usually resort to it. We would suggest that to put a stop to this the Islamic rule should be adopted and a person who gives false evidence should be declared to be incompetent to give evidence in any other case and a register should be maintained of such witnesses. The Courts before which false evidence is given should also have the power to punish the perjurer and not, as under the present law, only file a complaint. If this is done we shall get rid of stock witnesses and such witnesses as are in Punjab called *'wajtakar'* witnesses. Witnesses should also be administered the oath on the

Quran instead of the present practice of making only a solemn affirmation. The defendant in a civil case and an accused in a criminal case should also be required to take the oath.

59. The office of *Muzakki* should be re-introduced for keeping a record of the witnesses called before Courts and to make local enquiries as to their character and reputation. This will enable judges to make proper appreciation of their evidence.

60. The accused should be made a competent witness and should be allowed to be cross-examined as is the practice even in the United Kingdom. The law of evidence will also be required to be brought in line with the Islamic rules of evidence. With these changes our existing court system will be able to satisfactorily administer *Shariat* Law if the judges make themselves familiar with the *Fiqh* and the *Usul-ul-Fiqh* or Islamic Jurisprudence.

2

Codification of Law

The Jurisprudence

The *Shariah* is not to be understood in any static sense. The great Muslim political thinker, Ibn-e-Khaldun, in the early 14th century, had said of Muslim Kings that they should "act in accordance with the requirements of the Islamic *Shariah*", and therefore their laws were to be "composed of statutes of the *Shariah,* relation of right conduct, regulations which are natural for political association and other necessary things concerning power". These views were endorsed by Ibn-e-Sina and by Ibn-e-Rushd and indicate beyond question that in the views of these great political philosophers, the integrity of the Muslim State is bound up with adherence to the *Shariah.*

The *Shariah* is not to be understood in any limited sense, in fact, its meaning is almost synonymous with the expression *Fiqh* as appears clearly from the following quotations taken from the Preface to the *Majelle.* The *Majelle* is the work of a learned Commission appointed by the Sultan of Turkey in the last quarter of the 19th century to draw up a Civil Code of contemporaneous character. In the Preface, the members of the Commission spoke of His Imperial Majesty having "entrusted to His humble servants the important work, the production from the practical part of the *Shariah (Fiqh)* of the beneficial work so that it shall be sufficient for application to the transactions of people which happen everyday, according to the wants of the time". In submitting their report to the Sultan, the Committee stated that they had collected the opinions of the *Hanafites* and also "cases from the practical part of the *Shariah* about transactions'. They had submitted their work to the Sheikhul Islam and two other persons who had "sufficient knowledge of the matter and were skilled in the science of the practical *Shariah (Fiqh)*", and the suggestions which these learned persons had made have been incorporated in their work.

Today we have statutes covering to a very great extent the field of human relationships and transactions on the secular side, we have not paid enough attention to this aspect of legal development. It may be said that if the legislators, the Courts and the lawyers did not care to examine the question whether the laws which are being made and implemented in Pakistan are or are not consistent with the tenents of Islam, then their negligence would give birth to tendencies which would not be consistent with the dictates of Islamic Law and would be injurious to the full development of Muslim society Pakistan as a just society in the way of Islam. We didn't advocate any upheaval of the present system either of legislation or of the Courts. But simply suggest that there should be injected into the system, through the decisions of the Courts, the spirit and the letter of the principles of the *Shariah.* These are dynamic principles, based upon the dictates of Holy Scripture, drawn in accordance with the correct rules of jurisprudence and adapted to meet the changing requirements of the time, in particular the circumstances of each case coming before the Courts. Under our system, the law declared by the superior Courts has a binding effect on all subordinate courts. Inevitably if the superior Courts, care to make use of Islamic jurisprudence, the law they declare will become incorporate in the judicial system of the country.

Any one of you who desires to look into the *Majelle* will find instances of approach to legal matters significantly different from that to which we are accustomed. As an example, there is a law of pre-emption which is dealt with in the *Majelle*. Under a particular Article a demand for pre-emption has to be made immediately and the action to pre-empt must be brought within a month. The right to pre-empt can be destroyed if the pre-emptor delays in making his formal demand. The comparatively lengthy periods of limitation which we observe form no part of this law. And the very short period provided for bringing a suit is another indication that the intention is that the pre-emption should take any steps to his own detriment that could later be raised as a bar. In other branches of secular law too, there are similar differences of a significant nature, which seem to me to operate to minimise litigation, and in particular the abuse of the legal process.

All human activity can, in my submission, be likened to the function of cultivating a garden. In that garden, those plants and trees are most appropriate and therefore most beautiful which grow naturally out of the soil. The duty is to preserve the good and the useful, allowing them to grow to their full size and height, while at the same time discouraging everything in the nature of weeds and other obnoxious growth. We who serve the law and justice also have our garden and it is a great garden indeed. The present condition could perhaps be described somewhat as follows. Instead of maturing and developing the plants and trees of value which are natural to the soil we are engaged in maintaining a garden which is composed almost exçlusively of plants and trees which are of exotic growth. We labour incessantly to promote the growth of these foreign forms of vegetation. Many of us find our greatest satisfaction in having created this artificial garden and we require the whole population to take the judicial fruit from these foreign plants and trees and to be satisfied with it. Our own natural growth are allowed to become matters of dusty record in foreign countries, to be buried in libraries and. museums, while we diligently and with enormous labour apply ourselves to cultivate and promote the foreign vegetation with which we are seeking to populate our garden.

That is why we fail to produce the finest fruit of which our soil and our labour is capable. The fruit that we produce is a low-level product, compared to that of the gardens where such growth are natural, and it necessarily fails to satisfy the basic sentiments and requirements of our people. Our own plants and trees are relegated to the position of weeds and rough undergrowth in this process. When the master gardeners and their employers were all of foreign origin this was unavoidable. But today we cannot be content with the thought that our laws and our own principles of justice are relegated to a subordinate and indeed an almost irrelevant position, as if they have no place in the garden which we are engaged daily in nourishing. These principles are of the highest validity. The practices of justice based on *Shariah* and *Fiqh* need not give way to any corresponding rules that we found suitable in other countries. Therefore, legislators, Judges and lawyers alike should cultivate this garden with the finest trees and plants which belong to our own history and culture. Then only can the fruit have the true quality which is the basic necessity of the modern society.

Role of Languages

There is need for bringing all the processes of justice into the common languages of the people. That indeed is a part of the argument we have just been presenting, for it would be strange indeed if we were to become convinced that unless we use a foreign language, the propagation of our own laws and beliefs as to justice would not be successful. So far it is difficult to see any sign of departure from the course which we have been following, i.e., working for the development of law through the medium of English language. But as time goes on, it is becoming apparent that the substratum necessary to continue that state of affairs is beginning to fail. Interest in the study of, and more so, the mastery of the English language is steadily declining. It no longer approaches the degree of command necessary for the due appreciation and expression of the finer development of the law. Already judgements are appearing from the subordinate Courts whose faulty English clearly indicates that the entire thinking has been in the writers' language and that he would have been greatly assisted in making his meaning clear if he had allowed himself to use that language. That is an unmistakable sign of a change that is inevitable. It may not come in our time but it is certain to come.

The Conclusion : It is well-known that the whole operation of law is a continuous and endless stream in which all of us are merged. Our thoughts and deeds that have gone into the arguments, the judgements that have been written, have become an integral part of that stream. We ourselves are not originators. We have sat at the feet of learned teachers and seniors who in turn have received instruction at the hands of their elders. The whole body of law is a long record whose principles stretch back to the distant past when human beings first became aware of their duty as moral agents in the way of God. The earliest learned writings in law are based on these scriptures. We have used those writings and reports continuously in our work to maintain the steady flow of that great stream. The opportunities of correction within that stream of law are so numerous that the maintenance of its purity is indeed guaranteed. Although active engagement in the process of justice is not open to a Judge after he retires, he has a great satisfaction in knowing that in his time he has been a part of that living and moving stream and perhaps has been fortunate enough to leave a mark here and there which could serve as landmarks of justice. Though not in the main-stream, he may yet assist from the outside by contributions in writing to the better understanding of the laws. Speaking for ourselves we do not feel that we can ever become a stranger to this stream. We owe and hereby tender our very sincere thanks to my learned colleagues who have sat with me, and to the many lawyers whose labours have assisted in the accomplishment of any work that has passed through our hands.

Development and Growth

Islamic Law or *Shariah* is the Command of Allah revealed to the Prophet Muhammad (PBUH). Islamic Law, irrespective of the variety of its "sources", emanates from God and aims at discovering and formulating His Will. God's Will is not once and for all defined as a static system; rather it comprehends all spheres of man's life and is progressively unfolded'.

The Islamic concept of law is that God Almighty is the Sovereign. Who is Supreme and in Whom vests all controlling and absolute powers. The very opening Chapter of the Quran says: 'Praise be to God' Lord of the Worlds' (1 : 2). His Sovereignty is repeatedly asserted in various verses of the Holy Book. The Command is for none but Gods' (12:40). 'He is the best to Command' (12: 80). His is the Sovereignty of the Heavens and the Earth (57: 5). The concept of Sovereignty in Islam is therefore quite different than the one prevalent in a democracy whereby the sovereignty vests in the people. But in Islam He alone is the Creator and the real Ruler and the worldly affairs are to be run according to His Commandments. 'Verily His is the Creation and His is the Command' (7 : 54); And those who do not make their decisions in accordance with that revealed by God, are (in fact) the unjust' (5:47). This follows that the Divine Laws are perfect and are meant for all humanity and for all ages to come and the balance of justice cannot be maintained without obedience to His Commandments.

Islamic Law finds its chief source in the Will of Allah as revealed to the Prophet Muhammad (PBUH). It contemplates one community of the faithful or *Ummah* though they may be of various tribes, colour, caste or creed. Geographical integration is not an essential ingredient for the emergence as one *Ummah.*

Islam and not nationalism is the all-prevailing Force which binds them together.

According to Sir John Salmond the legal status of the man-made law depends entirely on the assumption that it enjoys the sanction of the tribal chief or head of the clan, or that a Court has enforced it, or that it has the recognition of a government. If it does not enjoy at least one of the foregoing sanctions it loses its legal status. The Islamic Law on the contrary has no such limitations or sanction behind it for its implementation or recognition of a government. It is Divinely Ordained, Universal in character and for the benefit of mankind not only for this world but for the Hereafter. It does not presuppose the existence of a State rather the State is subservient to it. Its superiority, its legal status is least effected if any court or government does not recognize it. But the court or the government itself would stand indicted for disobedience and rebellion.

> 'Whose judgeth not by that which Allah hath revealed; such are evil livers' (5 : 47).

This position is also supported by the terminology adopted by Islam for its law. One of the words used for Islamic Law is *'Kitab'* or 'the Book by which is meant whatsoever Allah hath written for us. Another name given to it is *"Sunnah"* by which is meant whatsoever the Holy Prophet (PBUH) has determined for us. The third is that well-known word *'Shariah'* by which is meant whatsoever Allah hath appointed for us. Likewise some other terms used for Islamic Law illustrate the same truth'.

> There is uniformity and consistency in Islamic Law as its origin does not lie in the traditions, customs and the habits of the clans and tribes. Identical law was revealed by Allah to all the Prophets. The Holy Quran has elucidated the consistency of the Islamic Law in *Sura Shura.* (42: 13)

> 'He had ordained for you that religion which He commanded unto Nuh, and that which We commanded unto Abraham and Moses and Jesus saying: Establish the religion and be not divided therein.'

Generally it is said that the Islamic Law originated with the advent of the Holy Prophet (PBUH). This is not the correct estimation. The Islamic Law took its birth with the arrival of Prophet Adam on earth. All the Messengers who preceded the Prophet Muhammad (PBUH) upheld and preached the same law. The distinction of the Holy Prophet (PBUH) in this context is not that this law originated with him, but that it was brought to perfection with him. The development of this law however kept pace with the advancement of society and its needs. Certain changes were made to meet the growing requirements. Islamic terminology for such change is *'Naskh'* (abrogation) or "amendment". But so far as the fundamental principles or basic values are concerned they have remained the same. The difference was in points of detail and not in essentials. *Shariah* remained the same throughout history from the beginning.

The law given to the Holy Prophet (PBUH) was not revealed in a single instalment. This was communicated piecemeal within a period of 23 years. Thus Islamic Law completed after its necessary amendments, came to be compiled finally before the demise of the Prophet (PBUH), 'It was now rich in all the potentialities which were essential to an ideal *Din* or Faith and was now fully equipped to steer mankind through the changing condition of life'.

> 'The development of Islamic Law has proceeded along defined channels and based on certain principles. It does march forward but in doing so it is invariably well anchored to its fundamental principles and basic values. Its track is identified and its boundaries well-known. There is no possibility of its going astray or its being unfaithful to its historic faith'.

There are four main recognised sources of Islamic Law, namely the Holy Quran, the *Sunnah, Ijma* (Consensus), and *Qiyas* (inference through precedent or analogy). The other sources of law are *Istihsan* or Juristic preference, *Al-Masalih al Mursalah* or unrestricted Interests and *Uraf.*

The period of the Prophet commenced with the beginning of his mission in A.D. 610 and came to an end with his demise in A.D. 632. During this period the Book (The Holy Quran) was the principal source of law. It was revealed by God as a guidance to the right path. The period of revelations extended over a period of 22 years, 1 2 of which were in Mecca before the *Hijra* and the remaining 10 in Medina.

The *Sunnah* is the second source of law after the Holy Quran. It comprises the sayings of the Prophet (PBUH) his deeds and his tacit approval. The Quran and the *Sunnah* are thus the primary sources of law.

The evolution of Islamic Jurisprudence can be divided into the following four periods:

The Period of the Prophet A.D. 610 to 632 : During the period of the Holy Prophet all judicial matters, decisions centered round the personality of the Holy Prophet (PBUH). During this period the foundation of Islamic Jurisprudence was laid on sound footing. Every issue relating to *Aqaid* (beliefs), *Amaal* (conduct or actions) and *Akhlaq* (ethics) was settled in accordance with dictates of Quran and the *Sunnah* and this was termed as *Shariah.*

So long as the Holy Prophet continued his preaching in Mecca, he gave all importance to the Declaration of Oneness of Allah Almighty and eradication of concept of *shirk.* The interpretation of Quranic injunctions started soon after the *Hijra.* The Jurists or *Ulama* during the time of the Holy Prophet (PBUH) were well versed in the Quranic verses and were known as *Qura.* This period was for the development of basic concepts of Islamic society and for the advancement of cause of Islam. The intention of the people was focused on *Jihad* and *Amal* (action). They had no time to give thought to other issues. They had direct guidance from the Prophet (PBUH) for the solution of their day-to-day problems.

The main fountain-heads of the Islamic Jurisprudence in this period were : (i) The Holy Quran, and (ii) The *Sunnah.*

> 'The Quran is the Book which contains the revelations made to the Holy Prophet in his capacity as the Messenger of God. These revelations are in God's own words as communicated from time to time in fragments called *'ayat'* or verses. Many of them laid down rules of law with reference to cases which actually arose. The other sources of law, the *Sunnah* is not only explanatory of text of the Quran but also complementary to it, for the Prophet 'never spoke of his own will unless it was a revelation revealed to him'. (Quran 53, 3 : 4)

The Period of Orthodox Caliphs A.H 11-40 (A. D. 632-661): During the lifetime of the Holy Prophet the Companions of the Prophet felt no difficulty as they had the advantage to seek direct guidance from him. After the demise of the Holy Prophet the Caliphs sought guidance from the texts of the Quran and the *Sunnah* and from their own *Ijtihad.* The Muslims subjugated the territories of Qaiser and Kisra. The peoples of Egypt, Syria, Iran and East Africa subdued before the Muslims. The people with different civilizations, castes and creeds gave birth to a number of new and novel political and socio-economic issues. Naturally a guideline had to be sought from the availability of the laws of the First Period for their application in the new spheres of human conduct. The Companions therefore in extracting the rules of law from the main two sources followed the principles of *Qiyas* (analogy) and *Ijma* (consensus). There was a specific indication in the Holy Book and the *Sunnah* to follow the methodology of the two. The Caliphs and the Jurists therefore extended the scope of these two principles to meet the desirability and the requirement of the time. The very first problem that confronted the Companions was the election of their Caliph. The Holy Prophet had asked Abu Bakr to lead prayers before his death. So the Companions decided to accept him as their leader on the analogy that he who is a leader in religious matters can shoulder the responsibilities to run affairs of the state. This election of Abu Bakr was upheld by the general public and thus attained the status of consensus. Analogy and consensus thus were regarded as the primary or original sources of law. 'It may be mentioned that infallibility of *Ijma* is proved by the saying of the Prophet;

'My followers will not agree upon an error.'

An analogical deduction by a qualified person becomes *Ijma* if it is supported by general agreement and analogy is 'an extension of law from the original text to a particular case by means of common cause or *ila'*.

> 'The period of the Orthodox Caliphs extending over about 30 years was eventful in that there was a revolt against Islamic Faith, which was put down with a heavy hand by Abu Bakr'.

During this period the work of collection of the Holy Quran was completed. Allah has declared that nobody can produce even a single *Surah* like that of the Holy Book.

There are two peculiar characteristics of this period. Firstly, the principles of juristic exercise of the companions *(Ray)* and *Ijma* were followed. This was done because it was the practice of the first two Caliphs Abu Bakr and Umar that whenever a new problem arose, they used to summon the Companions and used to make decisions on their consensus. Secondly, we notice extraordinary juristic capabilities of the second Caliph Umar who made revolutionary decisions confronting him with new victories and domination over new territories. Some of his decisions are as under :

(i) He stopped the share of *Muallafal Qaloob* (those whose hearts were concentrated) whereas this practice was established from the Quranic Nas but Hadrat Umar had his eye not on the *Zahir* of the injunction but on its *ila.* The purpose behind that concession was that it was allowed as a matter of necessity during the early days of Islam with a view to achieve the goodwill of certain sections of people in order to safeguard the Muslims from their *Shar* (ill will). When the Islam was strengthened, the *ila* of this necessity was therefore no more felt.

(ii) Hadrat Umar introduced his *Ijtihad* that suspended the punishment of chopping off the hands of the thieves during the year when the people were dying as a result of famine and instead he awarded punishment by means of *Tazir* because the people indulged in thefts under conditions of *Iztrar.*

(iii) Hadrat Umar allowed a woman to contract a second marriage if the whereabouts of her husband were not known for a period of four years and did not consider it necessary to wait for the news of his death or till the death of the contemporaries of her husband.

(iv) He disbanded the distribution of lands of Iraq and Egypt to the *Mujahidin.* The *Mujahidin* contended that these lands should be distributed to them as a part of enemy property after deduction of *Khamas* but Hadrat Umar declared that these lands were part of *Fai* and *Fai* is that portion of *Baitul-Mal* which is meant for utilization for the welfare of the existing Muslims as well as for their generations to come. And this decision was based on the Quranic text *(Sura Hashar).* So Hadrat Umar allowed the lands to remain intact with their original owners and levied *Kharaj* on them. The result was that the lands remained under cultivation and everyone benefited out of their produce.

The Period of the Umayyads A. H. 41-132 (A.D. 661-750) : This period starts with the rule of Amir Muawiyyah from A.H. 41 to the early period of second century *Hijra.* It was during this period that the political centre was shifted from Medina to Damascus in Syria. The Umayyads were more guided by their mundane considerations than spiritual guidance in the discharge of their functions in all spheres of life with the exception of Umar ibn Abd-al-Aziz who is well-known for his piety and rule strictly in accordance with the Quranic principles and the traditions of the Holy Prophet.

During this period there were two schools of thought amongst the Muslims. One was known as *Hijazi* and the other one as Iraqi. The first group of Scholars had their centre at Medina and of the second at Kufa. The Qadis or Judges enjoyed unrestricted power to decide cases in accordance with their personal opinion *(ray).* This group of Iraqi *Ulama* was called *Ahal-ur-Ray.* It was because there was less publicity of *Ahadith* in Iraq in the beginning and they were confronted with complicated problems and found no clear *Nas* for their solution. The second school of thought had the advantage that they had direct approach of *Aḥadith* at Hijaz and for that reason they did not deem it proper to use their own wisdom or *Ijtihad* in dealing with new matters. This group of *Ulama* was known as *Ahl-e-Hadis.* During this period the Jurists followed the principles of *Qiyas, Istehsan, Istislah,* etc. Some followeres of *Ahl-e-Hadis* group however opposed this practice. No schools of *Fiqh* were in existence during this period. Everybody was at liberty to seek guidance from whichever jurist or Mufti he liked. The *Kharjis* and *Shia* sects also progressed during this period.

Hadrat Umar ibn Abdul Aziz emphasised the necessity of collection of *Ahadith.* He wrote to the people of his country to "search for the *Ahadith* of *Rasool Allah* and collect them as there was apprehension of annihilation of knowledge and the *Ulama*". It was also because a practice to introduce false *Ahadith* also started and false stories and sayings were attributed to the Holy Prophet. Divine law was here subjected to reason which only served to deform and distort it. The Umayyads stood condemned as rulers for their disregard of the fundamental principles of law and in consequence the Abbasids came to power in A.H. 132 (A.D. 750).

The Period of the Abbasids A.H. 132-656 (A.D. 750-1258): The foundation of the fourth period had been laid down in the third period as the regular codification of *Fiqh* was undertaken in this period. The renowned *Imams* and Jurists whose followers spread all around the world are the product of this period. It is in this period that a number of schools of law sprang up, outstanding among them being the four *Sunni* schools, named after Imam Abu Hanifa, Imam Malik ibn Abbas, Imam Shafii and Imam Ahmad ibn Hanbal.

Imam Abu Hanifa

Imam Abu Hanifa was born in Kufa (Iraq) in the year A.H. 80/A.D. 699 and died in A.H. 150/A.D. 767. He was a great *Mujtahid* and possessed remarkable qualities of reasoning. He was the propounder of the theory of *Istihsan.* During his time Jurists were, broadly speaking, divided into two classes. Those of Hijaz or Arabia were called the 'upholders of traditions', and those of Iraq were known as the upholders of private opinion.

Imam Malik

Imam Malik ibn Abbas known as Imam Malik was born in A.H. 95/A.D. 713 at Medina. He was a great Jurist and the highest authority in *Hadith.* He is the founder of *Maliki* school and attached great importance to the customs of Medina on the presumptions and belief that they must have been transmitted from the time of the Prophet.

Imam Shafii

Muhammad ibn Idris al-Shafii, known as Imam Shafii was a pupil of Imam Malik. He was born in Palestine in the year A.H. 150/ AD 767 and died in A.H. 204/ AD 819. He is considered as the chief architect of Islamic Jurisprudence and his theories are noted for 'moderation of views and balance of judgement'. He discouraged the free use of personal opinion and projected the authority of the Prophet as the law-giver after the Quran.

Imam Ahmad Ibn Hambal

He was born in Baghdad in A.H. 164/ AD 780 and died in A.H. 241/ AD 855. His full name is Abu Abdullah Ahmad ibn Hambal. He strictly followed the traditions of the Holy Prophet and allowed a little margin to the doctrines of *Ijma* and *Qiyas*. *Musnad* is his outstanding work which contains more than 40,000 traditions.

After the establishment of the schools of law the period of *Taqlid* (conformity) began. This process was finalised in the fourth century of *Hijra*. *Ijtihad* within the framework of respective schools started and the process of original *Ijtihad* came to a standstill. In the medieval period a large number of commentaries on the works of the authorities or old masters were written and no original work was done. Consequently *Fiqh* became rigid and stagnant for want of original efforts in this field. A large number of problems have cropped up in the wake of advancement of science and technology. These are to be solved in the light of the Holy Quran and *Sunnah*.

The question arises as to who should exercise *Ijtihad?* This question is important because *Ijma* in the early period seems to be so informal that it is difficult to know whether on a certain point there was *Ijma* or not. We are of the opinion that *Ijtihad* should be exercised by the competent scholars in cooperation with the government so that it can be enacted into legislation; otherwise it would remain purely theoretical and the conflict between the scholars and the Government will continue. In fact collective *Ijtihad* is needed on an international basis by a select committee of Muslim Jurists of the whole world. Most of the problems discussed in the classical *Fiqh* are to be reviewed and up-to-dated. Law is meant for society and not *vice versa.* With the change of society necessary changes in the classical *Fiqh* can be made by mutual consultation to keep pace with the times.

Law in Force

Fiqh and Shariah : Here in Muslim society, the duty is to shape the laws in such a way that they become instruments for the manifestation and fulfilment of the will of Almighty, through the lives of the people and the organisation of their State. If that ideal is achieved, the laws would have a natural force to project and sustain them in the same way as its principles are maintained and universally accepted. It will become the delight of the community of Muslims to live according to their laws, and the divine wisdom, as embodied in the laws, will find its delight in providing guidance to the citizens of Muslim countries.

The law in Islam is called *Fiqh;* it is the name given to the whole science of jurisprudence because it implies the exercise of intelligence in deciding a point of law in the absence of a binding command from the Quran or *Sunnah. Fiqh* literally means "intelligence", and *faqih* is a jurist, a person skilled in the law. A *faqih* must possess the quality of independent judgement, *Fiqh* is the soul's cognisance of its rights and obligations. The Turkish Mejelle defines it as the knowledge of practical legal questions.

Fiqh is the knowledge of one's rights and obligations derived from the Quran, or the *Sunnah* of the Prophet, or the consensus of opinion among the learned *(ijma),* or analogical deduction *(Qiyas).* The Quran is the first source of *Fiqh, Sunnah,* the second, *Ijma,* the third *Qiyas* and the fourth source of *Fiqh.*

Fiqh is divided into two portions: The *Usul* and the *Furu.* The *Usul* are the roots of the law and the *Furu* are the branches. The science of *Usul* deals with the first principles of interpretation and the science of *Furu* deals with particular injunctions which really follow from the science of *Usul*. The science of *Usul* deals with the sources of law and its interpretation: while the science of *Furu* deals with the law as it is actually applicable in the courts of justice; for instance the law of *Waqf* or the law of inheritance.

In Islam the law preceded the state, both logically and in terms of time. The State existed for the purposes of enforcing the law.

Islamic law began with the activities of the jurists; it was not created by State legislation. Law was considered superior to the state, and hence not subject to state legislation.

While Islamic law is assumed to be unchanging, the impact of social change is so profound that it affects legal concepts as well as institutions.

The source of Islamic law is the will of God. Islamic law is an ethical or moral system of rules. There has always been a close connection between Islamic law and theology. Islam is a religion of both belief and action. Islamic law derives its source from the Divine Revelation through the Holy Prophet. Being Divine, these sources are believed to be sacred, final, eternal and hence immutable. Nothing can be qualified as good or bad except in relation to Allah's Will.

Islamic law is not amenable to change through legislation. It is a doctrine of commandments. There is much more emphasis on what one ought to do rather than on what one is entitled to claim as a right. Penalties and sanctions in Islamic law are religious and moral, not civil and legal. The term used for penalty is *Hudud* Allah (the limits fixed by God) which implies that a certain offence has been committed against God and that it is His prerogative to impose the penalty.

In a number of situations, some of the new practices may come into conflict with the teachings of Islamic law. In such cases, the jurists may in their *fatwa* make an attempt to reconcile the new practices with the Islamic law.

The Holy Prophet (peace be upon him) had said that moral values are the criterion of the Islamic law. He emphasised that one who lacked truthfulness and honesty is far from abiding the path of law.

The Holy Prophet brought forth the dawn of a new age—the age of realisation of *Shariah* – the age of emancipation from bonds of lawlessness and despotism—the age of a steady advancement towards perfection. He laid due stress on reasoning. He propounded the idea of social justice. It guaranteed for every individual, social and economic security.

History has never known a person other than Hadrat Muhammad (peace be upon him) to have spent his life fighting tyranny and destroying tyrants. The mission of the Holy Prophet was a complete revolution to liberate humanity, a revolution that encompassed all facets of human life and destroyed tyranny.

Islamic law never became divorced from social realities. For lawyers Islamic law consisted of enforceable legal rules; for traditionists it was a code of moral and religious duties. The concept of *"amal"* in Islamic law emerged as an instrument to modify and adapt the *Shariah* to meet the practical needs of society.

There has been no conflict between theory and practice in Islamic law. The reason for the lack of inconsistency and ambiguity is that the *Shariah* and the *Fiqh* are inseparably connected, *Shariah* being the law, and *Fiqh* the science of knowing the law. *Shariah* is, in the proper sense, the law of Islam. *Fiqh* is the science that deduces rules of law from the *Shariah*. Accordingly, *Shariah* is known through the *Fiqh*.

The *Shariah* is the central core of Islam; no understanding of its civilisation, its social history or its political system is possible without a knowledge and appreciation of its legal system. *Shariah* is the totality of Allah's commandments. *Shariah* embraces all human actions. It contains an infallible guide to ethics. It is a code of obligations. It exhibits a tendency to evaluate all affairs of life. All human activity is embraced in its sovereign domain.

Societal Angle

Shariah is the wider circle, it embraces all human actions; *Fiqh* deals with what are commonly understood as legal acts. *Shariah* reminds us always of revelation, that knowledge which we could never have possessed but for the Quran; in *Fiqh,* the power of reasoning is stressed. The path of *Shariah* is laid down by Allah and His Prophet, the edifice *of Fiqh* is erected by human endeavour.

In the *Fiqh,* an action is either legal or illegal. In the *Shariah,* there are various grades of approval or disapproval. *Fiqh* is the term used for the law as a science; and *Shariah,* for the law as the Divinely ordained path of rectitude. The criterion of human action, however, is the same both in the *Shariah* and the *Fiqh.* The criterion is meant for seeking the approval of Allah by conforming to an ideally perfect code.

Shariah is the social code of Islam. It aims at creating a society based on a deep sense of moral responsibility in which every citizen can develop his personality in accordance with his spiritual and moral traits. The main difference between the *Shariah* and the secular law is that the *Shariah* is based on revelation.

The highest religious and juridical office in an Islamic State could be that of *"Qadi-al-Jamaa"*. The historians stress that it was the noblest office in the polity of Islam. The evidence is to be found in the generous salaries, the ceremonial investitures, and the lengthy formal decrees of appointment given to the *Qadis.*

The *Fuqaha* may officially be attached to the courts as *Muftis* (jurisconsults) in Pakistan. They may also play the role of *Mushawirs* (consultants) and *Wuth thaq* (formalaries and notaries). The administration of religious and trust properties may be entrusted to them. Whenever the Government makes a donation for a special purpose, a *Faqih* may be appointed to supervise it. The inspection of trade and commerce may be made the responsibility of the *Fuqaha.* They may be given responsibilities for fixing prices and for the quality and weight of commodities in the market. The *Fuqaha* may be required to supervise the minting of coins. The status of *Fuqaha* may be sustained by their control of intellectual life. The institutions of legal learning may be placed under the administrative control of the *Fuqaha.*

On the level of the *Fuqaha* strictly religious matters including those of exegesis and theology may be referred to *Muftis.* On the level of notaries *(Wuth thaq),* the *Faqih* may be applied to register and validate various kinds of contractors and other types of legal documents. These *Wuth thaq* may be appointed also as *Muftis* and *Mushawirs.*

In matters of procedure the litigants may seek the *fatwa* of the *Muftis* in favour of their claims and may present them in the court. The judge may arrive at conclusions after consulting the notables in his court. The notaries could be given limited jurisdictions such as the attestation of a witness or a contract, yet they could not decide a case.

Great Achievements

The law in Islam is called *Fiqah;* it is the name given to the whole science of jurisprudence because it implies the exercise of intelligence in deciding a point of law in the absence of a binding command from the Quran or *Sunnah. Fiqah* literally means "intelligence", and *faqih* is a jurist, a person skilled in the law. A *faqih* must possess the quality of independent judgement. *Fiqah* is the soul's cognisance of its rights and obligations. The Turkish *Mejelle* defines it as the knowledge of practical legal questions.

Fiqah is the knowledge of one's rights and obligations derived from the Quran, or the *Sunnah* of the Prophet, or the consensus of opinion among the learned *(ijma)*, or analogical deduction *(Qiyas)*. The Quran is the first source of *Fiqah, Sunnah* the second, *Ijma* the third and *Qiyas* the fourth source of *Fiqah*.

Fiqah is divided into two portions : The *Usul* and the *Furu*. The *Usul* are the roots of the law and the *Furu* are the branches. The science of *Usul* deals with the first principles of interpretation and the science of *Furu* deals with particular injunctions which really follow from the science of *Usul*. The science or *Usul* deals with the sources of law and its interpretation, while the science of *Furu* deals with the law as it is actually applicable in the courts of justice; for instance the law of *Waqf* or the law of Inheritance.

In Islam the law preceded the State, both logically and in terms of time. The State existed for the purposes of enforcing the law.

Islamic law began with the activities of the jurists; it was not created by State legislation. Law was considered superior to the State, and hence not subject to State legislation.

The source of Islamic law is the Will of God. Islamic law is an ethical or moral system of rules. There has always been a close connection between Islamic law and theology. Islam is a religion of both belief and action. Islamic law derives its source from the Divine Revelation through the Holy Prophet. Being Divine, these sources are believed to be sacred, final, enternal and hence immutable. Nothing can be qualified as good or bad except in relation to Allah's Will.

Islamic law is not amendable to change through legislation. It is a doctrine of commandments. There is much more emphasis on what one ought to do rather than on what one is entitled to claim as a right. Penalties and sanctions in Islamic law are religious and moral, not civil and legal. The term used for penalty is *hudud* Allah (the limits fixed by God) which implies that a certain offence has been committed against God and that it is His prerogative to impose the penalty.

There has been no conflict between theory and practice in Islamic law. The reason for the lack of inconsistency and ambiguity is that the *Shariah* and the *Fiqah* are inseparably connected, *Shariah* being the law, and *Fiqah* the Science of knowing the law. *Shariah* is, in the proper sense, the law of Islam. *Fiqah* is the science that deduces rules of law from the *Shariah.* Accordingly, *Shariah* is known through the *Fiqah.*

The *Shariah* is the central core of Islam; no understanding of its civilisation, its social history or its political system is possible without a knowledge and appreciation of its legal system. *Shariah* is the totality of Allah's commandments. *Shariah* embraces all human actions. It contains an infallible guide to ethics. It is a code of obligations. It exhibits a tendency to evaluate all affairs of life. All human activity is embraced in its sovereign domain.

Shariah is the wider circle, it embraces all human actions; *Fiqah* deals with what are commonly understood as legal acts. *Shariah* reminds us always of revelation, that knowledge which we could never have possessed but for the Quran; in *Fiqah,* the power of reasoning is stressed. The path of *Shariah* is laid down by Allah and His Prophet (PBUH), the edifice of *Fiqah* is erected by human endeavour.

In the *Fiqah,* an action is either legal or illegal. In the *Shariah,* there are various grades of approval or disapproval. *Fiqah* is the term used for the law as a science; and *Shariah,* for the law as the divinely ordained path of rectitude. The criterion of human action, however, is the same both in the *Shariah* and the *Fiqah.* The criterion is meant for seeking the approval of Allah by conforming to an ideally perfect code.

Shariah is the social code of Islam. It aims at creating a society based on a deep sense of moral responsibility in which every citizen can develop his personality in accordance with his spiritual and moral traits. The main difference between the *Shariah* and the secular law is that the *Shariah* is based on revelation. That is why Islamic law does not accept the idea that whatever people determine on the basis of what appears useful to them, is good. For example, sexual relations based on free-will are allowed by secular law, while they are held to be a sin under the *Shariah*.

Usul-ul-Fiqah are closely related to those of *Shariah*. They have the same relationship to *Shariah* as the *Usul-ud-Din* (the principles of religion) have with *Deen*. *Shariah* is the light of knowledge. The Quran is the totality of *Shariah*, the fountain-head of wisdom. A rule of *Shariah* must essentially conform to the laws of human physical nature. *Shariah* has regularised as legal good what is considered to be good in social experience. The promise is that Allah has instituted the *Shariah* for the benefit of the people. The objective of *Shariah* is to bring *Mukallafin* out of the dictates of their desires so as to make them servants of Allah.

Fiqah is supposed to amplify and supplement the *Shariah* but not to supersede it.

Islamic law is the sum and substance of our faith. The purpose of this law is to bend earthly life to the purposes of God. We would interpret this step as signifying our allegiance not only to the Quran as a pure idea but also to the Quran as implemented. Islam is in essence the purposes of God for mankind as expressed in the Quran. Islam for Muslims is not an abstract idea but a system of law in operative practice.

In Islam, the goal of life is to attain eternal felicity through obeying the commands of Allah. Human reason is charged not so much with discovering unknown areas of facts as with uncovering the insights and the directions implied in divine or

Prophetic announcements. Islam expects of its followers to demonstrate readiness for subordinating emotional to rationally oriented insights.

Islam is the community that has come into being to transfer into actual living the imperative that is the eternal word of God. Before revelation, the essential law of Islam existed as a transcendent pattern. By revelation, the world has been made incorporated in history with the Muslim community as its keeper. The fundamental religious arguments in Islam have been concerned essentially with what shall be the direction in which the ongoing historical enterprise is to proceed.

The nature of man need be understood only in the light and according to the standard of Quranic revelation. The classical *Ummah* lives under divine law whose protector in the *Ummah* itself; the ruler is neither source nor guarantee of the law; his is only the executive power. The state guarantees the preservation and, if possible, the expansion of religion. Islam's real intellectual bond is the conviction that all believers are brothers. Islam does not reject scientific synthesis. It does not reject free interpretation of facts either. The Islamic legal system has developed from philosophical principles.

Three fundamental values are associated with the Islamic way of life. First, Muslims believe that the goal of life is seen to be other worldly. Any worldly achievement remains valuable only inasmuch as it will be subservient to the life after death. Second, Islam perceives man's existence here and hereafter as an indivisible unit. Third, Islam makes the community the guardian of the road to salvation. By introducing these valued judgements, Islam has introduced at least three fundamental questions: How to live correctly? How to think correctly; How to organise correctly?

The Quran encompasses spiritual and worldly matters and provides the possibility of a Muslim society. This society owes its comparative uniformity to the Islamic law. Grand as may seen to us some of the threads which *Fiqah* has woven around this society, a plausible interpretation can be found for it. To quote Allama Iqbal: "In the evolution of such a society even the immutability of socially harmless rules relating to eating and drinking, purity or impurity, has a life value of its own, inasmuch as it tends to give such society a specific inwardness, and further secures that eternal and internal uniformity which counteracts the forces of heterogeneity always, latent in a society of a composite character".

The Islamic law contains what in theory at least must be considered the most potent means of self-adaptation by recognising the consensus of the competent as one of its foundations. This *Ijma* of the local learned is neither postulative nor formative : it is merely verifying.

Theology and law, on the one hand, and the forms of conceptualisation, argument and presentation, on the other provided the most potent means of communicating a sense of cohesion in Islam. Canon law and customary law, canon law and executive law co-exist as an expression of divergent approaches to the social realisation of the ideal Muslim community. The history of the legal rites can to some extent be accounted for through an investigation of their relations to local cultural traditions.

The *Fiqah* covers a large field of human activities in a decisive and methodical way. It shares generously with local customs and discretionary judgement. It includes portions on public law and penal law as well as ethical precepts. The *Fiqah* has been very effective in transmitting the imperatives of Muslim spirituality into the real world.

The development of Islamic law illustrates in a most significant manner the interdependent phenomena of unity and variety in Muslim Civilisation. The essential contribution that Islam made toward the formation of its law emerges from the fundamental attitude that exists in the Quran. It pervades and unites its parts and has made of Islamic law a unique phenomenon suigeneris. Over elements of varied provenance that were retained in Islam, the central core of ideas exerted a strong assimilating power. Permeating them with what is felt to be the true Islamic spirit. This process resulted in the creation of a balance in Islamic law.

The Islamic society created the office of *Mazalim* (Ombudsman) for the redress of abuses. The administrative jurists have held in that the office of *Nazir Fil Mazalim* is of great significance in Islamic law.

The strength of Islamic law is in the extensiveness of approach which at its best is applicable to all situations. It does mean universality. It does imply immediacy in relation to the world of thought and perception which lends so much colour to it. The Islamic law possesses a quality of repose, of dignity and poise, which has developed as a result of the dynamic conception of an ideal society. Islamic law carves good life for Muslims and better life for posterity. It recognizes the supreme value of morality.

The Islamic law is at rest, and the Muslim is at rest within it. His immediacy to Allah and his acceptance of the divine order are not disturbed. A genuine submission to the Will of Allah is rewarded by the consciousness of fitting naturally into the great preordained scheme of things that embraces mankind. The Muslim finds happiness in attuning himself to the wishes of the *Rabbul Alameen.* Allah has revealed to him enough of the truth to understand what needs understanding and to trust divine wisdom where understanding ends.

The Islamic law asserts that man has been created for a purpose. His value is high and his dignity great. His body is temporal but his mind is divine. All wisdom consists in the divine law delivered to human beings. The Muslim stands secure in the centre of a wisely ordained system of law. The law teaches him his duties and his rewards.

Islamic legal system is omnipotent. It has qualities that can keep its identity under changed conditions. It continues to broaden its base within the framework of the Quranic text. It cultivates mental habits that promote legal research and the ability to discuss problems according to the categories of formal logic. It incorporates universal skills. The legal system of Islam maintained its liberal traditions of accepting information, techniques, objects and customs that are supported by logic.

Through emphasis on Quran as the primary bond between people, Islamic law and jurisprudence are capable of maintaining the intellectual unity of the area. A highly educated Muslim jurist is acceptable everywhere in Muslim territory. The dynamism of the Islamic legal institutions are responsible for the presence of component elements which makes Islamic system look like a great civilization. Abounding in its growth during the past fourteen centuries, it has appeared in the 15th Century *Hijra* as a system full of promises for the future. It has mobilized power of organizing the innumerable elements to an organizing idea more comprehensive than the desire for individual liberty.

The Islamic law showed its power in molding the forms and ethics of civic life. It is sympathetic to speculation *(Qiyas)* and it has furnished the Muslim mind with a great deal of imaginative and moralistic subject matter. This feature certainly adds a decisive trait to the cultural profile of Islam.

The originality of Islamic law consists exactly in the capacity of adapting the Quranic inspiration to its needs. Most of its conceptual contribution is either new or unique. Its style of interpretation is without a real precedent. Consequently, to understand the spirit of Islamic law, it is necessary to appraise its effectiveness. This effectiveness can be measured by the extent to which Islamic jurisprudence contributes to the welfare of Muslims.

It is fair to judge Muslim legal achievement by the outstanding accomplishments of Muslim jurists. It is fair because the unusual contribution remains to influence future generations. It is because the Islamic law is fundamentally a stable system of formal and material truths communicated to man.

We are inclined to admire Muslim jurists who broke the limitations imposed on the rational investigation of the universe. They should be accorded due respect for their intellectual boldness. These innovators have established their right to departure from the pre-Islamic system. The habit of *Ijtihad* encouraged the putting forward of opinions which are true and can be proved as facts properly integrated in a system which would assign them their proper significance.

The Islamic legal research continues what might be called an authoritarian tradition. The standards of credibility have been consciously evolved. A significant portion of the work is stimulated by Quranic revelations. The system has accorded recognition to observational and experimental methods of truth finding. To appreciate the Islamic outlook, it must be realized that the art of observation has all along been reasonable and whatever positive knowledge they have contributed is very reliable. The legal constructions are also based on deduction. No amount of logic can impugn them. The lawyers in an Islamic setting had developed precision in the observation and description of symptoms. The system enjoins empirical study. Its experimental spirit has been exceedingly sharp. Its importance as a method of a reorientation of the investigating mind is very considerable. It is necessarily sophisticated. The methods devised for experimental truth finding and some of the problems they are expected to solve are well chosen and soft.

With all the keenness of observation displayed in social studies, it is quite obvious that, on the whole, Muslim scholarship is superior in what is now called jurisprudence. There is infinitely more mental initiative in Muslim jurisprudence than in its obsequious refurbishing of ancient law. One cannot help the impression that the Muslim jurist's mastery of facts was solid and his presentation rational. He was prepared to register the minutest detail when it came to describe legal opinion, and he controlled a superb machinery of concepts and terms to help him organize his results. He can proceed with complete self-assurance: the technique is tested, and his sensitivity to shades of thought is delicately developed. The research acumen of Muslim jurists has always appeared at its best.

To appraise the effect of Islamic civilization on the development of law, three sets of facts must be taken into consideration. Firstly, during the past fourteen centuries Muslim legal scholarship is widely acknowledged. It has never stagnated intellectually. The present state of our knowledge regarding law permits a final judgement on the contribution of Islam to each branch of legal learning. It can be asserted with a fair degree of certainty that, by and large, Muslim jurists have consolidated the conceptual background of the material they took over. They have definitely surpassed their ancient predecessors. Scientific work in the field of law has maintained its vigour, and a great numbers of teachers and students are engaged in its promotion.

Secondly, legal scholarship as transmitter of Quranic thought has been a powerful inspiration for the entire world. And at times the west accepted avidly the concepts offered by the Muslim *Fuqaha.* Leading Muslim jurists are regarded with awe and might in non-Muslim settings.

Thirdly, when Islamic *Fiqah* as it has crystallized through the past fourteen centuries is analyzed for its main components, the extensive effect of its scientific influence is clearly felt. Islamic Civilization, one might say, contributed a good deal of detail, acted as a catalyzer and it did influence the fundamental structure of the legal institutions. There is hardly an area of legal reasoning where Islam has not enriched the universal norms. The concepts of *Ijtihad, Qiyas, Istehsan, Ijma Ibada, Ummah* and many others indicative of the full measure of Islamic contribution would take up many a pages without being even remotely complete.

Mastery of nature, public morality, and the condition of the common man have been suggested as measures of achievement of a civilization. It does not require elaborate demonstration that, by these standards, the Islamic legal system has a definite contribution to make. There has always been a concerted effort in Islam to put *Fiqah* and *Shariah* to such use as would ensure progressive control of the social conditions of life. The Muslim lawyers have paid attention to the problems of poverty. Islamic *Shariah* has encouraged individual charity and religious equality. The finest accomplishments of Islamic *Shariah* have spread to a wide circle. Legal consciousness has grown sufficiently strong to raise the value of human life.

Islamic legal system embodied in the concepts of *Fiqah* and *Shariah* have shown that overflowing abundance of ideas, that boundless fertility that is greatness of the vicegerents of Allah. It manifests itself in exuberant advance to all fields relevant to human life. This system is realistic. The mental effort of the jurists is directed toward ever subtler understanding of the cultural heritage, and toward ever more perfect expression of the familiar. Expansion of the range of control entails the use of proved varieties and procedures. The *Shariah* acts as an authoritative guide to progress. Quranic wisdom is trusted. *Shariah* is the fortress under whose protection Islamic life unfolds itself.

From the viewpoint of what they set out to do, Islamic *Fiqah* and *Shariah* have succeeded in making good their universalistic appeal. They have succeeded in providing the believer with a civilized and dignified form of life. Having been blessed with a divine origin, the achievements of Islamic *Fiqah* are extraordinary, and the great vitality of Islamic civilization emanates from the potentialities of *Shariah* to provide satisfactory answers to the basic questions that have been besetting the humanity on the face of globe.

The Islamic *Fiqah* promotes purpose—directedness of human existence. The *Shariah* pervades every sphere of man's activity, the technological or the economic as well as the political or the interpretative. Man is encouraged to strive for ends that have an objectively valid Orientation. No insight is considered scientific unless it is part of a context and unless this context is structured in accordance with a rational principle. The *Shariah* caters to the needs of the inner and the outer world. It promotes cultural self-understanding which is pragmatic and directly purposive. The Muslim *Faqih* would always determine the rank of his subject within the hierarchy of values by its relatedness to divinity.

The Muslim *Faqih* is aware of the need for mutual respect and for self-respect in matters cultural. The Quran projects the "exceptional value of man" as the most noble creature. The Quranic revelation tends to render man more truly human and encourages him to use the forces of the physical universe as instruments of self-liberation. Islamic humanism is based on the notion that man is destined for a transcendent life of eternal felicity whose attainment presupposes an earthly existence lived in communion with Allah.

Islamic society emphasizes legal continuity. There is a strong correlation between Islamic law and ethics, between law and society, between law and political structure. The cultural achievements develop either from definite legal situations or they may be viewed as responces to them. The very survival of Islam as an organized community under Allah depends on the existence of an adequate body of *Fuqaha* and *Ulama*. Also, integration in that community is indispensable if the individual believer desires to lead the correct life as enjoined by Quran and defined by the *Ijma*.

The science of law is an endeavour to collect and systematise what information the *Ummah* requires to realize its values. It is an effort to widen man's insight into the ways of Allah. Its ethical value depends on the area to which the law relates and on the intention *(Niyya)* of the *Faqih* who attends to it. To be fully relevant, therefore, the science of law must inquire into the data of revelation and of the *Sunna;* and it must adjust the believer systematically to this world. The law provides the hard core of the intellectual life by whose requirements the nature of legal scholarship and of the nature and function of the scholar are formed. The *Ummah* cannot continue without cultivating legal scholarship because it has its roots in fundamental needs. The science of law is directed to re-organizing, adjusting and to the initiation of exploration.

The methods of legal doctrinal utilization in Islam showed a tendency to cover the vital areas of learning as well. The *Faqih* is ever aware of the service of Allah. He demonstrates an element of civic virtue. The legal scholar sustains the framework in which the correct life can be lived. It is left to the canon lawyers *(Fuqaha)* to see to it that the government does not deviate too far from the essential demands of the *Ummah.*

The problem of the relation between co-existing lawyers of law is culturally identified with a civilization of universal "out-reach". This civilization is characteristically associated with legal aspiraions. It is largely developed from Quranic message claiming universal validity. The realization of this rationality presupposes the existence of a Muslim identification. Its resolution is attempted within the framework of universal culture.

The legal culture in Islam does not exhibit any conflict. It does not reflect any contradiction between the social forms of existence and the social forms prescribed by Quranic revelation. The *Fiqah* in Islam promotes the universal Islamic culture with which it is intimately affiliated.

A series of objective criteria borrowed from Islamic *Fiqah* can be discovered to form a leading civilization. It provides analytically obtained evidence. It is based on factual knowledge of concrete beliefs and mores. The *Faqih* demonstrates an adequate comprehension of the Islamic way of life. This phenomenon has facilitated the transcultural effectiveness of the Muslim mission. It permits the cultural patterns of Muslim life to exist in different parts of the world. These cultural patterns are sufficiently in tune with the ideal represented by the Quran and the *Sunna.* This factor is responsible for strong cohesiveness of the Muslim community.

The Islamic *Fiqah* devises methods of reaching solutions to practical problems. This gives the community a sense of structural permanence.

The Islamic *Fiqah* and *Shariah* speak of the equality with which Allah causes tolerance, freedom and love to prevail. They promote the devotion of Muslims to the essence of truth, virtue and beauty. They provide a rational guide to humanity. They keep the Muslims away from self-seeking *(Ananiyiya)* and lead them to service *(Ubudiyya).* They put every individual in human society in his proper place. They give hope to man and have developed the mood of humanity into active optimism.

The Islamic *Fiqah* steeps itself in the sciences to gain mastery of technology and commerce, and also of defence. Thus the Islamic *Fiqah* has established a tendency to integrate without a break in basic structure the social reformer and his contribution which is perhaps an important pre-requisite of an extended developmental continuity without loss of cultural identity. In this fundamental legal attitude there lie infinite possibilities of advancement of Muslim society.

3

Principles of Law

Significant Features

The Supreme Fundamental Islamic Principles are related both to matters of Faith and Law and, in conjunction with Islamic ideas, retain the distinction of immutability. The encompassment of the characteristic vision of an Islamic society is an attribute of these fundamentals. To view these as universal "process ideals" in law, so that, statutes ought to be interpreted in accordance with their purposes and meanings, is appropriate. The capacity of transforming the law into an activity, rather than allowing it to remain an entity, is thus apparent. Implicit in human responsibility for the acts is the capability for compliance, which is inclusive of the rational aspects of the law. These considerations together necessitate the law to be based upon an explicit "ila" which is extendable upon legal situations.

The immutability of the Supreme Principles remaining established, the demand for legal change is accommodated by the "process method" of "Ijtihad"; the legal features of the Supreme Principles provide its basis and direction, and establish the limits of legal change in conjunction with the relevant law. This, more than any other approach deserves to be designated as the foundation of an Islamic legal system, an assertion whose elucidation is provided in the subsequent portions of this discourse. Recognition is due to the fact of principles and rules being of a conceptually different order; the differentiation being that the former is not entitled to any exception.

The Supreme Principles are concerned with the interpretation and application of law, and are proximately related to the process of "law-making." In an Islamic social ethos, the conduction of administration in society and the governmental decision-making are spheres of national life, which also come within the scope of the functions of Supreme Principles, a measure that mitigates the cause for the establishment of administrative courts. Ascertainment of *legal validity the* recognition of law as a part of the Islamic legal system-is their juristic attribute.

The act of *legal adjustment,* whereby the legal harmonization of law with the remaining laws is attained to establish uniformity in the legal system, is another legal characteristic. Eradication of stationary quality of law, to introduce legal "mobility" through "finding" laws, is the additional feature of *legal supplementation.* All these desirable legal characteristics are maintainable due to the condensation of seminal concepts as inexhaustible source of legal values and ideas which are available in the Supreme Principles. On the analogy of seed harbouring a dormant potential, these concepts can find expression as a stupendous "tree" in the form of legal development, with the application of the Principles according to the Legal Method described in this discourse. Without the support of the legal attributes ascribable to the Supreme Principles, the law functions as a part of simple process, without imparting full legal expression to law, for a similar form of social order, which are not in conformity with the Islamic socio-legal objectives. Because, lacking this Legal Method, the general policy of Islamic Law remains unpromulgated.

Essentially, the basis of law and, hence, of society is established by the Supreme Principles, as the laws of the political constitution are themselves derived from their universal explanations. The primary purpose of the principles is to provide Islamic conceptual frame-work for the remainder law, inclusive of the formulation of the legal rules. To visualize these as the evolutionary elements in the Islamic Law which otherwise retains a dormant tendency of development, and the "character keel" of the legal system, to describe in the Platonic phrase, is the proper assessment. In the words of Shah Wali Ullah, originally meant to describe a related subject, within the confines of these "all-embracing principles" resides the solution to universal law. The terms of revealed guidelines and the exact scope of Divine "legislative will" for the law are contained in the Supreme Principles. The universal process-ideals, comprising these principles, underscore the necessity for the development of Islamic Law from the original sources, according to the Legal Method.

Procedure of Judiciary

The Quran : The juristic provisions in the primary source of Islamic Law are not exhaustively stipulated, and the grounds for the law in the various legal schools, and ever since, have come to lie in the explicit provisions of the Quran. The cessation of revelation, in combination with the preceding factors, necessitates the availability of principles within the framework of a legal methodology for the development of law. Due to these reasons, the possibilities of interpreting the sources of law in Islam gradually diminished. Therefore, search for the intensive general principles from the Quran, which encompass the particular laws, is imperative. For the maintenance of the universality of those principles, their preeminent meanings should not permit to be regarded as general in a secondary sense. A properly conceived formulation, resulting in the inclusion of such principles in a legal method, with the jurisprudential attributes for the demonstrable eradication of the aforenoted legal shortcomings in Islamic Law and to make it evolve into a comparable legal system, is justifiable.

The Shariah : The doctrine of the unity of Shariah law signifies the legal conformity in the interrelationship between rules. The existence of contradiction in law has the implication of the imposition of an impossible obligation. Accordingly, Shatibi also believed in the non-existence of disagreement in Shariah law. The Muslim legal theorists recommended the replacement of contradiction in the Shariah law by the supersedence of the superior statement over an earlier edict, with the inference of non-permissibility of "disagreement" in the law. On the contrary, the application of this concept upon Islamic Law means the unity of its intent, a subject whose import should not be unheeded. The prescribed Legal Method, incorporating the Supreme Principles, is operative according to present-day juristic idea of non-contradiction among the norms of law and, therefore, exercises a unifying influence upon the law's intent. This approach places reliance upon the doctrine of "pre-established harmony," to preserve the legal unity of the system. In this respect, a similarity exists between law and empirical sciences, where the issue of the compatibility of a particular law with the hitherto accepted facts in a system recurringly arises.

As a matter of fact, with the concomitant existence of Supreme Principles and the explicit rules in the Shariah law, the law remains heterogeneous unless a formulation for defining an interrelationship between the two becomes a part of Islamic jurisprudence. Realization is due to the fact that the Supreme Principles existed antecedently to, in actuality or in legal effect, and independently of, the other enactments of legal importance in Shariah law. As can be seen, the method for the development of the Islamic legal system establishes a relationship between revealed doctrine and practice of Shariah law. Lacking this approach, aspirations of an ascendant legal system will prove elusive; and the Shariah may remain in quest of itself. The fact is of far-reaching significance that the contemplation of Shariah in divergence from its implementation is in contravention of the jurisprudential dictates. Additionally, not to ignore the legal truism will be rewarding that the application of law is conducive to its own future creation.

Islamic Law **:** The Islamic concept of law as a derived code of ordained law for obligatory behaviour, founded upon the Supreme Fundamental Islamic Principles, which, within these limits, encompasses the aspect of legal change, is adoptable without any conflict in meaning with another realistic definition. The complexities due to evolved social situation, which require adaptive legal response, are the essential substitute in Islamic legal order for the social change, often alluded in literature in the context of law. In the opinion of Coulson, the traditional Islamic jurisprudence has relegated its provisions to the category of moral injunctions, in particular, concerning the status of women.

The distinction between legal and moral norms, and the concept of law intimately associated with sanctions, are relevant considerations in this respect. For the adoption of the revealed moral injunctions as a source of relevant law-making, and not the law *per se,* is a legal objective for the future, and it will foster a creative unity of purpose in society. As a matter of belief, as a requirement of wisdom and as a demand of legal system, Islamic Law is intended to be complete. With the understanding of Islamic legal history, a legal formulation such as would result in the uncurtailing of the formative potential in Muslim jurisprudence, in reversal of the self-inimical approach in law due to imitation or "taqlid" and due to the disuse of the juristic principle of "Ijtihad," is indicated. As an extension of the scope of Ijtihad, the individualization and concretization of law will produce enhanced instances of legal relationships and cause a reduction of the arbitrariness in law. In addition to the fulfillment of the requirements of the rule of law, this approach as a legal process imparts law the eminently wise character, an attribute which is impressively emphasized in the Quran." Within the meanings of the wisdom of law is the issue of the legal statutes that may produce results other than intended by the legislation, which evokes the subtle but functional distinction between the fact and the effect of law. For instance, the Islamic Law of inheritance of property could not have been conceived to create the issue of the status of women in society. Hence, in relation to Islamic Law, the preservation of the intent of the Law-giver remains a vital concern.

Pertinence of these evaluations is augmented by Plowden's analogy of the letter of the law as the body, and the sense and reason of the law as the soul. Desirable becomes the function of a legal method that satisfies the demand for the sense and reason of law. The observation by Mill, that political institutions are the product of deliberate efforts by men, finds a relevant application on other allied social systems as well. The same lesson is implicit in the traditional Islamic Law, which lost its institutionalized usefulness due to inadequacies in Islamic legal philosophy and legal methodology long after the Islamic schools of law came into existence. Any juristic formulation, embodying the measures based upon the same lesson, will be of benefit in the development of Islamic legal system, suited to an ascendant social order.

According to Fuller's theory, concept of law is comprised of certain implicit principles which constitute morality, and the law is lacking to the extent these principles are violated. Notwithstanding the issue of the place of morality in legal positivism, however, the preceding assertion finds relevant application upon the Supreme Fundamental Islamic Principles, with the differentiation of religio-legal for moral principles. Any legal formulation that addresses itself to the implementation of Supreme Principles, evidently brings to completion the higher functions of Islamic Law. The legal capacity to fulfill this and other aforementioned requirements of jurisprudence, delineated in this section, is available in the Legal Method explained during this discourse.

Islamic Values : The theory of Islamic value draws a distinction between instrumental and intrinsic values in relation to their role as means and ends, respectively. Perry explored eight realms of values, including religion and law. The subject of intrinsic value evoked varied responses, including pleasure from hedonists, harmonious self-realization from humanists and love of God from the Christians. On the other hand, Pluralists, and Perry among thcse, believe in the multiplicity of intrinsic values-any number of intrinsically valuable things. The correlation between desire and value identifies one or the other as of primary significance.

The idea of the independent mode of manifestation of the value, which is contained within a norm, is of interest. Adam Smith's classification of values in use and in exchange, an observation which is sometimes referred to as the "paradox of value," has remained the subject of explanation by the theories of value. Generally, the term value is applied to all those objects deemed to be worthy of human pursuits on various grounds. From a pragmatic standpoint, any ideal be it religious, legal or political, which has the purport of existing, prevailing or recommending itself to others, of necessity, upholds the objectivity of value judgments.

The formulated Legal Method is an approach by which legal system will give effect to the particular scale of values that ought to obtain in the Muslim society. In accordance with it, the judicial process becomes the instrument for giving scope to the development of and adherence to built-in values, and for removing the threat to those essential values such as may arise due to the administration of legal rules, within the framework of law. In this connection, it is often ignored and frequently forgotten that the application of laws also gives rise to values. All norms, legal or moral, can be viewed as a more or less imperfect reflection of some values, and a legal method for the improvement of their value-content, in effect, has its own desirability in an Islamic society.

A consummate value as a measure of all other values in terms of implementation is the "best community" for the Islamic legal system. Assuming a value system to have a somewhat hierarchical pattern and, while maintaining an ultimate value, which in Islam is identified as success or "falah" in a transcendent sense, it should be sufficiently composite of values for the attainment of diverse objectives. Enhanced possibility for the same is dependent upon the substantive nature of the included values, which can serve as the source of multiple derivative values. These substantive or superordinate values are inherently prior to all other values, and possess the attribute of stability in the sense of specificity of interpretation.

Such values are describable as preeminent Islamic conceptions of social reality. The classification of derivative values offers a further categorization into ordinate values, offering a certain desirable flexibility of interpretation, and subordinate values, allowing generous latitude of interpretation. The subordinate values are available for pursuance in case the other category of values prevails. With the correlation of norms and values already identified, the Supreme Fundamental Principles are recognizable as superordinate values, and the constitutional and statutory norms are describable as the derivative values-ordinate and subordinate, respectively, in the general sense.

The preceding discourse delineates the rationale for the Supreme Principles which, on the biological analogy of genetic system, retain the immanent potential of providing change through new mutants and, simultaneously, are the principal means of maintaining evolution control. Insofar as the inherent power of these Supreme Principles to influence the social order is concerned, the archetype of the Fundamental Principle of

"Tauhid" is citable. The derivative or ordinate value of fidelity to principles vis-a-vis personalities is an "instrumental value" as a necessary condition for creating a preeminent value of "Nomocracy," that is, government by laws! As an irony of history, the significance and practical realization of this particular value into meticulous socio-political expression has eluded the Muslim Civilization, and the type and development of constitutional law in Islam is citable in evidence, wherein the law was not distinctly preponderant to the interests of statecraft.

Rule of Law : In derivation of the injunction with the message for the observation of the revealed law, as an epitome of the Scriptural text, in conjunction with the fact of law and moral tenets in the original source of Islamic law being inseparable, immoral law is excluded from the observation of law. This requirement is a provision of the Islamic rule of law. With this in view, the Supreme Fundamental Principles, which are religio-ethical ideals, are to be transformed into operative legal ideals, and the Legal Method herein described is a most suitable approach for this purpose.

Due to the fundamental nature of these principles, as these underlie the purpose and provisions of revealed law in all their different aspects and developments, their legal influence should be traceable throughout the constitutional and statutory law in its application. As a further requirement of the Islamic rule of law, Divine intention in relation to the revealed law, embodied in the Supreme Principles, is not to undergo infringement or contravention during the future enactments. This is necessitated because the divine law, being an outline for guidance, is in requirement of the supplementation of law. Additional distinguishing legal features pertaining to Islamic rule of law have been enumerated at an earlier juncture, and those provide a persuasive part of the rationale for adoption of the Legal Method which is founded upon the application of Supreme Fundamental Islamic Principles.

Legal Validity of the Supreme Principles : Adoption of the definition of the validity of law as a rule court ought to apply, removes the difficulties in the way of its discussion. However, for the legal rule to be lawfully part of the law, that is, according to the legal norms or constitutionally in conformity with an established criteria, is an essential aspect of this consideration. The rule of recognition described by Hart is typically composed of a number of criteria which aid in the recognition of the validity of other rules. The validity of this rule itself, however, is beyond reproach, so that, there is no question of its conformity with higher order rules. From among the criteria specified to assess the validity of other rules, one criterion is supreme, and the rules identified by reference to it are rules even if in conflict with other criteria, while its exact opposite is not true.

The rule of recognition is not an extra-legal juristic hypothesis, but rather a rule of positive law. And the conformity with the rule of recognition is a sufficient but not a necessary condition for the existence of a valid law. In comparison, the Supreme Principles as a vital component of the Legal Method conform the rules of adjudication to the requirements of Islamic legal validity. The Supreme Principles are neither an extra-legal juristic hypothesis, nor a set of rules of positive law by any means. Conformity with these principles is both a sufficient and necessary condition for the validity of law. The very title of the principles settles the issue of their own legal validity. Nonetheless, moral validity of the principles resides in the rational justification, comprising the advantages in reference to the legal conceptions that accrue in conforming with, the drawbacks on similar grounds that ensue from the contravention of, and the innate legal merit that is characteristic of, the principles. And no legislative revision in the criteria of validness for the Supreme Principles is anytime obtainable, for the constitution and the political authority are reliant upon the principles. These distinguishing jurisprudential features of the Supreme Principles are understandable, as the Islamic Law, due to the ideological necessities, maintains a unity with religion. This fact itself affords the delineation of universal religious principles underlying all the legal rules.

In some systems, the ultimate criterion of legal validity explicitly incorporates the principle of justice, or substantive moral values. The Legal Method, due to its foundation upon the Supreme Principles, establishes a scrupulous conformity with absolute higher morality, including justice, in the criteria of legal validity. The Legal Method based upon Supreme Principles of absolute higher morality is verifiably then of universal validity, hence, the desirability for validation of man-made law according to this method is persuasive. The legal validity through this way acquires the meanings of the "ought," or the appropriate nature, of law. The subject is proximately allied to the consideration of a single law to cover all categories of theft, as an instance, in contrast with individualization of justice. In this legal context, the Legal Method appears a superior mode of justice in relation to legal validity of the relevant law. In this respect, realization is due that legal positivists usually adopt a relativist approach to moral values. The prospects of the Supreme Principles as a higher law with the universal application, therefore, are entertainable.

The eminent Muslim jurist, Shafii, maintained that in all matters which touch the life of a Muslim, there is either a binding decision or an indication as to the right answer. Correlation of this observation with matters pertaining to law indicates the desirability of distinguishing one situation from the other, and the criteria available is the Legal Method with Supreme Principles. This approach averts the self-imposition of limitations or subjectivity in Islamic Law. As a result, a binding decision will not undergo alteration to any extent. The underlying juristic measure is definable in terms of "*authentic interpretation,*" to mean construction of one revealed text by another. Importantly, the Supreme Principles do not deprive the interpreted text of all its legal effects in any case, for the former is not a repealing law, a function which will be contrary to the meaning and purpose of interpretation. It lends full credence to the proposition that interpretation is the discovery of the intention of the lawgiver with respect to the operation of a text in the significant sense. The realization, that the manner of interpretation of law and the character of legal change are indispensable, is a juridical maxim whereupon reliance has been reposed in the Legal Method. This method of interpretation is then also applicable to other than Islamic revealed texts on their acceptance as a supplementary source of Shariah law. The legal meanings and religious significance of this observation have proven elusive during the whole course of Islamic history, and the consummation of Islam as an essentially universal religion is contingent upon its fine intellectual apprehension.

Law-Making : For an Islamic legal system suited to an ascendant social order, reinterpretation of the law from its original sources is to be effected; a view which was also supported by Abdu and Iqbal, among others. With this proposition in view, and the realization that the legal system will be a product of sustained, purposive effort, then it is a matter of inference that, in essence, the Islamic legal system is to be established. For this objective of "law-making," the Islamic legal history spanning the initial two centuries, till the advent of the law schools, is available as a source of emulation. The sound approach, based upon the principle of revealed ordinance and juristic appraisal, produced the legal contents to result in the partial codification of the schools of law.

In describing ways of failure to make law, Fuller mentioned the enactment of contradictory rules and failure to achieve rules, among several other causes. The same author mentioned that a total failure in anyone of these directions does not simply result in a bad system of law, but it results in something that is not properly called a legal system. In this perspective, the laying of emphasis upon the necessity for the establishment of authoritative law-making procedures in a society is due. Some of the other notable suggestions for law-making included the envisioning of law as essentially a dynamic affair, elimination of the reductionist impulse and the need for the recognition of conceptual issues in law. The deficiencies in the credible interpretation and proper implementation of law are the recognizable causes of the inadequate lawmaking. Insofar as the last cause is concerned, the motivation to bring it about is noticeworthy Inability to maintain minimal conditions of literacy which are required for compliance of law, and to enhance the respect for law in society are the additional factors in relation to the defects in law-making.

A jurisprudential reconstruction of the legal system is the solution to overcome the aforementioned hindrances in law-making. The logical positivists set for themselves the task of rational reconstruction, and the principal interest was situated in natural sciences and mathematics. On the other hand, Kelsen applied the notion of rational reconstruction in the sphere of law. The idea of reconstruction, however, had its origin in antiquity with Euclid's development of geometry with the method of rational reconstruction. Afterwards, the most noticeworthy instance of reconstruction is the Principia Mathematica of Russell and Whitehead, preceding the logical positivist attempt at it. According to Euclid's rational reconstruction, the corpus of geometrical knowledge acquired a systematic order, relevant terms were defined with precision, and with the use of less than a dozen axioms and postulates, whose verity was beyond doubt, the truth of a multitude of complex theorems was ascertained.

With the Islamic legal history as a guide, the jurisprudential reconstruction should entail a judicial process, with emphasis upon the meaningful in law, for the jurist's law bears academic connotation. The method envisaging the adjunction of Supreme Principles, such as are an assumption in every single legal instance, for the individualization of law, engenders the transition form a law in quest of itself to a legal system for an ascendant social order. For without this adjunction, no legal norm, that prescribes sanction, can lay claim to be an Islamic legal norm due to the requirements of Islamic rule of law and lacking the legal validity of the full expression of Islamic Law. The paraphrasing of this methodological approach in the language of rational reconstruction will be the securing of guarantee about the inevident truth of the rule by deriving it from a set of fundamental principles with transcendent truth. A systematic reformulation of law with the instrumentality of Supreme Principles as the terms of Islamic legal reconstruction, and with the contribution of the juristic responsibility, are the conceptual features of the Legal Method. This approach is accommodative of the legal implications of the maxim that law cannot be laid down a priori, nor can it reside exclusively in the rules of enacted law. This reconstruction of law, while it avoids the shortcomings of the mechanical application of law; a barren jurisprudence can be described as the result-however, it retains the advantages of perpetual creativeness in law.

The reductionist concept of legal rule, as an instrument for the settlement of specific legal disputes, is often upheld in societies with adopted systems of law. However, as a part of the function of law, and as policy-directing aspect of law, the rule is a means to the organization of society in its original social milieu. In this perspective, the attributes of a rule underscore the significance of the methodological application of the Supreme Principles in an Islamic social organization. The conceptual justification of this approach furnishes a characteristic definition of the Islamic legal rule: As a part of the function of Islamic Law, inclusive of the dispensation of justice with equity, the legal rule is a means for the propagation of such values as are facilitative of the individual success (falah) in a social organization, with the objective of producing an Islamic society that is recognizable for its paradigmatic attributes, on consideration from internal and external viewpoints. The basic function of the legal rule as a means of adjudication according to Islamic injunctions in a litigational instance is recognized, and the rule thus is an extension or reflection of Islamic values. For the fulfillment of these functions of rule, a conjunction of the "general" and "particular" provisions of law in a judicial process is necessitated.

The Legal Method, based upon the use of Supreme Principles in the prescribed process, satisfies the aspirations for Islamic resurgence, a demand whose expression is a constitutional requirement for conforming the Law to the injunctions of Islam. Thus, Shariah law will remain no longer in quest for itself, and the jurists, inspired by the authority of a prospective major legal system, to be established with their own striving and ability, will make their universal contribution towards the ascendant cause. With these resources of legal development, the law will endure; and with the built-in capacity for Islamic reconstruction, the legal edifice will prove durable to outlast and to overcome the challenges of time.

Mandatory Application: The Supreme Fundamental Islamic Principles are of a compound nature so that their transformation in the form of conventional law is not easily codifiable. The legal characteristic of the recalcitrance demonstrated in the comprehensive framing of statutory law is not a unique attribute identifiable with the Supreme Principles, for the same legal trait is not uncommon with the basic constitutional elements, in general. The identity with the constitutional elements ends in the instance of the Supreme Principles on consideration of their religious origin which lays demand upon the obligatory legal application of the principles. Additionally, the social ramifications of those principles are of such a universal scope as to require each legal instance to acquire the benefit of assessment in accordance with their Islamic meanings and legal demands. These dual requirements are fulfilled by the application of the method in the form of the modified extension of Islamic injunctions upon the individual legal situation, so that, the dispensation of law is effected according to the distinct legal implications of the Supreme Principles for the full expression of Islamic Law, and the formulation of secondary rules for utilization in future. The mandatory nature of the Supreme Principles from the religio-ethical standpoint then alone is directly transferable for the socio-legal usefulness by the Legal Method.

Principle of Falah : The Islamic revealed law cannot but accord with norms of "higher morality" and, in this respect, it has some degree of identity with Natural Law which is synonymous with moral rules. The justification for the rules of morality in natural law was contained in certain aims of human life, which were determined by the desires of mankind, designated as "passions" by Hume, and no role was assignable to reason in this.

However, the norms of higher morality in Islamic revealed law are of transcendental nature due to their proximate affiliation with the revealed doctrine of Salvation and, although, their moral value is demonstrable by reason, yet the desires of mankind obviously have no determining role in relation to those norms.

In order to furnish a substitute for the natural law, the issue of discovering a rational standard to provide the means of judging the moral nature has proved intellectually engaging. The Kantian "categorical imperative" was the absolute rule of morality encompassed in the realm of "ought" rather than in "is." This postulation, however, proved to harbour limitations on empirical grounds, for particular problems could not assuredly find the resolution according to its dictates. With the similar purposes in view, Bentham formulated the principle of utility, which acquired acceptance and, later, it was to make the tangible conceptual contribution towards legal positivism.

The assessment of maximum stock of happiness of the largest numbers was the criterion of utility. This principle provided the measure for the evaluation of the moralness of law, and its main advantage was considered to be the distinction it offered between legal and moral obligations. In comparison, the Supreme Islamic Principle of Success or "falah" is of universal scope in the realm of morality due to its transcendent nature. As a juristic principle of reasoning, it has the conceptual profundity to furnish frame of reference for the evaluation and development of law related to the legal and social reformation.

The implications of the derivative principle of the right to equality for all human beings are of basic import concerning all the orders in a society, without exception. But, more importantly, this fundamental principle is not a metaphysical conception, for its reality can be demonstrated or proven while, at the same time, itself affording a usage as the standard of universal proof. Appropriately then, moralness of law for Hobbes resided in the law itself, to Bentham it reposed in the principle of utility, and in Islam it is identifiable with the Supreme Principle of Success or "falah." With these legal and moral attributes embedded in the Islamic Principle of Success, to ascribe this Supreme Principle as a higher law, adoptable by humanity, is a philosophically unassailable proposition.

Modern Legal Concepts : According to Hart, the union of primary and secondary rules is the key to the science of jurisprudence. The foundations of a legal system are constituted by the acceptance of the secondary rules with the criteria for the identification of the primary rules of obligation, in the setting of a complex social situation. In this view, the primary rules of obligation comprise of the legislative enactments, customary practices, general declarations of specified persons and judicial precedents in particular cases. In the description of Hart, the secondary rules are classified into the rules of recognition, rules of change, and rules of adjudication. The rules of recognition function to eradicate the "uncertainty" of the primary rules such as would not form a system. The rules of change are the remedy for the static quality of the regime of primary rules. And the rules of adjudication, intended to rectify "the inefficiency of its diffused social pressure" concerning the regime of primary rules, allow the "authoritative determinations" of the issue of violation of the primary rules.

In his appraisal of the dual distinctions drawn between the two types of rules by Hart, attention towards the ensuing features is drawn by Summers. The one type of distinction is characteristically between "duty imposing rules" and "power conferring rules." The other type of distinction is between the primary rules that impose duties and the secondary rules of recognition, change and adjudication. These distinctions, on more profound evaluation, were characterized as somewhat "hybrid" or "ambiguous" in the critique.

The essential significance of Hart's description of the two types of rules in their combination is the retrospective insight it lends into the organized legal systems. This is evident from the claim that the addition of secondary rules to a set of pre-existing primary rules marks the transition from the pre-legal into the legal world. The importance of legal obligation and of constitutional law in the context of vertical view of law-making is signified. In contradistinction, the Legal Method founded upon the Supreme Principles is of prospective nature, for it serves as a formulation for the establishment of a legal system.

The subscription to the legal idea of the vertical image of law-making is ascertainable to a certain extent, however, the combination of the full expression of Islamic Law and the individual judicial responsibility are the distinguishing legal concepts functional in the Legal Method. The formulation, therefore, places substantive reliance upon the characteristic Islamic concept of justice, which comprises of features in addition to the conventional authoritative determinations of the fact of the violation of legal rule. In this perspective, then, it is appreciable that the Supreme Principles are the rational standard which provide the means of Islamic adjudication. This approach is in obvious contrast from Austin's definition of the concept of a legal rule in terms of a notion of "command" and "habitual obedience," and is more in accordance with the legal realists view of the rule. As a matter of comparison, Islamic concept of the legal rule cannot maintain conformity with its elucidation provided by Austin, for then it is in contravention of the Islamic rule of law, wherein the legal obligation is contingent upon the consonancy of the legal rule with the Islamic injunctions.

A characteristic aspect of "Kelsenism" in law is embodied in the observation that the reason for the validity of a norm is always another norm and never a fact. The hierarchy of legal norms is thus based upon the scheme of justification and, as it constitutes the systematic character of legal system, it is considered to be an important contribution to the concept of legal system. A similar, if not the same, view is entertained about the constitutional rules in relation to their legal role in the law. In the opinion of an authority on this subject, the provisions of law issuing from various sources are situated in a hierarchy whose summit is formed by the constitutional laws. A matter of unanimous opinion, the constitutional provisions are of more substantive legal value than the ordinarily enacted laws, for being the means of controlling the constitutionality of enacted legislation.

Now, Kelsen's theory is considered not to be free from shortcomings, and not alone because it imparts a "misleading picture of legal systems. The systematic character ascribable to legal system then is not unexceptionable. The constitution that includes the basic rules of recognition for a legal system, cannot derive its authority from the system itself. In the opinion of Salmond, the constitution is "necessarily prior to the law" and it is a matter of fact and practice rather than of law in reality. In contrast the term validity "within" the system, which is central to the theory as well as to the concept of intramural justification of the legal norms, used by Kelsen, is an important step in the Legal Method founded upon the Supreme Principles for the organization of Islamic legal system. This particular notion of unexceptional validity is only entertainable with the use of the Legal Method, for the legal norm demonstrably valid in one system is not assumable to be valid in another system.

Another important contribution to legal theory, made by Kelsen, is the emphasis that in order to ascribe the characteristics of legal system to a set of norms, designated as secondary norms, in contrast with the genuine legal sanction-prescribing norms, there must also exist rules of different type, which enable to identify such norms as elements of an order. The basic soundness of the contribution notwithstanding, a profound assaying of this idea imparts a systematic character to the general content, structure and operation of a legal system, which lends itself to misgivings. Now the Legal Method based upon the Supreme Principles, in addition to "identifying" the "secondary norms," as a part of the general function of making norms to be the elements of an Islamic legal order in a systematic manner, provides in such instances the prescription of sanctions.

The imparting of the characteristics of the Islamic legal system to the "secondary norms" fulfills the function of the identification. And the legally important role of prescribing sanctions in the case of "secondary norms" is performed due to the legal authentication lent from the Quranic injunction, requiring "the wrong-doers who debar (or detract) from the way of Allah" that "such will not escape in the earth...." This measure resolves the difficulty in law due to the differentiation that exists between moral and legal norms, distinguishes the legal order from all other social orders due to the fact, that it regulates human conduct and exercises social control by means of a specific legal technique of sanctions, and also fulfills the requirements for a genuine legal norm, delineated both by Kelsen and Hart.

As its but one legal instance, the law pertaining to inheritance of property in Islam is citable. Devoid of formulation for the sanctions in the event of the violation of the relevant rules, in effect the laws of inheritance remain a matter of conscience alone, not possessing the legal means to uphold their religious sanctity and legal inviolability in the event of oftener than not breach. The prescribed Legal Method ascribes the characteristics of the Islamic legal system to the cited "secondary norm," and maintains the legal jurisdiction to transform it into a *"genuine legal norm"* by prescribing legal sanctions in the event of its violation.

In distinguishing between law and jurisprudence or the science of law, Kelsen assigns the function of "representation" of the law produced by the legal authority to jurisprudence. The law, whose "description" is given as legal norms which, in their "specific connection within a legal order," are viewed as the "ought" representation of the law. The emphasis is laid upon the distinction to be drawn between the "legal norms" the "prescriptive" elements of the law of community-designated to be the "objects of jurisprudence," and the representation by the theorist of law, designated as the "statements of jurisprudence." Now, in accordance with the requirements of the Legal Method, and with the usage of Kelsenian descriptive terms for the purpose of legal comparison here, the "objects of jurisprudence" are the legal rules, the Supreme Principles and the legal features in an individual instance of adjudication.

The "ought" of law, as a result of the method, is the juristic form as the representation of the Islamic "rightness" of law. In other words, the Islamic legal character of the legal rule is its "ought" juristic form as determined with the utility of the Legal Method.

The determination of the Islamic law relevant to the legal rule during judicial evaluation is the fulfillment of the requirement of a Supreme Principle. In addition to the Islamic "groundnorms" of Tauhid, the consummate legal concepts of "public beneficence," "best community," and success ("falah"), are the wellspring for the elements of Islamic legal character.

No less significant are the superordinate legal concepts of justice, equity and vicegerency, the components that by no means exhaust the enumeration. With the individualization of the process of "representation," though of a circumscribed legal scope, the Supreme Principles are to be imparted, through concretization of a general or abstract law, a characteristic Islamic legal expression, which has the potential for influencing indeterminately large instances and aspects of the law. Consequent to the juristic conjunction between two types of laws, designated here as general and particular rules, the methodical approach for the individualization and concretization of a composite law imparts the legal system an "open" texture.

The U. S. Constitution incorporates by positive enactment certain value judgments or principles. This approach makes explicit the underlying main assumptions of the legal system, and it renders these into obligatory or "overriding" legal norms, capable of being enforced by the legal process. In comparison, the Supreme Principles represent the multifarious fundamentals which underlie the religious and legal structure in Islam and, hence, in general serve as the determinants of the values in religion, jurisdiction of laws and legal development in the legal system. Due to the contrasting fact of the Supreme Principles constitutionally not being upheld only in their legal breach, but their legal functions are also availed through their systematic exercise, the Legal Method constituted of those fundamentals acquires the following distinguishing functions:

(1) The administration of justice is fundamentally altered to its appropriate Islamic requirements.

(2) The role of judiciary in the structure of legal system is altered from the simplistic ascertainment of the violation of law to its feasible creative function.

(3) The effectiveness of the law is extended and enhanced to the full Islamic scope of its application.

(4) The Supreme Principles viewed as the indispensable fundamental Islamic values, in conjunction with the law through the process of adjudication, in accordance with the demands of Legal Method, transform the law into a constant medium for the propagation of those values in the society.

(5) The invaluable legal notion of the "separation of powers," with the distinct implication of the indepe-ndence of judiciary, finds its logical expression in the application of the method, for the extra and vital dimension of the independence of judiciary in its comprehensive sense is manifested in the universal exercise, to an extent, within a predetermined framework of law, of the individualization of legal judgments.

(6) The judicial latitude accrues from the fact that the Supreme Principles carry the legal validity of confirming the "norms for decision," assigning to them new authority or imparting to them equitably different effect from that which had been previously attributed to them.

The issue of any similarity of the Legal Method with the existence of "general legal principles" in the constitutions of other states as, for instance, affirmed in the preamble of the French Constitution itself, is relevant. The Spanish Civil Code enumerates among the possible sources of law the general principles deduced from the Spanish codes and legislation.

The series of judicial judgments in the GFR stipulated that the constitutional law is not limited to fundamental legislating texts, but is also made-up of "certain general principles which the legislators have not rendered in the form of positive rules." Now the consonancy of law with the fundamental principles and values of the constitution is a common legal aim in all the legal systems, at least on a theoretical basis. However, the mandatory creative objective underlying the Legal Method has distinct differentiation from the preceding feature recognized in all legal systems.

The Islamic legal system is to address itself to the substantive issues of Islamic legal concepts including the legal rules, legal positivism, and the Islamic concern for the just social order. The implications of the last issue entail the legal rules which would not be socially unjust and, by the same token, there is no divergence between law, justice and equity in accordance with Islamic requirements. The *result-orientation* of the Supreme Principles, in contrast with mere process-orientation, in their application is an Islamic legal characteristic, which is ensured through individualization and concretization of the legal implications of the superordinate principles, describable for clarity of apprehension as legal *constellation-concepts.* In summation, the Legal Method represents the present stage of Islamic legal theory, which does not lend itself to sufficient similarity with any other theory of law in promulgation.

The conventional elements in the constitution are also known as its understandings. And other functional designations such as the constitutional and political ethics, and constitutional morality depict the nature of constitutional conventions. In describing the salient characteristics of the understandings which make the constitutional morality. Dicey identified one common quality, that is, determinant, in general, of the mode in which discretionary powers belonging to the political sovereign ought to be exercised. Noticeworthy is the translation of the discretion into reasons for use in juristic preference by the court. In contrast with the constitutional law, the conventions of the constitution are not in reality enforced by the courts.

The legal binding force of the latter, then, is derived from the fact that their breach should necessarily reflect in the violation of law, finally. On comparative evaluation, the Supreme Principles belong to a different category as explained earlier. The realization is due that one essential principle of the constitution is obedience to the deliberately expressed will of the lawgiver, however, the Supreme Principles are a set of religio-legal maxims, meant to secure deference for this principle in the context of the primary source of law. The legal concepts and values that ensue from the Supreme Principles necessitate their individualization due to the religious basis of Islamic Law. This then becomes the expression of the connection between the law and the Supreme Principles, however, no ascertainment of the nature of connection between the law of the constitution and the constitutional conventions, if at all, can be made with exactitude.

The reiteration of the observation by Gibb to the effect that Islam is to be evaluated essentially in its own terms, is pertinent at this juncture. This legal nexus relating to the Supreme Principles and the law, as the former are the superordinate concepts and consummate values, is applicable by conscientious interpretation to all claims, relationships and conflicts of interest. No symmetrical analogy in legal history is available to explain the legal usage of the Supreme Principles as formulated in the Legal Method. Nevertheless, the effect of equity law on the stationary medieval English Common Law, and the Ordinance on Civil Justice of 1900 A.D. in the Sudan to provide the necessary development of law, are citable to impart some idea of the legal usefulness of the Supreme Principles.

The definition of legal system or the correlation of rules to legal system is of relevance. Kelsen considers the identification of legal system to reside in its systematic character due to the common denominator of basic norms for the rules. These norms in the analogy of reconstruction are the initial maxims for the derivation of subsequent propositions. The law emanating from the same sovereign is also viewed as the characteristic of legal system. In Austin's opinion, "a legal system is a system of rules within rules." In this description, a general habit of obedience was not attached significance, but the acceptance of a set of constitutional norms for the identification of the rules of the system is its characteristic. Hart considered the union of primary and secondary rules to be the criterion in addition to its conforming with the requirements of moral nature of laws as the definition of legal system. In Salmond's observation, Hart and Austin, like many other legal theorists, described a working model of a standard legal system.

In this perspective, the important juristic issue of the determination of the constitution of a state by law, if at all it can be accomplished, remains. According to Rawls' description, constitutional rules are logically prior in existence to that of the institutions defined by those rules. Salmond has addressed this engaging issue in the following terms: Constitution includes basic rules of recognition of a state's legal system which cannot derive their authority from the legal system itself. Further, a poignant query is raised by the same source. Does this mean that the state and its constitution are necessarily prior to the law, and that what passes as a constitutional law is in reality not a law, but a matter of fact and practice?"'

Against this background, the definition of a legal system stays in want of completion, for the constitutional rules are non-derivable basic norms in the legal system. In this respect, the Legal Method removes this legal deficiency, so that the Supreme Fundamental Islamic Principles are situated prior to the state and the constitution.

Opinions of other Islamic Jurists : The conflict was natural to arise between the antithetical viewpoints concerning legitimacy of standards for society to be set by law and the law as the outgrowth of the experience of society. The reconciliation of the differences between traditional law and the demands laid upon it by the social change were engaging the interests of Muslim jurists. The advocation for the reinterpretation of the principles embodied in the divine revelation by the great Egyptian jurist, Abdu, at the end of nineteenth century, was in response to legal reformation.

Another Islamic thinker of eminence, Iqbal, emphasized the revitalization of Ijtihad and described it as "the principle of movement in the structure of Islam," with the same objective in view. Adopting the line of thought that the founders of the Islamic schools of law could not have envisaged finality for their legal reasonings and interpretation regarding the sources of law, the same thinker underscored the need for re-interpretation of the Islamic legal principles in consonance with the newly emerged social and empirical demands. However, the onus of this far-sighted response was both substantive and intricate, for it required a legal formulation as a framework for systematic Ijtihad. Without such an essential basis the reality of Ijtihad would have remained a mere aspiration. Yet the irreducible minimum requirement for such a formulation was for it to stay indisputable in accordance with Islamic religious as well as modern juridical criteria.

In the absence of these antecedents, the challenging task of reinterpretation of the primary sources of Muslim law, that is, independent of the traditional Muslim juristic construction of the law, has since existed unattended and incomplete. The Muslim theologian, Shah Wali Ullah, has pointed out the prophetic aim, including all-embracing principles in the sublime teachings, with the view to satisfy the requirements of different times, peoples and places. These principles, in practical effect, are of usefulness in the construction of "Universal Shariat." An Islamic legist of incomparable vision and wisdom in his times, whose legal theories did not find assimilation into the traditional legal system of Islam, Shatibi propagated the comprehensive legal concept of "Masla." This juristic principle was deemed to find a wide applicability in law as the objective of Shariah, and as a method of legal reasoning. These legal uses of Masla, or public welfare, would have proven to be the precondition for the reintroduction of Ijtihad in the Islamic legal system.

The "habit" of adherence to the respective school doctrine among the legal scholars constituted the "science of jurisprudence" according to Ibn Khaldun, as referred to before. This obviously indicated a need for reform in this lingering approach. A similar view was formulated by Fazl-ur-Rahman, who pointed out that Islamic scholarship during the past a few centuries had been more or less mechanical and semantic rather than interpretative or scientific. And his suggestion for the re-exercising of Ijtihad as a prerequisite for ensuring an honourable place for the Muslims in the community of "progressive, dynamic and living nations of the world" is intellectually engaging.

The following observation attributed to famous Muslim jurist, Shafii, is reiterated to a similar interpretation: On all matters which touch the life of a Muslim, there is either a binding decision or an indication as to the right answer. On the basis of hierarchy of law, the juristic criteria for the evaluation and differentiation of the alternatives in law according to Shafii should also be ascertainable from the same sources. This subscription to the idea of "all-embracing" principles in the present-day legal terminology is paraphrasable as a legal formulation, representing the hierarchy of law, for the ascertainment and validation of legal rules.

Ideological Necessity : The term ideology is credited to Tracy for utilising it at the end of the eighteenth century. Viewed as a science of ideas, the power to demonstrate the relationship between ideas and experience on the one hand, and reality and well-ordered human world on the other, was ascribed to it. However, Marx become popular for using the term ideology in literature. Another notable theorist, Mannheim, is recognized for making original contribution to the concept of ideology. It is to be realized that the term ideology has triple differential characteristics that impart distinct applicability to its each classical concept. Now, the recognition of a new concept, with its definition according to a neologistic term, and the existence of its dynamics antedating to that discovery are not extraordinary. Accordingly, the Islamic definition of the ideology is distinct and its identifying criteria of a coherent world-view, rationale of its pursuit, and the justification to establish an identifiable social order as well as to reform the world were available preceding the advent of the term ideology. With this in view, the assumption that the adoption of ideology somehow guarantees the attainment of ideological objectives in the society is erroneous as it is not borne out by historical experience.

An interrelated fact is the furnishing of directions for the achievement of ideological objectives, which is not a recognized function of ideologies. The significance of human factor in the successful implementation of ideological theories, therefore, is worth of mentioning. On another level, the ideological objectives remaining constant, ideological theories should necessarily retain adaptability for rational reconstruction and reinterpretation in the light of new experience on the analogy of law. The proposed theory of law, founded upon the Supreme Principles, is in fulfillment of the pointed out ideological necessity which is further emphasized by the primal importance of law in the Islamic social order – an ideological fact which yet awaits its full realization.

Throughout the course of legal history, ideas have served as legal values, as basis of legal reasoning, as criteria of interpretation and as framework of standards. Greek thought developed into and centered upon the idea of social harmony, with characteristic meanings, which would be of equal utility even today. The Roman jurists adopted the idea of social control as a constituent of the legal theory. The Islamic legal concern focused upon "Masla" or public interest, a legal principle which was markedly elaborated by Shatibi subsequently. During the Reformation, the individual self-assertion emerged as the preeminent legal notion.

In this succession of legal ideas, the engaging concepts of economic infrastructure and the end of law held ideological sway. The competing idea of legal value, the maintenance of strength and efficiency in an organized society, was to emerge. To maintain the evolving sequence of ideas, the Islamic Civilization for its *new legal age* is anticipated to subscribe to the concept of "best community." According to Pound, application of standards and legal interpretation are done with reference to received ideals, while ideals are described as the authoritative pictures of social order, and are viewed to be as much a part of the law as rules and principles, conceptions and techniques. The relevance of these aspects in relation to the Supreme Principles as ideological and legal foundations for the Islamic Law is evident, and the resolution of the juristic and political dilemmas, which have historically stalled the evolution of the corresponding systems in Islam, appears conceivable.

The juristic issues of the reintroduction of Ijtihad for the establishment of legal system, to sustain the desirable legal development in order to cope with the requirements of evolving social organization and to reconcile the conflicting demands of stability and change in law, find the suitable response. On the other hand, development of the political constitution, rule of law and matters related to the legal concept of sovereign and subject, issues with substantive political ramifications and proximately interrelated, find their appropriate resolution through Islamic system of Nomocracy. Noticeworthy is the definition of rule of law as projected by the remarkable Greek genius, Plato, and according to it the law is not to serve the interests of the ruler, but the reverse ought to be true. The political view of sovereign and subject expresses only one aspect of the relationship between state and individual. In that instance, the sovereign will as expressed in legislation may be arbitrary, despotic or irrational. A consideration which may not be within the ambit of its validity as law, the social and moral content of such an expressed will is not unlikely to be deficient.

The passive reception of orders is the political distinguishing mark of such a legal relationship. Now, due to the singular fact that the Supreme Principles are situated prior to the constitution which finds its validity from the principles, and not conversely, therefore, the type of constitution, its continuation in force as a legal document and development of constitutional law are reliant upon the former. A modern constitutionalist, Dicey, ascribes noticeable legal value to this sequence of constitution with the law in context, of human rights. The fundamental legal concept of Islamic rule of law as a constituent of the Supreme Principles is then immune from amendment, abridgement or abrogation due to any imaginable constitutional uncertainties. And this rule of law, finding its diverse implications in the law and expression in the legal precedents, provides a double guarantee against its own violation in the specific Platonic context, which is relevant to the immediate purpose of present discourse.

Moreover, due to the characteristic attributes of Islamic rule of law, the political distinction between sovereign and subject is legally not valid, for the contractual ground between the ruler and the populace is formed by consonance with the provisions of Islamic Law as a condition for political allegiance. The judicial independence is a logical deduction from the Islamic rule of law as a source of impartial arbitration, for without its surety in advance, the rule of law is theoretically unsustainable and, indeed, more often than not, may prove a hollow principle. The same issue of sovereign and subject is relevant in the context of Austin's legal concept of command and obedience. However, within the meanings of the Quranic rule of law, allegiance to the political authority cannot legally be construed as subordination which is reserved for law as a common denominator, both for the ruler and the citizens.

The consideration of political authority itself, under the command of an external source as a sovereign, will be then a contradiction in terms. Hence, the Islamic legislative texts are guides rather than commands, for the latter emanate from the political sovereign, considered strictly according to the demands of Islamic rule of law. A matter of far-reaching significance, the source of essential definition and limitation of political authority in Islam is not the political constitution, but the Islamic Law, a fact that confers the valid designation of "Nomocracy" upon the Islamic political system, with the basic differentiation of real obedience in Islam being to legal principles and not to political authority. This legal relationship between the political authority and the populace in Islam is demonstrable, on theoretical grounds, to become the antecedent of the "end of law" in society, a utopian objective entertained in the communism, provided the law is deemed as man-made and society is construed at the zenith of its evolution, so that, the primary source of Islamic Law will then suffice.

Various Aspects

Source of Law : Any Supreme Principle is comprised of *Islamic constellation-norms,* and each can result in the deduction of a legal system. This substantive observation emphasizes the legal value of the principles as an inexhaustible source of law. Representing Islamic religio-legal fundamentals, these principles offer themselves to be systematically analyzed, reconciled with maxims available in modern knowledge, and developed along rational lines consistent with legal modes of reasoning. The last designates a more intense and systematized form of ordinary human reasoning, according to Lloyd. Due to the creative religio-legal concepts in the Supreme Principles, the prodigious potential for the opening of new vistas of legal creativity is to be realized.

The judicial interpretation of law is within the legal framework of the Supreme Principles as prescribed by the Legal Method, and all of these legal factors will lend incentive to the work of legal scholarship as well. The legal importance of this last effect resides in the fact that the products of legal scholarship were the fundamental source of law in Romano-Germanic system for a prolonged period. Legal scholarship is, therefore, of fundamental value, for it creates ideas and initiating bases for the juristic output. With these legal advantages in relation to the source of law, the formulated Legal Method can be envisaged to be the *"principle of legal development"* in the Islamic legal system.

Interpretation of Law : In Kelsen's view, jurisprudence or science of law is the "representation," that is, rational reconstruction, of the law of community." According to Amos, the French utilise this term to mean interpretation, which is not essentially different from the former. This fact, no doubt, underscores the significance of the interpretation of law as a process in a legal system. A pronounced accentuation of this conclusion is observed in the instance of religious fundamental laws which possess special authority in the related communities.

These set of laws, considered as exceptional legislation, then, are in need of interpretation with the aid of methodology and principles which are different from those utilised for that purpose in "conventional" legislation. A more profound appreciation of this view is acquired by realizing that the usual legislative concerns-the provision of all the necessary regulations not feasible during the legislation, with the result that the usual outcome is the statement of principles and general rules pertaining to a relevant area-are augmented in religious law." Additionally, the interpretative approach must take into account the identification of law with a juridical objective. The law in the Western Civilization is identified with the safeguard of individual rights in the community, the socialist law identified itself with the omnipotence of state which, in traditional Islamic Law, is equated with religion. This last view merged substantive discipline of law into the "science" of religion, and omitted to grant it the due recognition as a distinct "science."

Now the practical value of any enacted law depends upon the technique of its application, an outcome which is intricately associated with the antecedent of a process of interpretation, whose real importance has proven elusive in the traditional

Muslim Law. The identification of Islamic Law is not suited to any other objective, on the basis of knowledge of religion or legal reasoning, than with the Supreme Principles and, in particular, its more tangible-in the sense of concrete-objective of "best community." From this discussion it can be concluded that the interpretation and application of the Supreme Principles, as a fundamental part of the religious law, are of essential juridical value.

The singular characteristic of the Supreme Principles is their interpretative inexhaustibility due to the lack of complete definability of legal relationships under various associable circumstances, and due to their prodigious explanatory powers. To reiterate, one essential principle of the constitution is obedience to the deliberately expressed will of the law-giver. From the religious viewpoint, the abiding obligation towards the essentials of religious faith and morality is derived from the same principle. However, from the legal viewpoint, the Supreme Principles are a set of maxims, meant to secure respect for this principle. The necessity for the methodical application of the Supreme Principles is further reliant upon the justification that the violation of the principles is a proof of the particular legal norm not being identifiable with Islamic Law to the extent of its divergence from the requirements of those principles. In other words, with the application of the Supreme Principles, with the interpretative function of the measure of the essential Islamic religio-legal values, deficiency from the provisions of Islamic religious law is sightable.

The legal controversy that exists between rule and the law demands a serious attention in the instance of a religious law. The conventional interpretation of rule, under an ordinary legislation, usually results in a narrowly materialistic, in the sense of worldly, application of law, which is not justifiable in the case of a religious law. The desirable avoidance of mechanical deductions from rules with predetermined meanings, without reference to all the attendable legal relationships envisaged in a religious law, is exercisable through the systematic interpretation of law in accordance with the legal formulation described. Due to the manner of interpretation of law and character of legal development are recognized to have an indispensable linkage, the legal approach embodied in the Legal Method in relation to the former objective is denotable as the *Islamic juristic method* for the interpretation of law.

Composite nature of the objectives in a religious law is recognizable, yet the literal interpretation of the legal rules is rather routinely exercised, and due to the synonymity of the process of adjudication with the dispensation of law or administration of justice, the intention of the Law-giver is not necessarily considered. This outlined variance between the law and the legal rule concerning the religious law, in particular, is averted by the legal approach comprising of Supreme Principles. Moreover, law at times, is insufficient and incomplete, and the same approach is of assistance in that ascertainment and supplementation. Against this perspective, the law may be deemed as a well-defined *juridical framework* which the act of interpretation, with the use of the method, will complete. Additionally, in the routine application of law, the possible inconsistency of the statutes with each other, a counter to the concept of legal system according to Fuller, is remediable with the legal use of a systematic standard of superordinate principles.

Islamic Jurisprudence : The jurists consider the characteristics of legal system to be the fundamental elements through which the rules to be applied are themselves discovered, interpreted and evaluated. These elements are viewed as determinants of the social objectives to be achieved with the assistance of legal system, and the place of law itself within the social order. In the instance of German Law, the general provisions of law are allowed to neutralize the more specific provisions. As a result, without changing the meanings of the text, the new demands upon law are fulfilled. In order for the comparison to emphasize the distinction between fundamental elements and Supreme Principles, the latter represent the law's Islamic religio-legal conceptual structure and are the embodiment of the theory of the sources of law. The Supreme Principles epitomize the idea of the universe and society that ought to permeate the law. In essence, then, the Supreme Principles reflect the specific ideological outlook the law is founded upon, comprised of religious, philosophical and socio-political dimensions. The consideration of Islamic economic and defensive frameworks of society is the prominent aspect of the law.

The scope of social objectives to be achieved with the assistance of legal system, thus, is evidently extensive, and the place of law within the social order, considering it as an indispensable part of religion, is indeed of primal importance. Insofar as the methodological approach is concerned, the fundamental elements of law, as part of the general provisions, are allowed to prevail over the special provisions for the juridical advantage of consideration to constant and more fundamental elements rather than the less stable legal rules. This primary legal function is described as subordination of law to the commands of essential legal principles, and standards of higher morality, in one constitutional system, and as the overriding influence to certain elements in law in another system.

The Legal Method relying upon the Supreme Principles basically purports to impart full effects to Islamic Law, whereby the juridical notions of "subordination" and "overriding influence" in law find a primarily contrasting substitution of conjunction and supplementation of law. The reiteration of the fact is due that Supreme Principles comprise of *constellation-concepts* and, viewed strictly in terms of law, constitute its Islamic purposes, whereas the instrumentality of the Legal Method is the source of their implementation. And the overall purpose of Islamic Law is none other than the establishment of a social order suited to the organization of such a society as is definable in revealed Islamic terms. The intricate and pervading concepts of individual success ("falah"), the dispensation of justice with its undissociability from equity alongwith other Islamic attributes, and the characteristic requirements of Islamic rule of law are prominent distinguishing legal features in such a society.

The valuable legal notion of sociological jurisprudence is credited to Roscoe Pound. Among its objectives are the quest for means of making legal rules effective and individualization of legal decisions. In connection with the legal rules, the important question of terminology, whether rules of conduct or laws is settled, for the legal discrepancy between the two is resolved by the usage of the Legal Method. The Supreme Principles confirm the "norms for decision," assign new authority and impart equitable Islamic effect to them in the face of competing legal values. The explanation resides in the fact of the Supreme Principles being both more fundamental and wider in scope than the statutes and enactments which are to be construed in conformity with those principles.

The approach is essentially to be looked at as means to avoid the resignation to serviceable substitutes in law, given the Islamic desirability for the use of high juridical standards. In resultant, as the law becomes devoid of any possibility for social injustice, so the Legal Method becomes a way to a just social order. On the basis of another consideration, any legal measure that augments the principle of social interdependence, designated as solidarity ordinarily or, conversely, eradicates the potential for social friction, it can be deemed to enhance the effectiveness of legal rules. And, more importantly, the effectiveness of legal rules is inseparable from the position for the law in the social order and its general reverence. A direct correlation apparently exists between the immediately preceding reason for the effectiveness of rules and the availability of the constitutional guarantees for the individual rights towards their enforcement.

Due to the vital fact of the preeminent characterization of Islamic society being a Nomocracy, as ascertained from the primary source of law, the essential requirement for Islamic rule of law extends the safeguard to the continuity of constitution and, simultaneously, establishes the lawful grounds for the legal enforcement of individual rights. According to the requirement of the Islamic rule of law, the abrogation or abridgement of the individual rights, granted in Islam, is not without legal infraction. The legal attainment of individual rights is fortified by the demands of the rule of law, which make it incumbent upon the individuals to attend to the legal obligations and, as its necessary counterpart, the attentiveness to the legal rights is ever kept within social consciousness. In this background, the rationale to give the Supreme Principles a mandatory legal expression, as prescribed in the Legal Method, is obvious. And the same legal formulation is a means for the attainment of the other objective of the sociological jurisprudence.

The maintenance of political constitution and the judicial independence are among the legal consequences ensuing from legal application of the Supreme Principles in the Legal Method, which becomes the justification for the adoption of the formulation. If one is the consequence of, then the other is the only effective guarantee for, the pivotal requirement of Islamic Nomocracy—the observance of law—as epitomized in the previously referred Quranic injunction. For not finely apprehending the legal value of the Islamic juristic truism, that Islamic fundamental of the rule of law is the basis of the law of constitution and not its result, the muse of history has exacted a heavy toll from the incautious, and repeatedly.

The resolution of the rule and law controversy has its demonstrable desirability in Islamic Law, and it is attainable through the prescribed legal approach. The right of inheritance available in Muslim laws is identified with Islamic concept of social values, whereas it is a distinction which indeed is legitimately owned by the Supreme Principles. The considerations of the *ratio legis,* with the special meaning of the adaptation to wholesome experience of society, and the rare possibility of the provisions in a code may be a "dead letter," also demand a suitable legal formulation.

A matter of fundamental significance, law in Islam is a means towards a certain defined end, and not the latter *per se,* which is explicit from the illustration in political jurisprudence. As an instance of "neologism," this category of jurisprudence is more suited to Islamic Law due to its comprehensive nature than, perhaps, to any other legal system. And Islamic economic laws can afford to be included into an independent type of jurisprudence. Since law in Islam is based upon the ordained set of revealed injunctions, then jurisprudence is deemable as the science of understanding and ascertaining that law, as suggested by Coulson, however, this objective is lent specificity by enhancing its scope to defining the "ought" or rightness of Islamic Law. And the present legal formulation endeavours towards the attainment of that redefined juridical objective. In consonance with this description, the Islamic political jurisprudence is the definition and limitation of political authority within the Islamic scheme of state and society. The basic differentiation from other constitutional forms that exists in Islam is the political identity of the society, which emanates from its *legal personality,* and not *vice versa.*

The invaluable distinction denies the political authority to supersede over legal sovereignty. An instance of legal history, in the domain of Muslim public laws, political interests necessitated additional jurisdiction and, hence, the politico-legal doctrine of "siasa Shariah" was evolved, whose inimical consequences upon the Islamic legal and political systems have already been dwelt upon. However, the legal formulation envisages to forestall the legal ramifications of the traditional doctrine in the new age of Islamic Law for an ascendant social order. On the same grounds the philosophical correspondence that exists between obligations and rights, the political jurisprudence will provide a legitimate accommodation to the latter. The Supreme Principles furnish the adequate conceptual basis for the balancing addition of individual rights; it is a legal measure whose value cannot be over-emphasized as it is overdue and consonant with the demands of Islamic rule of law.

The primary right of the ruled to opt for the political authority ensues from the mandatory provisions of Islamic rule of law, and it is inherent in the qualified right to refusal of the authority's obedience. This essentially is the legal basis for the security of political freedom in society as a universal religious requirement of "Tauhid." The belief, and not just the recognition as is provided for in the Universal Declaration of Human Rights of 1948, in the common source and hence equality of humankind, is the foundation of Islamic political freedom. This heritage of religious belief, translatable in legal terms, hence, claiming cumulative weight for implementation, is an Islamic political distinction which, as an invaluable legal concept, should not remain without full recognition or complete legislative expression. Alternatively, the denial of political freedom in Islam will convey the religious implication of the abrogation of a Supreme Principle.

The fact is to be granted that the general principle of justice finds diverse application for the idea in various legal theories. However, Islamic concept of justice is inseparably allied with the legal notion of equity. The Legal Method provides utility for the principle of equity, without the need for autonomous rules or courts of equity. Besides, it is a practical means for the desirable alternative to the traditional Islamic approach of dual court system comprising of "Qadi" and "Mufti," and allows its effective unification. And the potential for the legal formulation to furnish a substitute for administrative and constitutional courts, as are available in some legal systems, cannot be underestimated.

"Best Community": End of Law : The juridical features of the legal system in "best community" are as follows:

(1) The "ought" or rightness of law is a constant objective.

(2) The practical manifestations of law, rather than the theoretical content of the legal precepts, draw attention.

(3) Law due to the requirements of its science, is regarded as an improvable social institution as well as in constant need of improvement.

(4) Law is not merely an instrument of social control but, being of primal significance in the social order, it is the means to social ascendancy.

(5) Due to the essential differentiation that exists between law and rule, the legal rule is definable as to give full individual expression to the requirements of Islamic Law, rather than remaining the simple and artless instrument of settling the individual legal controversies.

(6) The past of Islamic Law is deemed to reveal ideas and principles in inductive, historical and empirical terms and the law is thus not only found but also developed.

(7) In accommodation of the teleological view of law, and with the attainable ends of law in sight, accessibility to an established criteria for the "adjudication" and "supplementation" of "law" is available.

(8) Law is oriented towards serving the interests of the Islamic rule of law in juxtaposition to the interests of the political authority.

An Aspect of "Jihad" and Law : The right to the ownership of firearms is cognate to the individual Islamic obligation of Jihad and, therefore, is an indispensable Islamic right. The legal issue of the correspondence between rights and obligations is involved in this instance, and the juristic consideration of capability as an antecedent of legal obligation is no less important. An appropriate analogy from the evaluation of legal history belonging to other systems of law becomes available to be drawn. The 18th century jurist, James Wilson conceived that a moral right, due to its moral nature, is also legal. The right of the citizen to keep arms was deemed necessary against the historical perspective of the encroachment upon political liberty, and it was viewed to be a palladium of the liberties of a republic. As another instance, a guarantee in the first bill of rights was the right to bear arms, which was secured to the king's Protestant subjects by the English Bill of Rights. This was necessitated against the background of James II, who had sought to hold down a Protestant majority by disarming them while allowing a hostile minority to bear arms.

The reluctance to vividly recall the episodes in the historical experience, that led to the usurpation of Islamic political sovereignty during the 18th century in the subcontinent, has manifested in the perpetuation of those policies and enactments, in effect. An allusion in this regard is appropriate that the constitutional privilege allowing a citizen the initiative of submitting the petition for the conformity of a law in promulgation to the injunctions of Islam was availed by this author. In respect of the relevant appeal in that instance, it is suggested that the constitutional provision of empowering the court to take cognizance on its own, of any law in force which is contrary to the Islamic injunction, should have proven facilitative in the adjudication of the appeal that contained a set of comprehensive arguments.

Judicial Virtues : A not so rare mistake of equating the display of judicial virtues with legislative activity is made. In the opinion of Hart, these virtues besides including the impartiality and neutrality, in surveying the alternatives and consideration for the interests of all who will be affected, additionally consist of the concern to employ some acceptable general principles as a reasoned basis for decision. The inference that the judicial process in an advanced legal system entails creative functions of the courts is, therefore, inescapable. In the instance of Islamic Law, the judicial interpretation of the legislative enactments is indicated due to the legal value in the full expression of law, rather than the rule alone, in the individual legal decision, as a process.

It is not inexplicable, for it is recognized that each legal system has concepts through which its rules are expressed and legal decisions are made. In Islamic Law, perhaps, more than in other legal systems, the legal rules are not deemable as complete, and only as the "fragments," without conforming to the original intent of the Lawgiver, which may require their "recasting" in that direction. Lacking the assimilation of these considerations into the legal process, the identity of Nomocracy in Islam will remain incomplete without the use of law as a source of societal reformation, and this is an objective whose achievement is inconceivable unless the court is transformed into an organ of Islamic social purposes. An exercise in abstraction in the realm of idealism, no doubt, has its definite role. However, to impart a tangible form to the preceding conclusion, a legal formulation in concrete, to serve as a framework to define the role of the jurist and to provide a desirable direction for the juristic efforts to adopt, is necessitated.

The issue of correct judicial decision in the context of judicial virtue is unavoidable. In routine understanding, simply the application of a formally valid law to the legal facts of a case is recognized as its definition. However, the controversy that exists between law and rule is more pertinent in the instance of Islamic legal system. Fulfillment of the requirements of justice according to the prescribed legal norms, and propagation of the original intentions of the Lawgiver in relation to the law, will be the constituents of such a judicial decision in Islam. Islamic legal concepts, as a characteristic of the legal system, own features which are not completely identifiable with the same concepts in other systems of law. And justice is but one such example of the legal concepts whose differentiating attributes have been outlined earlier. In addition, importantly, judicial decisions often involve a choice between moral and other legal system-characteristic values, which is a demand upon the decisions in excess of the mere application of some single outstanding value or principle.

Now, an appraisal of the Supreme Principles is demonstrative of the desirability for such an approach in a judicial decision, for the demands laid in the balancing of competing claims in respect of various principles, that is, the derivative concepts and values, are to be met in order to satisfy the integral dispensation of the Islamic Law. The precedents for this distinctive Islamic juridical demand for the law are the fundamental Islamic Principles in a setting of the circumscribed individualization of legal decision. As a matter of high legal import, the valuable legal doctrine of the "separation of powers," which is reflected in the judicial independence, is less than adequate in accordance with the meanings of the outlined demand. Not without establishing the "judicial balance of power," the Islamic juridical demand can be unequivocally satisfied. Now, the understanding of a principle, viewed in the light of its opposite, is critically enhanced. The attainment of the highly valuable objective under review is not imaginable according to the dictates of the doctrine of Siasa Shariah, whereby the political authority has the power to control the jurisdiction of the courts.' In contrast, the Legal Method comprised of the Supreme Fundamental Islamic Principles has the demonstrable potential to suitably fulfill the positive Islamic demands laid upon the law.

Acceptance of the crucial proposition for the reinterpretation of law in Islam from its primary sources will rely upon the judicial vision for an auspicious denouement. The measure of such a vision will become available from the following: (i) juristic awareness of the status of Islamic Law in the social order; (ii) the role of law in imparting ascendancy to the social order in future; (iii) juridical insight to read into revealed law the universal socio-legal conceptions; (iv) the recognition of the fact that implicit in the proposition for the reinterpretation of law is the construction of an Islamic legal system *de novo;* (v) to be inspired by the enterprising task of organizing an original legal system in the world; (vi) a profound appreciation for the unifying role an Islamic system of law potentially has in the Muslim world; (vii) the realization of originality as the paradigmatic key-factor in the formation of traditional Islamic schools of law, and exemplified in the juristic endeavours of eminent Abu Hanifa; and, (viii) an owning of the consciousness that the manner of interpretation of law and the character of legal development maintain a productive correlation.

Legal Change : In the agreeable opinion of Coulson, the attitude of detached idealism dominated Shariah Law in the past." The desirability for the purposive nature of law has already been emphasized and, in the case of Islamic Law, it is inseparably allied with the Scriptural standard of "best community," thus, setting for itself a definite social objective. In the attainment of this purpose, the law is required to cope with dual demands laid upon it. The maintenance of balance between legal stability and social change, and the ascertainment of those "social desiderata" which are desirable as well as achievable for the law to satisfy. In delineating the factors causative of the "rigidness" in the traditional Islamic Law, Coulson mentions the ethical mould, concept of "taqlid" as blind orthodoxy in law and literal interpretation of law.

A legal formulation such as can satisfactorily incorporate the demands for the adaptability of law, obviates the causative factors underlying the stagnation of legal development, and demonstrably is founded upon principles underlying the Islamic religio-legal tenets, is suited for adoption. The additional commendable features of this approach should include the fostering of the evolution of law through self-creative process, substantive contribution of judicial responsibility and the reorganization of a comparable legal system suited to the Islamic genius. The stability of the law is preserved as the new law-making is developed within a legal framework and, therefore, the process is neither uninhibited nor unguided. Obviously, then, the Islamic legal framework, essentially based upon primary Islamic sources of law and, importantly, in accord with the higher principles of modern jurisprudence, is the incontrovertible prerequisite of a contemporary legal system, and the Legal Method provides a formulation for the attainment of these ends.

The Legal Method is founded upon the doctrine of the full expression of Islamic Law in individual instances and the Supreme Principles represent the time-honoured wisdom of the Scriptures where prolific contents are conveyed in laconic form. Islamic legal history is a testimony to the vision of Shafii and the originality of Hanifa as the insubstitutable instruments of legal change, and it should become the guiding principles of any legal process that aspires to establish a contemporaneous legal system.

The prospective salient benefits ensuing from the Legal Methodology are enumerated hereunder:

(1) A systematic form is imparted to Islamic jurisprudence.

(2) Consistency, with the elimination of antinomies, in the principles of revealed law is restored.

(3) The long-standing and staunch recommendations of renowned Muslim jurists, thinkers and other legists in the reformist mould, that is, the reinterpretation of revealed Islamic Law, the reintroduction of "Ijtihad," and the reorganization of a process of legal development find an institutionalized expression.

(4) Systematization of the invaluable Islamic juristic principle of "Ijtihad" is an attainment, while the principle in no other way can find an exit from the mere ambit of juristic aspirations.

(5) With a demonstrable potential for the organization of an "original" and at least comparable Islamic legal system, with evidently surpassing juridical merits, the legal methodology brings the establishment of such a legal system within the scope of realization.

(6) Due to the interrelationship of basic significance that exists between the law and society in Islam, an original legal system, organized and developed along the parameters prescribed in the legal methodology, will exercise its causative influence upon the effecting of an ascendant social order.

Juristic Methods

All modern Islamic jurists committed to legal reformation concur about the dispensing of "Taqlid," and the reintroduction of Ijtihad, described often in terms resplendent with imagery such as of door to be thrown open. This is considered necessary for the evolution of laws required for meeting new facts and situations that may emerge in the Islamic social institutions. The persistence of this appraisal over a prolonged duration, however, is not the representation of an exactly appropriate outlook. The adoption of the legal means and the method for the utilization of Ijtihad to its full juridical benefits in the society is the real issue. Many a time in life, the dilemmas are resolvable only by developing the correct approach which can claim the benefit of profound insight, for the definition of the attainable objective may otherwise remain an inert inference for an indefinite period. Noticeworthy, however, is the critical point that Ijtihad is not to be misconstrued as the independent exercise of juristic opinion. The legal acumen underlying Shafii's equation of Ijtihad with "Qiyas" or analogous reasoning is comprehensible in this perspective.

On the other hand, Ijtihad and Qiyas are considered two essential conditions for participation in Ijma. Now, the Supreme Principles utilized in the Legal Method are viewable as the determinants of the jurisdiction for the terms of Divine Will on religio-legal aspects and, in the final analysis, are usable for the validation of the interpretation of primary sources of Islamic Law and the results of analogical reasoning. The emphasis is to be made that the Islamic legal concept of validation, besides its reliability as the standard for the full expression of law, is a fortiori the case where the legal principles of interpretation and construction are involved.

In this regard, invaluable lessons are available to be drawn from the legal precedents set in the initial period of Islamic history. As a chronicled fact, Caliph Umar and Abu Yusuf are associated with many a legal decision which, though prima facie seemed contrary to the strict letter of law, nevertheless, those were more in harmony with the underlying principles of the accessible primary source of law. With this in view, it is evident that the legal formulation, prescribed in this treatise, is a reliable expression of the juristic desire for the revitalization of Ijtihad and, more importantly, it is adoptable as a process within the delineated framework of its application. If this approach embodies the vital principle of optimal legal development, then, it also is decisively exclusive of any consideration of the independent expression of the juristic opinion in matters of Islamic Law. Additionally, it is also appreciable that the criterion for academic research and intellectual effort, as the suggested requisite of Ijtihad, is satisfactorily fulfilled with the implementation of the legal formulation.

Appropriate definition of the various juristic principles of legal utility has been provided at other junctures during the course of this treatise. However, an abbreviated account of the fact of their incorporation in the functions of the Legal Method, founded upon the Supreme Principles, is to be furnished here. Equity is described by Aristotle in the "Ethics" as a correction of legal justice. The construction of equity as anintrinsic ethical superiority of law has also been adopted. The fact of Islamic

Law transforming the Islamic principles of beneficence, repentance and moral rectitude, through the individualization of the dispensation of justice, in contrast from a tendency of their universalization generally existing in law, has already been dwelt upon, and it will be an Islamic expression for the granting of formal recognition to the legal notion, already known to the latter-day social jurisprudence.

Among the other juristic principles, Istihsan and Istislah are basically doctrines of equity and if the former is identified with juristic preference, then, the latter is credited to the Muslim jurist Malik for its legal applicability as benefit to the community. This legal notion of Istislah was further markedly developed and the scope of its juristic application was extensively enlarged by Shatibi under the general designation of "Masla." And the juristic principle of "Istihsan" is in the nature of future juristic exposition and development of Islamic Law. Now due to the simple reason that the Supreme Principles are of wider and fundamental legal scope, the aforementioned juristic principles will discover evident expression through the formulated Legal Method.

Difficulties Ahead

Notwithstanding the repleteness of legal literature with the usefulness of Ijma, which has been adequately dwelled upon during the earlier course of this discourse, the all-important issue of an efficient method for the utilization of this source of law-making in the present-day is in demand of a convincing response. Ijma can be viewed as an organized form of Ijtihad; Iqbal also subscribed to this viewpoint and suggested that the only possible form Ijma can acquire in modern times is the adoption of its role by the legislative assembly. According to this suggestion, the Islamic religious doctors are considered as the "vital part" of a legislative assembly for matters related to law. Adherence to this opinion was reflected during more contemporary times from the observation made in a legal precedent: A prerequisite for every member of a legislative assembly should be a fair amount of knowledge of law-making in Islam. The variance of academic viewpoint from reckonable socio-political realities is not the only issue that arises after a profound evaluation of the previous observations. The criteria for the merit of reason in the assignment of legal authority to lima is another issue which is as substantive as it is of historical relevance.

The eminent Muslim jurist, Shafii, is credited with the original contribution of Ijma by extension of the principle of agreement on matters of law into a source of law-making. The most notable quotation associated with the legist's name in this respect, to reiterate, is: whatever the community of Islam has agreed upon at any time is of God! If this juristic principle incorporates the underlying concept of consensus without the concurrent inclusion of the merit of reasons, then, an important prototypical issue, adoptable to be the augury for the consideration of far more weighty matters, whether the common political error can lay claim to Ijma, is to be seriously addressed. In the opinion of Coulson, the elected office of the Caliph as the basic article of Muslim constitutional law, is not derived from any text in the primary sources of law or analogy therefrom, but from the agreed practice of the early Muslim community. Two points of immediate and substantive significance arise.

Firstly, the issue of the source of political authority of the Caliph in Islam is to be responded. The characteristic requirements of the Islamic rule of law, the legal expression of the Quranic idea of political allegiance, and the Scriptural precept about the mutual consultation as a means to the conduct of affairs are affirmative indications concerning the consent and consensus as the requirements for the conduct of political matters. In addition, the Quranic ideas of the vicegerency of man, collective evaluation of a nation, and the fundamental prerequisite of self-determination in the sense of individual freedom of informed choice, in matters related to religious obligations, in general, and to the participation in Islamic defensive war ("Jihad"), in particular, are no less contributory towards the legal concept of political authority in Islam. Noticeworthy is the historic fact in this connection, the role of later Ijma in respect of the political tradition for the office of the Caliph was consonant with the political convention established during Omayyad and subsequently in Abbasid dynasties, rather than with the political prerequisite of allegiance ("baiya") for the office of Caliph, which was in practice during the early Islamic community.

The inference is of significance that it was a matter of fact, and not of law in consonance with the Islamic requirements of the rule of law as alluded to before, which was sustained through the "informal" Ijma or consensus in the Islamic society. And, secondly, the much professed value of Ijma as a source of law has not resulted in its institutionalization with the delineation of well-defined criteria for its legal authority.

The proposed Legal Method has the demonstrable advantage of compensating the shortcomings outlined in relation to Ijma. The judicial implementation of the method will equate with the satisfaction of the underlying concept of consensus or the Ijma of jurists, that is, special Ijma. However, its ratification by common Ijma will await the popularity of the Islamic legal system. But the most important requirement of the "merit of reasons" for the legal authority of Ijma is constituted by the set of Supreme Fundamental Islamic Principles as the foundations of the Legal Method. The juridical contribution of the method will repose reliance upon the approach that the conversion of a Fundamental Principle into a secondary sense will violate its universality, thereby, granting it the superseding hierarchical legal role in respect of the legal enactments.

Unity Factors

The legal formulation provides the basis for the consensus concerning the definition of Islamic legal rule, and the legal conceptions in the Islamic Law. In addition, the relationship of the law to the Supreme Principles, by allowing Islamic legal scope to the individualization of judicial decisions, will foster a community of common legal outlook. The exercise of juristic discretion will repose reliance upon the Fundamental Principles, derived from the primary sources of law, which, by establishing a framework of legal reasoning, further fortifies that outlook. The vital judicial dimension, a constituent of the "separation of powers," in its purposeful sense, that is, the exercise of legal judgment in the arrival of individual judicial decisions, will prove facilitative. And judicial decisions, acting as legal precedents, in addition to imparting stimulus to juristic scholarship in Islamic societies, are likely to engender similar results.

The need for a formulation to furnish a wide basis for the uniformity of laws in Islamic countries has been latent since the legal "sectarianism" that surfaced consequent to the various schools of law. And the fact that the blind legal orthodoxy or "taqlid," a juristic dogma which is exclusive of "Ijtihad," stymied the legal development in Islam further, is citable as its testimony. The role of "Ijma" assignable to the Islamic legislative assemblies, as envisaged by some renowned Islamic legists and allusion to this effect has been made in the preceding sections, is also identified with a drawback in the performance of that function by the assemblies independently of each other. This had led to the justifiable apprehension that the resulting variations in lima will undermine the Islamic unity.

In contrast, the Legal Method establishes a genuine basis due to the available criteria for the foundation of lima, and relocates it to the juristic realm where it essentially belongs according to its definition. This uniformity of approach in relation to Ijma, insofar as the justifiable criteria of its application and the source of its exercise-the consensus of the learnedare concerned, can be an antecedent of unity in different Muslim societies. As an impact of the Legal Method upon the scope of law-making and adaptability of law, the influence of the legal system upon other parallel social systems and institutions will be positively enhanced. This becomes a determinant factor in allowing a primal role to the legal system in the social order. The crucial issue of the adaptability of law finds a judicious response in the legal formulation, which allows accommodation to the vital aspects of "stability" and "change," and reconciles the dimensions of Faith and law as indispensable requirements for the reconstitution of Islamic legal system.

This establishing of a set role for law in independent societies will improve Islamic unity. The legal system will be comparable with other leading systems of law in the world. The verification of this assertion is demonstrable on theoretical grounds and it is the onus of this discourse. As a matter of fact, the envisaged Islamic legal system will consist of certain salient legal features ensuing from the concept of law, which bestow upon it a relative superior merit. The operative ideals of a genuine Islamic society are to find legal expression towards the organization of Islamic Nomocracy. The legal formulation entails an approach which guides towards a judicial direction, nearly in diametric opposition compared with that made available by the constitutional requirements in some Muslim countries. In the latter instance, the mere demand of the law not to be repugnant to the Islamic injunctions results in the orientation of law to the past, in the sense of the law being incapable of facing to the future, and the reductionistic definition of law whereby it is a corpus of rules, hence, imputing to the legal system an artless form.

From the foregone, the conclusion of an insufficient legal development is available. The serious dual drawbacks of this outcome are the law not being contributory to the formation of an ascendant Islamic legal system, and the law tending to impart the characteristics of a "closed society." The latter drawback is indicative of the law resembling with a municipal setup, wherein individual interests are suppressed by the society.

In contrast, the Legal Method embodies the principles of self-sustaining legal creativity, which becomes a precursor of the reconstitution of the legal system. The law no longer becomes so much a process of external imposition, as it represents the internal development from within the law *per se.* And the individualization of legal decisions, as a pronounced feature of the emphasis upon individual interests in the law, will serve both as a distinguishing juridical characteristic of the new era of Islamic legal system, and the vital means for the organization of an "open society." These and other interrelated social and legal objectives, attainable with the application of the Legal Method, represent the uniformity of attributes associated with an ascendant social order, which will acquire the new basis for Islamic unity.

In essence, the continuous social movement from being to becoming in the realm of law, caused with the application of the Legal Method, has the convincing constituents of an ascendant society, with its potential of lending vehement impetus to the concept and reality of Islamic unity.

4

Commitment of Crime

Basic Perception

Before deciding whether or not a criminal should be punished, we must determine the extent of his responsibility for the offence he committed. It is to be noted that Islam takes this into account when it considers the question of crime and punishment.

Role of Judiciary

Islam holds the balance of justice in the right manner and insists on examining all conditions and circumstances connected with the offence. On studying a crime Islam takes into consideration at the same time the viewpoint of the criminal and that of the community against which aggression took place. In the light of such considerations Islam prescribes the fair punishment which is in accordance with the dictates of sound logic and wise reasoning.

A person commits crime because he knows that he can escape the grip of law for lack of evidence; he may succeed in getting acquittal through the influence of persons or wealth. Last of all, if he is punished, the punishment will be much less than the magnitude of injury he has done, or the wrongful gain he has made. But the one who believes in the existence of Allah, and the life Hereafter may even in the thick layers of darkness, desist from committing crime because of the fear that permanent witnesses appointed on his shoulders by the Sovereign are present and cannot be avoided in any way. He will not be able to abscond and escape punishment. However secretly a man may plot, everything is known to Allah. His recording Angels are, by at all times and in all places, to prepare a record of his deeds for his own conviction when the time comes for final judgment. The Holy Quran says :

> "Or deem they that We cannot hear their secret thoughts and private confidences? Nay, but Our envoys, present with them, do record." (43:80)

Not only Allah is having track and full record of everything going on in this universe but also according to Islam, this record of events is being preserved and will be presented on the Last Day. Each and every individual is answerable to Allah on that Day and everybody will be either rewarded or punished according to his deeds performed during his or her life tenure in this universe. He may escape punishment of any crime committed by producing false evidence in this world, but in the next world he or she is bound to face the consequences. The Holy Quran says:

> "And every man's augury have We fastened to his own neck. On the Day of Judgment .We shall bring out for him a scroll, which he will see spread open. (It will be said to him :) "Bead thine (own) record : Sufficient is thy soul this Day to make out an account against the." (17 : 13, 14)

Again the Holy Quran says :

> "And thou will see every sect bowing the knee ; Every sect will be called to its record. This Day shall ye be recompensed for all that ye did. This Our Record

> speaks about you with truth, for We were wont to put on record all that ye did."
>
> (45 : 28, 29)

Now this comprehensive system of belief in the Unseen (One Allah), accountability on the Day of Resurrection and Allah's Own Guidance about right and wrong makes the behaviour and living of a man quite distinct from the one having any other conception about man's status in this universe.

Human behaviour over thousands of years endorses this fact that the people who do not consider themselves as answerable and responsible to Allah, who act on this presumption that life is but of this world only, who measure one's success or failure according to the attainments achieved in this world in respect of wealth, power and popularity, who depending upon their materialistic views reject Allah's Guidance, do become a symbol of wickedness. They live like animals paying least regard to any moral values.

Actually their moral values follow the footsteps of their desires and selfish ends. To achieve these ends, they commit every sort of cruelty and injustice. Their misdeeds convert the whole universe into a hell for others. All the mischief was introduced by Evil. The Holy *Quran* says :

> "Mischief has appeared on land and sea because of (the meed) that the hands of men have earned."
>
> (30:41)

Actually a man devoid of Allah's Guidance and the conception of accountability in the life Hereafter may be a great man otherwise, but is bound to behave like a beast. He runs after the benefits, lusts and comforts of the world and succumbs to temptations. He is so overpowered by avarice of these low desires that he discards all the moral values. He transgresses all the limits that he ought to have observed. Such human beings are no doubt like animals. The Holy Quran says:

> "Many are the Jinns and human beings We have made for Hell. They have hearts wherewith they understand not, eyes wherewith they see not, and ears wherewith they hear not. They are like animals – nay, even worse, for they are heedless (of warning)."
>
> (7:179)

It is but natural that man not believing in the Unseen, Day of Resurrection and Likes and Dislikes of Allah should behave like an animal. After all, if a human being does not possess the conception of accountability on some day and thinks that he is not going to be rewarded for his good deeds and punished for his bad actions, why should he act rightly, why should he make sacrifice for others and why should he undergo any sort of moral restraints ? It is the fear of Allah, surrender before His Almighty Power and fear of the Day of Judgment that makes man to save himself from all sorts of crimes.

Roots of Evil

Inner Urge : Islam works for removal of sins and thereby removes the chances of brewing crime. Every crime is sin but every sin is not a crime. If the sin is removed the brewing of crime will be minimised, but if the sin remains unattended and the society is not secured from the sinners who have indulged into the sin due to the inner urge, crime will be rampant, and no punishment will be useful in curing the criminals. Therefore, the basic question is to reform the society from the sinful life.

Secondly, Islam strives by various means to preclude circumstances that may lead to crime. There are sins which emerge out of the inner urge and environments create cause for it : such as false suspicion, envy, malice, sneaking whisper and the desire of godhood. It is the lust for power and desire for exploitation that prompts him to project himself on other people as god and extract their obedience, force them to bow down before him in reverential awe and make instrument of self aggrandisement. Although no one can be punished for any of these sins by any human society for the reason that none of these can be brought in a judicial court and none can be proved by documentary or circumstantial evidence, yet a person who is under influence of such sins may commit crime by causing injury to the society or to the individuals in one way or the other. Therefore, Islam takes notice of these sins and tries to remove them from the society.

Environmental Influence and Incentive of Crime : Man as a species of the living creature is in need of food, clothing, shelter, comfort and other things connected with the security of life and security of his race. He labours and exerts for getting his needs. If he can get his needs without any hindrance, discrimination or preference for any person or a group then there will bo no inducement for a man to act unlawfully. Islam takes full responsibility to see that the basic needs of life are provided, and takes care of the needs of the destitute. It manages to provide equal privileges and opportunities for every citizen to enable him to seek economic livelihood. Then social atmosphere is created in which none is compelled by force of circumstances to steal. To remove adultery and suppress the desire of sexual intercourse, marriage has been made easy. Mixed gathering of men and women and public appearance of painted and pampered women are completely prohibited.

In the society so organised, having love for virtues and hate for evils and sins, it will not be tolerated by the society that any person may be sinful or may disturb the economic system, or cause difficulties for the citizens to earn their livelihood through-honest and legal means. In such a society if any one would insist to carry on the evil designs, try to encroach upon the right of others, pollute the social atmosphere and commit crime when there was no incentive for doing so, it becomes absolutely essential to isolate, eliminate, exterminate and annihilate such elements for security of the social set up. It is for such elements that punishment is to be inflicted and law should operate.

The Sentences

The punishment prescribed by the law cannot be reduced or increased even under sentiments of mercy. The Holy *Quran* says:

> "And let not pity for the twain withhold you from obedience to Allah, if you believe in Allah and the Last Day. (24 : 2)

From the above verse of the Holy Quran, the following conclusions may be drawn:

1. If the guilt is proved, the culprit must be punished at all costs.
2. There should be no mercy in inflicting the punishment.
3. The prescribed punishment cannot be replaced : (a) if the change is due to the sense of mercy, it is disobedience, (b) if it is due to the sense of cruelty, it is denial and defiance and only a hypocrite can imagine or say so.

The Holy Prophet (peace and blessings of Allah be upon him) is reported to have said:

> An officer will be produced on the Day of Judgment who reduced a stripe from the punishment. He will be questioned for the reduction. "On the ground of mercy for Thy slave", will be his reply. "Were you more merciful than Myself", Allah will cay unto him, thus he will be ushered to be taken to the Hell.

Another officer will be produced who enhanced the punishment by one stripe. He will be questioned for his doing so. "To stop them from disobedience", will be his reply. Allah will say unto him, "Do you stand wiser than Me"? and he will be ordered to be taken to Hell.

The above was the decision of the case when punishment

was changed either way, but if reduction or the enhancement is in view of the status of the man it will become worst.

Aishah (Allah be pleased with her) reported Allah's Messenger (peace and blessings of Allah be upon him) as saying : "O people! the nations have gone, who were destroyed for the reason that one of status if he committed theft was overlooked and when a poor powerless committed theft he was punished."

Object of Punishment : Humiliation for the convict and the lesson for the public is the purpose of punishment. Thus the object of punishment is :

1. To award punishment to the culprit equal to the magnitude of his guilt.
2. To prevent him for repeating the crime.
3. To serve as a lesson for others so that inclinations of crime be removed through this operation and none may dare commit crime.
4. Punishment be given publicly so that the officer may not favour any one while inflicting punishment. This public display will have deterrent effect, and all those in the public who had inclination of committing crime will know that they will have to endure such punishment if they commit a crime.
5. *Protection of honour and chastity :* In the modern system very little value is attached to the honour of man and chastity of woman. We find that fornication is no crime under the modern systems. Adultery is a crime to the extent that the adulterer has infringed the right of the husband.

   Islam assigns priority to the value attached to the chastity of women and to the respect and honour of men. Therefore, it takes strong measures to preserve this value. Thus we see that the severest punishment is prescribed for persons who molest a woman, or dishonour a man. Therefore, punishment is prescribed in this respect by Allah and it has not been left to man to impose punishment for such crimes at his own discretion. Islam differentiates between fornication and adultery. For the former hundred stripes, and stoning to death for the latter, are prescribed. For false accusation, the punishment of eighty stripes is also prescribed, and the criminal cannot escape punishment unless he produces four witnesses to prove accusation.

6. *Preservation of Life* : In the modern system apparently importance is attached to the life of a man but the State has become a party in all such cases instead of satisfying the aggrieved. Therefore, the State punishes a criminal unmindful of the fact that the revenge exists or is washed out of the mind of the aggrieved. Under this legal system neither revenge is removed nor the recurrence of crime is checked with the result that a long chain of murders and crimes continues between the parties.

Under the Islamic Legal System, an equal right of revenge is permitted. Eye for eye, ear for ear, limb for limb and life for life is the law. But this is the right of a person who received injury or of his heir and not the State as is seen in the other legal systems. Therefore, the aggrieved can forgive the accused or demand compensation instead of revenge. Islamic Law is clear and natural that if this law is enforced the chain of crime which continues between the parties involved for generation by generation will be finished. The basic object of Penal Law of Islam is eradication of grievance from the heart and mind of the aggrieved party.

. ***Preservation of Property*** : In the un-Islamic system highest value is attached to the property and there is distinction between a man of the upper class and a common man. In order to protect machines and palaces, sometimes hundreds of persons are shot dead; and there is nothing in the so-called modern legai system to redress the aggrieved. No such class distinction exists in Islam.

Islam distinguishes between theft and dacoity, embezzlement, bribery, dishonesty and criminal breach of trust in prescribing punishments. Punishment for theft and dacoity are prescribed by Allah and no one can make any change in it. As regards punishments for embezzlement, it is left to the discretion of the Qadi. There is also distinction in the crime of theft of eatables, i.e., fruits, vegetables etc., in regard to inflicting prescribed punishment. A person who steals to appease his hunger cannot be punished if he steals an eatable to keep his soul and body together.

Significant Features

Punishments prescribed by Islam have been severely objected to by the opponents of Islam. Punishments in Islam include amputation of hand, flogging and stoning to death and are thus considered very severe. But apart from being severe these punishments have some prominent characteristics which are not usually taken into account while making this objection. Some of the chief characteristics are :

1. These punishments are inflicted as a last resort.
2. These punishments are inflicted to serve as an example to others.
3. These punishments are reformative.
4. These punishments are retributive, and redressive.

Punishment, Last Resort : Islam does not remain in search of any victim committing offence and as soon as it comes across one it inflicts the punishments immediately. Actually Islam leaves no stone unturned to block all the channels leading to a sin and it is in very rare cases that one commits sin and is thus exposed to punishment. For example we take adultery or fornication and see how Islam imposes checks to wipe out their very possibility.

Internal Checks : Belief in the Hereafter is the backbone of these checks. Islam explains that every action major or minor of every human being is recorded very accurately and this record will be placed before each and every individual on the Day of Resurrection, thus rewarding or is rewarding him depends upon the nature of actions. An act done in the thick layers of darkness may remain a secret in this world but cannot go unresponded in the life Hereafter. Even the feelings and passions taking turn in the very corner of any heart, is known to Allah and cannot go unnoticed. In this way apart from external checks Islam establishes a permanent sort of internal checks in the very heart of each of its followers. This is the greatest check in the way of incentives leading to sins.

External Checks : Then Islam imposes external checks, which are again of two types:

Marital Life

1. In the first instance it induces the individual to marry and makes the institution of marriage as easy as possible. Celibacy has been condemned and it has been ordained that unmarried people must be brought into the bondage of marriage. Bachelors if nothing else do, generally start taking interest in spreading foul news. Thus in the Holy *Quran* it is said :

"And marry those among you who are single, and those who are pious among your male slaves and your female slaves ; if they are needy, Allah will make them free from want out of His Grace ; and Allah is Ample-Giving, Knowing. And let those who cannot find a match keep chaste until Allah makes them free from want out of His Grace." (24 : 32, 33)

Hadith also lays great stress upon living in a married state. The Holy Prophet (peace and blessings of Allah be upon him) is reported to have said, "0 assembly of young people ! Whoever of you has the means to support a wife, he should get married, for this is the best means of keeping the looks cast down and guarding chastity, and he who has not enough means, let him keep fast, for this will act as castration."

(Bukhari)

According to another Hadith the Holy Prophet (peace and blessings of Allah be upon him) said : When a servant (of Allah) marries, he perfects half (his) religion ; and let him fear Allah in regard to the remaining half. (Mishkat)

2. Monasticism as well as celibacy is disallowed.
3. If a man is not satisfied with one wife, he is allowed to marry upto four ladies.
4. A widow is allowed to remarry as and when she deems fit (except for a short period after the death of her husband).
5. If a couple gets fed up of each other the provision of divorce has been made, which can be exercised by either of them.
6. After separation there is no restriction if any one of them wants to remarry (except for a woman who is required to wait for a few months till the end of pregnancy).
7. Early marriage has been encouraged. Reward in the Hereafter has been announced for those fathers who marry their daughters as soon as signs of puberty appear.
8. Whereas the illegal sexual act (fornication) between man and woman is said to be severely punishable, the legal sexual act (through marriage) is reported to be a part of devotion.

Restrictions on Free Mixing of Men and Women : Secondly, Islam puts restrictions on the general mixing of men and women:

1. Women's activities have been restricted within the walls of the house. Even when coming out of their houses for certain necessities of life women are forbidden to display their beauty and make up and to wear ringing and attracting ornaments. The Holy *Quran* says:

And stay in your houses and display not your finery like that of the Times of Ignorance." (33 : 33)

2. The institution of 'veil' is the corner-stone to guard the chastity of the women. The Holy *Quran* says :

"O Prophet! say to thy wives and thy daughters and the women of the believers that they should cast their outer garments over their persons; this will be more proper, that they may be known (ladies of reputation); and thus they will not be given trouble."

(33 : 59)

3. Even when coming across, men and women are not allowed to gaze at each other lustily : The Holy Quran says:

"Say to the believing men that they should lower their gaze and restrain their sexual passions. That is purer for them. Lo ! Allah is aware of what they do. And say to the believing women that they should lower their gaze and restrain their sexual passions and should not display their ornaments except what appear thereof." (24 : 30, 31).

Islam does not allow that a man should cast eyes upon women except his own wife or Mahrams (the women of the prohibited degrees, closely related to a man like mother, sister, daughter, etc.) in full gaze. The first surprise look is naturally unavoidable, but the second sight upon ladies except those mentioned above is not allowed. Such a sort of looking at is tantamount to fornication according to a saying of the Holy Prophet (peace and blessings of Allah be upon him) who said that a man can commit fornication through all his senses. Staring is a fornication of the eyes ; passion-arousing and artificial type of talk is a fornication of the tongue ; to enjoy the voice is a fornication of the ear, and to touch and walk for an illicit act is the fornication of the hands and feet.

4. Islam lays great stress upon the privacy of home-life. In the first place entering other's house without permission is forbidden. The Holy *Quran* says :

"O you who believe ! Do not enter houses other than your own houses until you have asked permission and saluted their inmates." (24: 27)

Another verse of the Holy *Quran* runs thus :

"O you who believe! Let those whom your right hands possess, and those of you who have not attained puberty ask permission of you three times : before morning prayer, and when you put off your clothes at mid-day in summer and after the prayer of night. There are three times of privacy for you."

(24 : 58)

Privacy of home-life is not limited to the entering of other houses only. But there are clear *Ahadith* of the Holy Prophet (peace and blessings of Allah be upon him) which forbid to peep into the houses of others and to stay in front of the doors of other's houses while calling them out. As a corollary, reading the letters of others without their permission is a sin. Further the instructions not to enter into houses without the permission of their inmates are not limited to the other's houses only, but even entering into the house of the mother or sister without seeking her permission is not allowed. Once a man asked the Holy Prophet (peace and blessings of Allah be upon him): I am required to go to my mother frequently as there is none else to look after her except myself, so should I seek her permission each time I have to go to her ? The Holy Prophet (peace and blessings of Allah be upon him) said, "Do you like to see your mother naked otherwise" ?

5. Islam does not allow talking of men and women face to face (with the exception of *Mahrama*). The Holy *Quran* says :

"And when you ask them (the wives of the Holy Prophet) for anything you want, ask them from behind a curtain, that makes for greater purity for your hearts and for theirs." (33 : 53)

It is thus clear from the above verse of the Holy Quran that when men and women are forbidden face to face talk, the question of mixed gatherings, co-education, and their working together in offices and factories does not arise. Even when talking from behind a curtain the women should speak firmly, so that someone having bad intentions may not feel inclination in the talk.

6. Last but not the least is the overall system ordained by Islam to keep the general atmosphere of the Muslim Society pure of false rumours and lustful talks. Islam does not allow that its followers should propagate sexual news and enjoy by playing with the character of others. A false accusation of adultery (*qadhf*) is punished almost as severely as adultery itself. The Holy *Quran* says :

"And those who accuse free women of fornication, then do not bring four witnesses, scourge them with eighty stripes, and never admit evidence from them; for such men are indeed transgressors. Except those who repent after this and act aright, for Allah is Forgiving, Merciful. (24 :4, 5)

It may be seen here that while in ordinary matters two witnesses are required, in case of an accusation of adultery four witnesses must be produced. Thus a case of adultery can be established on the strongest possible evidence.

In view of this comprehensive system of internal and external checks, one can easily visualize the general environment in which committing of an offence itself becomes almost impossible. The last nail in this system, however, is thrust by the fear of a severe punishment.

Thus the Penal Law of Islam curbs fornication and adultery by force as a last resort. Whereas the moral teachings of Islam cleanse man within so that he does not feel inclined towards sinning; its penal law regulates his external behaviour so that in case the moral teachings remain ineffective, his evil inclinations taking practical shape may be suppressed by force.

> The Holy Prophet (peace and blessings of Allah be upon him) said : Protect the Muslims as far as possible against the application of the Law. Let the culprit off if he can possibly be let off. For the Imam making a mistake in forgiving is better than his making a mistake in applying the Law. (Tirmidhi)

Punishments are Exemplary : Now one can easily think of the social set-up in which such a comprehensive plan of checks is exercised. But in spite of all these internal and external checks if one still commits a crime, severe punishment should be inflicted on the convict because he has no excuse or justification. Even while inflicting punishment, Islam still plans to make use of it in one way or the other. By inflicting exemplary punishment to a stubborn wrong-doer Islam carries out psychological operation of all those in the society having criminal intentions and trends. This is the object of gathering the masses on the occasion of punishing the adulterers. This is why hands or feet are cut off and this is why a punishment like stoning to death is carried out in open day light. Hanging somebody in the late hours of night as is prevalent in many present days' so-called civilized countries is not allowed by Islam, because it does not serve as an example to others.

Punishments are Reformative: It may be noted that whenever in the Holy Quran the punishment has been prescribed for an offence, it has been concluded either by advice or by a threat of punishment in the life Hereafter mentioning Great Attributes of Allah Almighty. For example, in cases of murder, the Holy Quran says:

> "And he who does this shall (not only) receive the punishment (but) the chastisement shall be doubled to him on the Day of Resurrection, and he shall abide therein in abasement." (25 : 68, 69)

Further, the Holy *Quran* says:

> "And there is life for you in the law of retaliation, 0 men of understanding, that you may guard yourself!" (2: 179)

In case of theft, the Holy *Quran* says :

> "But whoever repents after his iniquity and reforms himself, Allah will turn to him mercifully, for Allah is Forgiving, Merciful." (5 : 39)

In case of Qadhf, the Holy *Quran* says :

> "......And do not admit any evidence from them ever, and these it is that are transgressors. Except those who repent after this and act aright, for Allah is Forgiving, Merciful." : (4, 5)

Actually an individual who commits a crime never gets rid of its bad consequences even after he receives punishment in this world until and unless he or she also repents and acts aright.

Punishments are Retributive : Islamic punishments, in the fourth place, are retributive as laid down in the Holy *Quran*:

> "O you who believe ! prescribed for you is retribution in case of the slain : the free for the free ; and the slave for the slave ; and the woman for the woman. And if something is remitted for him (the offender) by his brother (who has suffered the loss of his near one)

then let this remission be adhered to with fairness,
and let its payment (be made) in a goodly manner."

(2 : 178)

Its object is, therefore, to satisfy that emotion of retributive indignation which in all healthy communities is stirred up by injustice.

Refutation of Criticism

Punishments prescribed by Islam are criticized on the following grounds :

1. Punishments are severe, inhuman and bar-barons.
2. A criminal being the victim of society is entitled to medical treatment rather than punishment.

Severity of Punishments : The Holy *Quran* provides for punishments for murder, dacoity ; adultery ; theft and accusation of adultery. The punishment for murder is death but an option is given to heirs to accept compensation instead. Dacoity is punishable with death, or amputation of hands and feet or imprisonment. Theft is punishable with cutting off of hand. For adultery the punishment provided in the Holy Quran is flogging for unmarried and stoning to death in the case of married persons.

The above punishments especially those prescribed for theft and adultery have been condemned severely by the Western people. They often say, "Can we apply today the same barbarous punishments which were inflicted long ago in the desert. Is it permissible to cut a thief's hand for five shillings" ?

It is rather astonishing that this objection is raised by those who justified most inhuman act of history, the subjection of mankind to nuclear weapons whereby hundreds of thousands of men, women, children and even babies, all wholly innocent persons, were within no time put to death. How is it that the twentieth century permits the slaughter of forty thousand innocent people in North Africa but condemns the rightful punishment of one single criminal!

Whatever view be taken of the extent of enormity of this act those who have justified it have subscribed to the proposition that the inhumanity of an act is to be decided not with reference to the act itself but with reference to its consequences. They have subscribed also to the proposition that in determining whether an inhuman act is justified the innocence of the person who is subjected to it and even the tenderness of his age is irrelevant. But if these two propositions are accepted all concentration camps, purges, genocides, third degree methods, and mass slaughtering of innocent persons are justified provided only that the person who perpetrated such inhumanities alleged that he was acting for the human welfare. It is surprising to note that while the twentieth century claims to be an advanced and civilized century not even a hundredth of the inhumanities witnessed by it were witnessed by any previous century.

It must be explained in the first instance that the amputation of hand is the maximum punishment for theft. It is admittedly not to be imposed if the theft be of a property less than *nisab*. It is also not to be awarded, in accordance with the practice of the Holy Prophet (peace and blessings of Allah be upon him) if fruit be stolen with a view of satisfying hunger. It is not applicable when the property stolen is not kept in a properly protected place. Further such punishment is never inflicted where there is the slightest doubt that the thief was impelled to commit crime due to starvation or hunger.

This is evident from a rule laid down by the second Caliph, Hadrat Umar ibn al-Khattab (Allah be pleased with him), who is considered as one of the most prominent Jurists of Islam. Hadrat Umar (Allah be pleased with him) was known for his rigidity in enforcing the rules of Shariah ; therefore it cannot be said that he was lenient in the interpretation of the law. It should be remembered that Hadrat Umar (Allah be pleased with him) did not carry out the punishment prescribed for theft i.e., amputation of the hand, during the year of famine when there was some doubt that people might be impelled to theft by hunger.

The above-mentioned rule is best illustrated by the following episode :

> "It was reported to Umar (Allah be pleased with him) that some young men in the service of Hatib ibn Abu Baltaa had stolen the she-camel of a man from the tribe of Muznah: When Umar (Allah be pleased with him) questioned the young men they admitted the theft, so he ordered their hands to be cut. But on the second thought he said, "By God I would cut their hands if I did not know that you employ these young men and starve them to that they would be permitted to eat that which is prohibited unto them." Then he addressed their employer saying : "By God, since I have not cut their hands I am going to penalise you with a fine that shall pain you," and he ordered him to pay double the price of she-camel."

This punishment is redressive. It also illustrates a very clear and express principle : Punishment will not be inflicted where there are circumstances which impel the criminal to commit a crime." This principle is supported by the saying of the Holy Prophet (peace and blessings of Allah be upon him): "Avoid the execution of punishment by doubt."

Secondly, the punishments provided by the Shariah are applicable only when and where a proper Islamic State exists. These punishments are a part of Islamic system and if applied apart from that system may be wholly inappropriate. The Islamic State strives to ensure a fair distribution of wealth. It is responsible for the support of every citizen, regardless of his creed, caste, race, language, colour or social status. The State is also responsible for ensuring suitable job for all citizens.

Where job is not available or if an individual is incapable of working, aid will be given to him from the *Baitul-Mal* (Public Treasury). According to a saying of the Holy Prophet (peace and blessings of Allah be upon him), "The Government is the guardian of the people."

Thirdly, the criticism for determining the propriety of a punishment is whether the infliction of the punishment will lead to the public good. This good as to be assessed with reference to what happens to the convict and what happens to the society. The most important consideration is the deterrent effect of the punishment to frighten those individuals who have no reasonable motive for crime yet feel a strong yearning for committing crimes. However strong their desires may be, the punishment will surely make them think twice before committing any crime. Even in accordance with the principles accepted by modern jurisprudence a very severe punishment is justified if it will have deterrent effect.

Here an extract is given from Salmond's *Jurisprudence,* a standard work on analytical jurisprudence, wherein the learned author justifies burning alive as a punishment for all offences major or minor if such punishment would in fact deter persons from committing offences :

> "In considering the measure of criminal liability it will be convenient to bestow exclusive attention upon the deterrent purpose of the criminal law, remembering, however, that the conclusions so obtained are subject to possible modification by reference to those subordinate and incidental purposes of punishment which we thus provisionally disregard.

"Were men perfectly rational, so as to act invariably in accordance with an enlightened estimate of consequences, the question of the measure of punishment would present no difficulty. A draconian simplicity and severity would be perfectly just and perfectly effective. It would be possible to act on the Stoic paradox that all offences involve equal guilt, and to visit with the utmost rigour of the law every deviation, however, slight, from the appointed way. In other words, if the deterrent effect of severity were certain and complete, the best law would be that which by the most extreme and undiscriminating severity effectually extinguished crime. Were human nature so constituted that a threat of burning all offenders alive would with certainty prevent all breaches of the law, then this would be the just and fitting penalty for all offences from high treason to petty larceny."

It appears that the criticism on the severity of punishments is due to a failure to realize the spiritual nature of punishment. A punishment is not cruelly inflicted by one man on another. It is a sacrifice offered by Society for maintaining the purity of its moral life and it is also, at least so far as Muslims are concerned, an atonement, and both these, that is, the sacrifice and the atonement are acts of the highest spiritual merit.

"Obedience to the law" is the basic characteristic of a true Muslim Society. Dr. Iqbal says : "The life of a Muslim is from law alone." That is the whole substance of the teachings of the Holy Prophet (peace and blessings of Allah be upon him). There are instances of guilty persons who came to the Holy Prophet (peace and blessings of Allah be upon him) and forced him to inflict punishments, even capital punishments on them, though no one had charged them with any offence, and though the Holy Prophet (peace and blessings of Allah be upon him) made efforts to avoid listening to them.

That the amputation of hand does in fact prove a deterrent will appear from the conditions prevailing in a country in which it is now in force, that in Saudi Arabia. It is well known that in that country you can leave your house open and go to another town, and you can leave your shops, even jewelry shops unguarded when you go away to say your daily Prayers. Gordon Gaskell says : "Foreigners consider this a horrible punishment but even they admit that it has made Saudi Arabia – the country with the lowest crime rate in the world."

Further it is not only in Islam that severe punishments are prescribed. Even in other religions certain crimes are punished severely. According to the Old Testament 12 offences were punishable with stoning to death. These included Sabbath-breaking, unchastity (not adultery), blasphemy, striking or even reviling a parent, false pretension to prophesy, witchcraft, idolatry and false evidence. Burning alive had been in pre-Mosaic times punishment for all adultery but in the Old Testament it was confined to adultery committed with the priest's daughter. Death by sword or spear was also the punishment for some offences. Jesus Christ said :

> "And if thy right eye causeth thee to stumble pluck it out and cast it from thee: for it is profitable for thee that one of thy members should perish, and not thy whole body be cast into hell. And if thy right hand causeth thee to stumble cut it off, and cast it from thee; for it is profitable for thee that one of thy members should perish and not thy whole body go into hell!.'
>
> (Matthew, 5 : 29, 30)

This passage may mean that the offending eye or hand is to be severed or it may mean that the offending member of society is to be eliminated. In either case it is a severe punishment.

The severity of punishment is determined mainly by the indignation which the criminal act causes, the importance of the need for preventing its recurrence, and the capacity for endurance, generally of the members of the society which imposes the punishment. All these three factors are on the decline in the present age. There is the greatest indulgence for sin, the need for purity of society has greatly diminished in importance and the capacity for endurance is much less than it used to be. It is agreed that the punishment provided by the

Bible relates to a particular period of human development, but it is to be observed that they were much severer than the punishments ordained by the Holy Quran and if they were justified then, the Quranic punishments are justified now.

In the case of fornication and adultery, the Islamic Law differs radically from the Western law. The Western law does not hold fornication by itself a crime ; it becomes a crime only when it is committed forcibly, or with a married woman. In other words, according to the Western law fornication by itself is no crime ; the real crime is rape, or the act of encroachment on the rights of the husband. Contrary to this, the Islamic Penal Law looks upon fornication by itself as a crime, and regards rape or the act of encroachment as additional crimes. This basic difference between view-points of the two systems of law gives rise to the difference in the punishment of the offence.

In case of rape, the Western law rests content with the sentence of imprisonment only ; in case of fornication with a married woman it requires the fornicator to pay compensation to the husband. This punishment cannot serve as a deterrent, it rather encourages the people. That is why fornication is on the increase in the countries where this law is in force. On the other hand the Islamic Penal Law punishes fornication and adultery so severely that the society is automatically cleansed of this crime for a long time. That is why it has never become common in the countries where the Islamic punishment for it is imposed. Once the punishment ordained by Shariah is carried out, it so deters the whole population that no one can dare commit it for years to come. In a way it performs a psychological operation on the minds of those having criminal tendencies and this reforms them automatically.

The Western people abhor the infliction of a hundred stripes. This is not because they dislike the idea of physical torture. It is because their moral sense has not yet fully developed. At first they regarded fornication as something indecent; now they look upon it as a fun, as a pastime, which amuses two persons for a little while. Therefore, they want that the law should tolerate this act, and should not regard it seriously unless the fornicator encroaches upon somebody else's freedom or legal rights. Even in the case of such an encroachment they regard it as a crime affecting the rights of one person only. Hence, they think that a light sentence or payment of compensation is sufficient punishment for the crime.

Obviously, a person who holds such a view about fornication will look upon a hundred stripes for it as a cruel punishment. But if his moral and social sense had developed, he would realize that fornication, whether it is committed with consent or force, and whether with a married woman or with an unmarried one, is in each case a social crime that affects the whole society. This will naturally make him modify his view about punishment, so that the society is saved from the ill-effects of fornication. He will have to admit that since the motives leading to fornication lie deep in the animal nature of man and since they cannot be eradicated by mere imprisonment or inflicting of penalties, strict measures have to be adopted for their complete eradication For it is better to subject one or a couple of persons to severe physical torture for the purpose of safeguarding hundreds of thousands of people against countless moral and social evils than to inflict light punishment on the criminals and so jeopardise the well-being of net only the society but also of the coming generations.

There is another reason for regarding the infliction of a hundred stripes as cruel. As pointed out above, the Western civilization emerged as a result of the urge of favouring the individual against the society, and it has been built up on an exaggerated notion of the rights of the individual. Therefore, even if an individual harms the society to his heart's content, the Western people do not feel ill at ease ; they rather put up with it willingly in most cases. But when the individual is proceeded against with a view to protecting the rights of the society, they shudder with horror and all their sympathies go with the individual as against the society. Moreover, like all ignorant people, the Western people also have the special characteristic of regarding feelings as more important than reason. Therefore, when they see the individual, as in a particular case, being severely dealt with, they feel outraged at the sight of his suffering. But they do not seem to comprehend the far-reaching effects of the damage that is done to the society and the coming generations, too.

Islam recognises the strength and importunity of sex but it tries to satisfy the sexual instinct through legal means i.e., marriage. Therefore, Islam advocates early marriage and provides aid from the Baitul-Mal (Public Treasury) for those who wish to get married yet cannot afford to do so. On the other hand, Islam purifies society from evil temptations which excite the passions. It also prescribes lofty and noble ideals which exhaust excessive vitality and direct it into the service of public interest. It prefers that leisure time should be spent in trying to become closer and nearer to Allah. In this manner Islam eradicates all temptations that may lead to crime. Nevertheless Islam does not hasten to inflict punishment unless the criminal has disregarded traditions and degenerated to animality by committing adultery so openly that he could be seen by four eye-witnesses, or he willingly confesses.

It may be said that the present economic, social and moral conditions make it difficult for young men to get married and consequently they are led to adultery. There is some truth in that. But when Islam is truly applied there will be no maddening craze, evil temptations which lead young men to corruption, and there will be no pornographic motion pictures, newspapers or songs. No exciting temptation will be walking along the streets. There will be no poverty which prevents people from marriage. It is then and only then that people may be called on to virtuous and they can be virtuous. In such a case punishment may be inflicted on offenders because they have no excuse or justification. Thus Islam, in the first place, tries to wipe out all circumstances and motives that may lead to crime.

When considering the question as to whether punishments provided by Islamic Law are inhuman, it will be appropriate to compare such punishments with the punishments which were in force in the Western countries till early nineteenth century. The punishments prescribed by Islamic Law were imposed in the 7 th century A.D., and from what has been stated above it will appear that death penalty was provided in four cases i.e., murder, dacoity, apostasy and adultery.

It should be remembered that in Islam murder is a crime which can be forgiven through compromise. And death sentence is awarded only when the slain's relatives demand it. Sura Maida verse 33 recommends four punishments for dacoity, and death sentence is awarded only when the dacoit commits murder along with robbery. As for adultery (by married persons) the Holy Prophet (peace and blessings of Allah be upon him) ordered stoning to death for it. And throughout the Rightly-guided Caliphate this was done.

The Hanafite school of thought are unanimous on this. But what were the punishments provided by the Western countries? To take as an example the case of one of them, that is England, upto early nineteenth century there were two hundred and twenty-three offences, the penalty for which was death. These included theft when the value of stolen property was more than one shilling, rioting, destroying banks, bridges, or floodgates, offences against administration of justice, offences against public health, offences against public revenue, rape, forcible abduction and other sexual offences. Treason was severely punishable. Even new in the case of treason the sovereign can order that the head of the convict be cut off while he is still alive.

It will be observed that in severity there is not much difference between the punishments prescribed by Islam and those in force in England till early 19th century. Even at the present time there are countries where punishments are much rigorous than those prescribed by the Shariah. In Soviet Russia for instance, there is death penalty by shooting for some categories of theft, professional counterfeiting, aggravated forms of rape and acceptance of bribe.

It is because Rome Europeans have not studied the reality of the Islamic concept of crime and punishment that they consider the punishments prescribed by Islam as barbarous and degrading to human dignity. They wrongly imagine that such punishments—like the European civil punishments — will be inflicted every day and on a mass scale. They also fancy that the Islamic society indulges in daily execution of flogging, hand-cutting and stoning to death. But the fact is that such deterrent punishments have been executed very rarely. The fact that the punishment for theft has been executed only six times throughout a period of four hundred years is a clear proof that such punishment was primarily meant to prevent crime.

Concept of Mental Sickness : Western countries regard the individual as the centre of life. Such countries straiten the state right to restrict the freedom of individual. This attitude is reflected in their concept of crime and punishment. They sympathize with criminals and treat them gently because they are victims of corrupted circumstances, psychological complexes and nervous disorders which they could not overcome. Therefore such countries are inclined to reduce penalties until—especially in moral offences—they are no longer regarded as punishment.

At this stage psycho-analysis comes in to justify or explain away the crime. It will be noted that Freud was the champion of the historical change which regarded a criminal as the victim of the sexual complexes resulting from the repression of the sexual instincts by society, religion, morality and tradition. Later all schools of psycho-analysts followed Freud's example but many of them did not agree with him that sexual instinct was the centre of life. All such schools regard a criminal as a passive creature who is the victim of general and personal circumstances amidst which he was brought up. They believe in what is called "Psychological determinism" that is to say, a man has no freedom of will or action with respect to the psychological energy which acts according to a predetermined manner.

Thus the public opinion in the West (which is considered to be the fountainhead of law there) and the legislators and courts have been much influenced by the concept that in fact crime is not a deliberate act but is the result of the criminal's mental sickness, who instead of being punished should be treated sympathetically. Although this impression has not resulted in the replacement of prisons by mental hospitals but it has definitely led to a softening of attitude towards moral crime and to a great extent this is responsible for the increasing rate of crime in Western countries.

Apart from the soundness of the argument put forth in support of this concept when one sees crime spreading with alarming rate in the countries where this concept has been accepted and almost extinct where Islamic regulations are in force, one is forced to ask that after all what sort of a "mental sickness" is this which is increasing in the West and receding in Saudi Arabia? If crime is actually a sickness and punishment is no cure for it then in Saudi Arabia too its patients should increase with the same rate as they are in the West. But when we see that in Saudi Arabia crime has almost disappeared then surely this fact shows that the proper cure for this sickness is not the one recommended by the Western people ; and a surer cure is that Qisas (retribution) should be meted out to the murderers in the open, the hands of the thieves should be chopped off in a public gathering, and those who commit adultery should be whipped in public. This would work as psycho-therapy on the minds of those who harbour criminal tendencies.

Crimes and Punishments

Crimes : A criminal act is defined as one that infringes public right: a right whose infringement leaves wider repercussions on the society.

From the viewpoint of Islam when certain primary public rights are violated the wrong is called *Masaat*, that is, crime or offence ; and it gives rise to certain substitutory public rights in the form of *Uqubat* or punishments. *Uqubat* denotes the punishments instituted in the Holy Quran and Traditions of the Holy Prophet (peace and blessings of Allah be upon him).

According to the Islamic Law criminal offences mostly concern :

1. Person
2. Property
3. Honour
4. State
5. Religion
6. Public peace and tranquillity
7. Decency or morals

Punishments : The Penal Laws of Islam are called Hudud (plural of *Hadd*) in Hadith and *Fiqh*. Hadd means prevention, hindrance, restraint, prohibition and hence a restrictive ordinance or statute of Allah, respecting things lawful and unlawful.

Punishment is divided into three classes : (1) *Hadd*. (2) *Qisas*, (3) *Tazir*.

Hadd : The Hadd is a punishment the limits of which have been defined by the Holy Quran and the *Sunnah*. The following belong to this class :

1. Adultery : Punishment for adultery is stoning to death (*Rajm*) in case of a married person.
2. Fornication (*Zina*): For an unmarried person punishment for fornication is one hundred stripes.
3. False Accusation (Qadhf): Insinuating a false charge of adultery against a married man or a woman for which the offender must receive eighty stripes.
4. Apostasy (*Irtidad*) : Renunciation or abandonment of Islam by one who professes Islamic Faith. It is punishable with death.
5. Drinking Wine (*Khamr*): For which the offender must receive eighty stripes.
6. Theft (*Sarqa*): It is punishable with cutting off the hand.
7. Dacoity, Robbery (*Qatal-Tariq)*: For robbery only, the loss of hands and feet, and for robbery with murder, death either by sword or crucifixion.

Qisas : Qisas stands for the return of life for life in a case of murder. Retaliation (*Qisas*) is that punishment which although fixed by law, can be remitted by the person offended against, or in the case of a murdered person, by his heirs. It is applicable to cases of murder and wounding.

Tazir : *Tazir* is the punishment which is left to the discretion of the court in regard to the form and measure in which such punishment is to be inflicted. It is applicable to those crimes for which *Hadud* and *Kaffara* have not been prescribed.

The punishments described above are the maximum punishments for the above mentioned crimes. These can be reduced keeping in view the circumstances in which the crimes were committed, the nature of evidence, and the motive of the criminal with which he committed the crime.

Islamic Penal System

The Islamic Penal Law recognizes three types of punishments i.e., Fixed punishment *(Hadd)*, retaliation *(Qisas)* and discretionary punishment (*Tazir*). Hadd and qisas are restricted to offences for which punishments are prescribed in the Holy Quran and the Sunnah. Under tazir comes the punishment for all offences not covered by Hadd or Qisas. This chapter will be limited to a discussion of the definition, origin and kinds of *tazir* punishment.

Definition : The word *tazir* is derived from the verb *'azar* which means prevent; to respect and to reform. The verb is used in its first and second meanings in the Holy Quran. However, in Islamic legal terminology *tazir* is a punishment aimed firstly at preventing a criminal from committing further crimes, and, secondly, at reforming him. Ibn Farhun, in his well-known book Tabsirat al-Hukkam, tried to specify the purpose of *tazir*, by saying that it is a "disciplinary, reformative and deterrent punishment." This indicates the fact that the two aspects i.e., reformative and deterrent, are combined here. To deter is the real basis of *tazir*, while reformation comes, in fact, as a means thereto.

However, *tazir* is defined as "discretionary punishment to be inflicted for transgression against Allah, or against an individual, for which there is neither a fixed punishment nor a penance or expiation (*Kaffara*)." This definition excludes all sorts of crimes for which specific punishment is prescribed in the *Quran* and the *Sunnah.*

Tazir is not mentioned in the Holy Quran, and Hadith has very little to record about it. This necessitates to trace out the possible origin (*asl*) of *tazir* punishment in both the Holy Quran and the Sunnah.

Tazir in the Light of the Holy Quran and the Sunnah : We find in the Holy Quran and the Sunnah reference to some types of crimes for which there is no fixed punishment and where it is left to the discretion of the Qadi to decide what sort of punishment to impose, and how to inflict it. An instance of this is the Quranic verse which reads:

> "If two men among you are guilty of lewdness, punish them both." (4 : 16)

Another verse in which the authority to punish is given in the Holy Quran in similarly flexible terms is as under:

> "As to those women on whose part you fear disloyalty and ill-conduct, admonish them (first), (next), refuse to share their beds and (last) beat them (lightly)." (4 : 34)

This verse is concerned with the treatment of wives who disobey their husbands. Although the methods of dealing with such disloyal wives are laid down and are to be used consecutively, a lot is left to the discretion of the husband, who is the head of the family. He is to have a free hand in deciding how to use his discretion.

It is this discretion which some jurists considered as the origin of the *tazir* punishment (*al-asl fit-tazir*). This view is based on *Qiyas* (analogy). That is to say that the husband as the head of the family, the basic unit of society, has been given such discretion in order to safeguard the interests of his family and its members. Consequently, the ruler of the whole society and his representative e.g., the judges, must be given the discretion to safeguard the interests of the Society when these are threatened by actions or omissions which fall outside the limits of the fixed punishments *(al-Hadud)*, and the punishment of retaliation *(al-Qisas)*.

Accordingly, it cannot be said, as it has been, that the Holy Quran does not know this kind of punishment. On the contrary, the Quran laid down the principle from which the *tazir* punishment is deduced. By paying more attention to the above verses of the Holy Quran one can say that the legal principles of *tazir* are expressed in the Holy *Quran*, implicitly, if not explicitly.

In the Sunnah, more examples and cases of *tazir* are found. All these cases have later been used, in one way or the other, to construct the juristic formulation of *tazir* as a part of the Islamic Penal Law. So far as the jurists are concerned, they are indebted to these Ahadith for their knowledge and understanding of *tazir*. It is true that the decisions of the Companions of the Holy Prophet (peace and blessings of Allah be upon him) relating to *tazir* appear more frequently in the manuals of Islamic Law, especially the decisions of Hadrat Umar (Allah be pleased with him), but these decisions in turn, are based on the Prophet's traditions and practices.

The following are some of the traditions dealing with cases of *tazir* :

1. Once a Companion of the Holy Prophet (peace and blessings of Allah be upon him) injured his slave, as a; punishment for his having had sexual relations with a female slave. When the Holy Prophet (peace and blessings of Allah be upon him) saw the injured slave, he freed him. This was a punishment for the Companion's misconduct.
2. Muslim and Abu Daud related a tradition according to which the Holy Prophet (peace and blessings of Allah be upon him) deprived a man of his share of the spoils of a war because of a misdeed committed against the Commander of the army.
3. After the Prophet's return to Medina from the battle of Tabuk some of the Companions who had not gone with him confessed that they had no real reason to stay at Medina and not join the army. The Holy Prophet (peace and blessings of Allah be upon him) ordered the Muslims to avoid any contact with them ; their wives

were not allowed to share their beds. Fifty days later, a Quranic verse was revealed saying that Allah had forgiven them and accepted their repentance. This Prophet's order to avoid and ignore the men, was a *tazir* punishment imposed upon them for their absence from the Muslim army.

4. For the theft of fruit of a value of less than that for which the Hadd punishment is inflicted, the Holy Prophet (peace and blessings of Allah be upon him) said that the thief must pay "double its value and be liable to punishment." Here in this case the "double value" is a fine which may be interpreted as *tazir*. A more obvious reference to *tazir* is the last statement of the tradition : "and be liable to punishment." Punishment here is left entirely to the discretion of Qadi.

5. Regarding Zakat, the Holy Prophet (peace and blessings of Allah be upon him) said : "Who gives it will be rewarded by Allah, and who refuses to give it, from him it will be taken, and we will take one half of his property, not for Muhammad (peace and blessings of Allah be upon him) or his family but for the Baitul-Mal (State Treasury)." This imposing of fine upon the offender is also a sort of *tazir* punishment.

6. It is a Quranic Command that if a debtor is in financial straits, the creditor must give him a chance to pay his debt. The Holy Prophet (peace and blessings of Allah be upon him) accordingly commanded that when a rich man refuses to pay his debt, he should be punished. In this tradition again, the Holy Prophet (peace and blessings of Allah be upon him) did not explain what kind of punishment he meant to be imposed for this deed or its amount. The justification for allowing *tazir* punishment here is that such a situation should be dealt with keeping in view the circumstances of both

the creditor and the debtor, and the general financial condition at a given moment. What is important, however, is that this tradition represents a case for which the Holy Prophet (peace and blessings of Allah be upon him) ordered *tazir* punishment.

In the light of the above discussion, one can easily conclude that *tazir* punishment is based on the above mentioned Quranic verses, and traditions of the Holy Prophet (peace and blessings of Allah be upon him). It is true that the development of this system of punishment took place at a comparatively later stage by different Schools of Law. Nevertheless, the claim that the Holy Quran does not know it, and the Sunnah has very little to record about it is totally unfounded.

Kinds of Tazir Punishment : Unlike the Hadd or Qisas punishments, *tazir* punishments are not specific. The judge, in cases of offences for which *tazir* punishment is prescribed, has a wide range of punishments from which he can select any one suitable for the particular crime, keeping in view the circumstances of the criminal, his record, and his psychological condition. The authority of the judge is limited by his obligation not to order a punishment which is not allowed by Islamic law. Here the punishments allowed as *tazir* will be discussed briefly; but the most important ones will be dealt with in more detail. These punishments represent what was known, and actually used, in Islamic legal texts and practice. They are by no means exclusive.

Admonition (al-Waz) : Admonition means calling the transgressors attention to the fact that he has acted unlawfully. The purpose of admonition is to remind the offender or to inform him of his misdeed. For example, as the first stage in dealing with wives in cases of disobedience, the Holy *Quran* says :

> "As to those women on whose part you fear disloyalty and ill-conduct, admonish them (first)." (4 : 34)

This sort of treatment of the offender must be restricted to those who commit minor offences for the first time, provided the judge thinks that it is enough to reform the offender and prevent him from any further transgression.

Reprimand (al-Taswbikh) : Reprimand may be through any word or act which the Qadi feels sufficient to serve the purpose of *tazir*. Jurists usually refer to some specific words and acts as a means of reprimand. Means of reprimand, however, may vary according to the offence and conduct of the offender.

Threat (al-Tahdid) : Threat is a *tazir* punishment which is supposed to serve its aims by making the offender fear the punishment with which he is threatened. It may be carried out by threatening the offender with punishment if he repeated what he had done, or by pronouncing a sentence against him and delaying its execution till the offender committed another offence (within a short period). Besides the normal condition of the suitability of the *tazir* punishment, the threat must be sincere.

Boycott (al-Hajr) : Boycott as a *tazir* punishment is recommended by the Holy *Quran* as under :

"Refuse to share their beds." (4 : 34)

It was practised by the Holy Prophet (peace and blessings of Allah be upon him) in the case of those men who did not attend the army in the battle of Tabuk. It was also inflicted by the second Caliph Hadrat Umar (Allah be pleased with him).

Public Disclosure (al-Tashhir) : *Al-Tashhir* (stigmatising) has been known as a punishment since the early days of Islam. By means of tashhir the Holy Prophet (peace and blessings of Allah be upon him) punished a man who, after collecting the Zakat, divided it into two portions of which he took one for himself ; claiming that it had been given to him as a present.

According to Shariah, a well-known Qadi who served during the reigns of Hadrat Umar and of Hadrat Ali (Allah be pleased with them), the false witness must be publicly identified so as to warn public not to trust him. On this point all the jurists are agreed. The means of tashhir were usually the taking of the offender, by some of the judges representatives to every part of the city and telling the people that he had committed an offence for which he had received a *tazir* punishment. The purpose of this punishment is to call the attention of the public to the fact that the offender is not to be trusted.

Fines and Seizure of Property (al-Zharamah wal Musadarah) : Fines were imposed as punishment in cases of tazir during the period of the Holy Prophet (peace and blessings of Allah be upon him). The jurists are however, divided into three groups as to its legality. According to some it is illegal to punish by fine or by seizure of property. Others regard it as legal, while a third group regards it as legal only if the offender does not repent.

The first view is held by the Hanafi School and some of the Shafiis. According to the Imam Malik, the Imam Ahmad b. Hanbal, the Imam Abu Yusuf [the famous Hanafi jurist), and some of the Shafiis, financial punishments are allowed as *tazir*. The Hanafi jurists explained that the view of the Imam Abu Yusuf means that the Qadi, or the Ruler, should keep the offender's money away from him until he has repented. They support this view by saying that nobody is allowed to take another's property otherwise than for a legal reason (*bi-sabab Shari*).

If it seems afterwards, that the offender will not repent then the Ruler may order the money to be spent on public requirements. The reason they give for this explanation is that to allow the Qadi or the Ruler to take the offender's money for the Baitul-Mal (Public Treasury) straight away, would be open to abuse by unjust Qadis or Rulers.

On the other hand the jurists who deny financial punishment as a legal *tazir* punishment claim that it was legalized in the beginning of Islam but abrogated afterwards. Tahawi was the first jurist who expressed this view in his famous book "Sharh *Maani al-Athar.*" This abrogation claim of al-Tahawi was strongly rejected by the Imam Ibn Taimiyya and his successor Ibn al-Qayyim on evidence taken mainly from the Prophet's practices and from some of his Companion's decisions. Ibn al-Qayyim added:

> "These are well-known cases which have been truly related. Those who claim that financial punishment was abrogated are wrong. Their view may be refuted by the cases ascribed to great Companions of the Holy Prophet (peace and blessings of Allah be upon him). Neither the Holy Quran nor the Sunnah can help them in supporting their claim, nor is there any consensus about it. Even if there was a consensus, it would have no power to abrogate the Sunnah. The best they may say is : in our School's view it is not allowed ; that means they take their own view as a standard of what is accepted and what is not."

Similarly other Hanbal, Hanafi and Malik Commentators hold this view and defend it mainly in Ibn al-Qayyim's words. In the light of Ibn al-Qayyim's views, both kinds of the financial punishment (i.e., fine and seizure of property) are allowed in the Islamic Penal Law. In some of the cases amount of fine was determined by the Holy Prophet (peace and blessings of Allah be upon him) e.g., in the case of theft where a stolen property does not reach the minimum *Nisab* required for imposing the hadd punishment; failure in paying Zakat etc. In other cases it is left to the discretion of Qadi to decide how much the offender should be fined. Hence it is incorrect to say that there are no financial punishments prescribed under the Islamic Penal Law and that the Islamic Penal System does not recognize it.

***Imprisonment (al-Habs)*:** There are two types of imprisonment in Islamic Law: imprisonment for a definite term and imprisonment for an indefinite term. Imprisonment for a definite term may be inflicted for minor offences, as the jurists prefer flogging as the punishment for major *tazir* offences. The minimum period for imprisonment is one day, and as to the maximum period, there is a difference of opinion among the jurists. The Malik, Hanafi and Hanbali Schools do not fix a maximum period for the *tazir* imprisonment as it varies for each offence and from one individual to another.

According to the Shafii School, the maximum period of imprisonment is one month for investigation and six months as punishment and in any case it must not exceed one year. This view is based on an analogy or qiyda to the punishment for adultery committed by an unmarried person. Banishment for adultery (a hadd in Shafii's view) is for one year. Therefore, *tazir*, if it is to be by imprisonment, must not exceed that which is a hadd. However among the Shafii jurists there is another view which is similar to that of the other three Schools. The majority view, therefore, is that the Qadi is free to determine the maximum period of a definite term of imprisonment. It is allowed, according to all the Schools of Islamic Jurisprudence, to inflict imprisonment as an additional punishment if the circumstances so require.

As for imprisonment for an unlimited term, it is imposed on habitual criminals who, in the view of the Qadi, cannot be reformed by ordinary kinds of punishment. This punishment may last either till the criminal's repentance or his death, in the case of a dangerous criminal. This kind of imprisonment is similar to that of the hadd punishment for armed robbery (hirabah) where one of the punishments prescribed is banishment (interpreted as imprisonment), to be inflicted till the criminal's repentance or until his death. *Tazir* imprisonment for indefinite period can only be ordered so long as reform of the offender by another punishment is impossible. It is only on this occasion that unlimited imprisonment is justifiable.

Flogging (al-Jald) : Flogging is a common punishment in Penal Law of Islam. It is prescribed as a hadd punishment for the crime of qadhf (eighty lashes), and for adultery committed by an unmarried person (hundred lashes). It is also prescribed for many *tazir* offences. The point at issue here is the maximum number of lashes allowed as *tazir*. The problem, for Muslim jurists, is whether *tazir* punishment may exceed the hadd punishment.

The most liberal view in this regard is that of Malik. According to the Imam Malik, *tazir* punishment may exceed the hadd punishment as long as the Qadi or the Ruler thinks that there exist such circumstances which require it. The opposite view is held by the *Zahiri* and *Zaydi* Schools, and part of the Hanbali School, who believe that flogging as a *tazir* punishment cannot exceed ten lashes. Compromising views are held by the Hanafi and Shafii Schools and some Hanbali Scholars. There is no unanimity about the maximum number of lashes to be inflicted.

This controversy is based on two Ahadith. In the first, the Holy Prophet (peace and blessings of Allah be upon him) forbade more than ten lashes to be inflicted except in cases of hadd punishment. This is related by the Imam Muslim and the Imam al-Bukhari. The second which is related by al-Baihaqi is to the effect that the Holy Prophet (peace and blessings of Allah be upon him) labelled those who exceed the limits of the hadd punishment, in a "*non-hadd*" offence, as transgressors "*mutadun*."

The dominant view about the first tradition is that it was abrogated ; this is deduced from the fact that the Companions of the Holy Prophet (peace and blessings of Allah be upon him) did not act in accordance with it. It is related that Hadrat Umar and Hadrat Ali (Allah be pleased with them) inflicted more than ten lashes in cases of *tazir* with no objections from the other Companions, so the tradition, according to the majority view, must have been abrogated.

Another interpretation of this *Hadith* was given by Ibn Taimiyya and Ibn al-Qayyim. They hold this tradition as relevant to the relations between father and son, master and servant and the like, i.e., relationships in which one may need to use some means of punishment for disciplinary reasons. In such cases if the proper means is flogging, it must not exceed 10 lashes. But this tradition has nothing to do with the relationship between the individual and the state, and the number of lashes allowed as *tazir* punishment is left to the discretion of the authority concerned. According to this view there is no need for the abrogation claim as the tradition is not relevant to the case in question.

The second *Hadith* although incompletely transmitted (*mursal*), was accepted by all the *Sunni* Schools except the Malik. Those who accepted this tradition interpreted it in different ways, and so their views vary about the maximum *tazir* punishment. The first interpretation is that this tradition forbade *tazir* punishment to exceed the minimum limit of the hadd punishment. The second interpretation is that the tradition forbade *tazir* to equal the hadd punishment in cases of incomplete crimes for which, if they were completed, a hadd punishment would be prescribed. That is to say a crime of theft, for which the hadd punishment cannot be inflicted, may result in *tazir* of one hundred lashes. A sexual relationship (which has not involved sexual intercourse), should not reach 100 lashes if the offender is unmarried because his original hadd punishment is 100 lashes.

The minimum number of lashes allowed as *tazir* was also discussed ; some jurists fixed it at 3, but the majority does not agree with this view as it contradicts the main feature of *tazir*; i.e., its variation from one crime to another according to the offender's conduct and other circumstances.

However, the view expressed by Ibn Taimiyya and his companions is the most relevant view both practically and logically. In practice, they allow any suitable punishment and avoid the strict limitation imposed on the Ruler's power to inflict *tazir* punishment. From the logical point of view they limit the tradition about the number of lashes allowed for "non-hadd" punishment, to a particular area and are, therefore, not forced to use the abrogation claim as other Scholars do. This is also in harmony with a principle of Islamic Law, recommending the application of every legal verdict rather than its neglect.

Death Penalty (Al-Tazir bil-Qatl) : *Tazir* is a part of Islamic Penal Law which deals with the less serious offences. The death penalty is usually imposed for the most heinous crimes. According to Islamic Penal Law it is the punishment of two hadd offences and, as a retaliation, for homicide. The jurists, accordingly, are normally against its infliction as a *tazir* punishment, but exceptional cases in which *tazir* by the death penalty is allowed are mentioned in the texts of almost every School.

According to Hanafi texts the offences in which death penalty is imposed are adultery, dacoity, the murder wherein qisas cannot be imposed and those offenders whose harmful conduct may not be stopped by other punishments. For the Malik School, the principle that the *tazir* punishment should fit the crime, the criminal, and the victim is of absolute application. Thus the death penalty is permissible in certain cases, where either the offence itself is of a very heinous nature, such as spying for the enemy or propagating heretical doctrines or practices which split the community, or where the criminal is a habitual offender and there is no other effective method to stop his wickedness. The Shafiis and Hanbalis hold a similar view.

However, it must be noticed that there are some traditions

which allow the death penalty as a *tazir* punishment The different views must be measured by these traditions. However, capital punishment should always be regarded as an extraordinary *tazir* punishment. Thus, it could only be imposed in cases of absolute necessity.

Various Criminal Acts

Tazir offences may be either of the same essential nature as the *hadd* offences or of a less serious degree or may qualify simply as "transgression." In both cases determination of the punishment is at the discretion of the Qadi. But in the case of a "transgression" it is usually said that the Ruler or the Qadi has to determine the offence as well. This view is absolutely wrong. To see how accurate this view is one must refer to the definition of *tazir* as a punishment to be delivered, for which there is neither hadd punishment nor *kaffarah*.

The right to determine what is a transgression and what is not is reserved in Islamic Law for Almighty Allah only, as the Muslims believe that Islamic Law is the final Will of Allah. Allah's Will is expressed in the Holy Quran and in the Sunnah. The Holy Quran and the Sunnah contain many statements which forbid some types of human activity and classify them as sins (maasi). For these forbidden activities the Ruler's or Qadi's task will be merely to choose punishment applicable in each case, but he has nothing to do with the determination of the offence as it has already been determined by the Holy Quran or the Sunnah. Examples of such oases are innumerable. Following are some of the most important ones:

Usury (al-Ribd): The Holy Quran forbade usuary in various verses in *Surah al-Baqara*, and *Al-Imran*. One of the verses runs:

"But Allah hath permitted trade and forbidden usury."
(2: 275)

Another verse says :

"O ye who believe! fear Allah, and give up what

remains of your demand for usury, if ye are indeed believers. If ye do it not, take notice of war from Allah and His Apostle. (2 : 278, 279)

Again the Holy *Quran* says :

"O ye who believe ! Devour not Usury, doubled and multiplied ; but fear Allah ; that ye may (really) prosper. (3 : 130)

Usury therefore is a prohibited activity ; its doer deserves punishment which has not been fixed in the Holy Quran or the Sunnah. Duty of the Qadi is to choose the proper punishment for it, but he does not determine the offence. Jurists are not unanimous about what may be considered usury and what may not. In this respect the Qadi may simply determine whether the offender's act constitutes prohibited conduct or not. Such is the role of any court in relation to any crime : to establish, in light of the evidence provided, the offender's guilt, after which the penalty can be pronounced.

A person who accepts Riba (usury) ceases to be an *'adl* and loses his competency for evidence.

False Testimony (Shahadat al-Zur) : False testimony has been condemned in the Holy Quran and believers are directed to state the truth when testifying. One verse says :

"O ye who believe ! stand out firmly for justice, as witnesses to Allah, even though it be against yourselves, or your parents or your kinsmen."

(4 : 135)

Another verse describes believers as :

"Those who witness no falsehood." (25 : 72)

Another verse orders the believers

And shun the word that is false." (22 : 30)

The jurists have said quite e lot about the punishment of a false witness, but the offence has been defined in the Holy

Quran and what the jurists said applies to the stage of choosing the punishment for the offence rather than its determination. For Libel and slander (or vituperative remarks) against a person, the case should be referred to the Qadi under and the Qadi can both inflict punishment (*tazir*) and pass decree of redress.

Breach of Trusts (Khiyanat al-Amanah) : The Holy *Quran* says:

> "Allah doth command you to render back your Trusts to those to whom they are due." (4 :58)

Another verse runs:

> "O ye that believe ! betray not the trust of Allah and the Apostle, nor misappropriate knowingly things entrusted to you." (8 : 27)

It was on these verses, and many others, that the Muslim jurists based their treatment of this offence. Noteworthy is the fact that the Holy Prophet (peace and blessings of Allah be upon him) equalized *Khiyanat al-Amanah* with theft.

Insults (al-Sabb) : To insult a human being, according to the Holy Quran, is forbidden even if the insulted person is an infidel, or as the Holy *Quran* says :

> "Abuse not those who pray apart from Allah." (6 :109)

As for the Muslims among themselves the Quranic Command is :

> "O' believers, let not any people scoff at another people who may be better than they ; neither let women scoff at women who may be better than themselves. And find not fault with one another, neither revile one another by nicknames. An evil name is ungodliness after belief." (49 : 11)

Accordingly insult is classified as a *tazir* offence.

Bribery (al-Rishwa) : As the Holy Quran forbade usury and considered it an unlawful way of making money, all means of making money by dishonesty are therefore, forbidden. About bribery the Holy *Quran* says:

> "Consume not your property between you in vanity, neither proffer it to the judge, that you may sinfully consume a portion of other man's property intentionally." (2 :188)

No punishment has been fixed for bribery, thus it is classified as a tazir offence, for which the authority may impose a punishment.

No Appeal against the Sentence Pronounced by a Qadi: In Islamic Law there is no (*murafaa : appeal*) against the sentence of a Qadi. The punishment is executed without delay and without any resistance. The Qadi enjoys the sanction of the Quran, for he has been accepted as the (*Hakam* : arbitrator) by virtue of professing Islam, and the Qadi decides the case strictly in accordance with the Laws of the Quran and the Sunnah. Hence the convict cannot prefer an appeal to the Ruler.

After that the punishment has been inflicted, the convict may complain against the Qadi, in which case the Ruler may investigate into the facts. If the Ruler finds that the Qadi has wrongfully punished the appellant, the punishment will revert to the Qadi (e.g. if the appellant had been flogged 80 stripes, the Qadi will receive the same number of stripes) and *ipso facto* will be deposed.

If the appellant is found a liar, he will undergo a further sentence of a *tazir* for lying.

Contempt of Court : Since the Qadi is an *'adl* and of reputed integrity, any statement or remark against his judicial actions is a cognizable offence. The offender shall have to produce evidence and prove his assertion, or else shall be convicted and punished for lying and defaming the *'adl*.

Introduction of Innovations in the Laws of Islam : Should ever a person try to introduce innovations in the laws and dogmas of Islam, he will be held accountable before the Qadi or the Ruler. Theologians and other Scholars will be invited to debate with the innovator, and satisfy the Qadi.

A sorcerer (magician) belongs to the same category, as he is likely to mislead the public and to play with the convictions of the Muslims in general.

A person claiming in (*Dawa*) i.e., the power of inviting the spirits, or (i.e., divination) or fortune, telling by palmistry and astrology is to be punished severely.

The only admissible form of such incantation is i.e., a formula pronounced repeatedly to counteract the ill effects of an evil eye and seeking assistance of Allah alone.

These examples are enough to show that *tazir* offences are mainly determined in the Holy *Quran* and the *Sunnah*. It is by no means claimed that the Ruler has no right, outside the province of the Holy *Quran* or the *Sunnah*, to establish offences and their punishments ; but this right is limited to what is necessary for the achievement of the aims and ends approved by the Islamic Law. Nevertheless it is quite unjustifiable when it is contrary to the Holy *Quran* and the *Sunnah*.

5

Legal Process

For the last several years there is a great enthusiasm in the country for enforcement of Islam and Islamic system in every walk of life. Sufficient advancement has been made in this behalf in different directions and several experiments are being made. Steps towards the enforcement of *Hudood* and promulgation of Ordinances in this behalf are also in pursuance of the same policy.

In order to achieve the desired positive result, there are certain prerequisities which are as follows:

(1) Real conception of the problem in question;

(2) Determination of right goal and destiny;

(3) Determination of right time;

(4) Sincerity of purpose;

(5) Proper procedure; and

(6) Appropriate working personnel.

Presently we will deal with point number 5 only. When we examine the question of enforcement of *Hudood* and *Tazeerat* in connection with the establishment of Islamic judicial system in muslim countries, in the above perspective we come to know that all that has been done is that Islamic *Hudood* and *Tazeerat* connected therewith which were already existing in the shape of substantive law. have been codified and promulgated as the law of land.

Let us see as to what guidance we get from treatises on *Fiqh* for the formulation of procedure for enforcement of *Hudood* and *Tazirat.* It is provided in *Al-Tatarkhania* that, "No accused is liable to imprisonment in *Hudood* and *Qisas* until the witnesses give their evidence, and when the witnesses have given their evidence, the accused will he detained in custody until the truthfulness of witnesses is proved by purgation. According to Imam Abu Hanifa, the accused would be detained in custody when one truthful witness has given evidence and according to Sahibain (Imam Muhammad and Imam Abu Yousuf), the accused would not be kept in confinement except in *Hadd* of *Qazf* and *Qisas".*

The evidence is defined in *Fatawa-e-Alamgiri* as, "giving of true information with the word of evidence for proving a right, in the court proceedings before Qadi is called evidence".

According to *Hidaya, "Zina* is proved with the evidence of witnesses or plea of guilt by accused but this proof must be before Imam (Judge) because *Zina* will not be proved in any way by statement of witnesses and plea of guilt anywhere other than before Imam (Judge)".

It is provided in *Altabieen* that if a *Zani* pleads guilty even for four times before any person other than Qadi, who has no authority to enforce *Hadd,* his plea of guilt is of no consequences because evidence of such plea of guilt is not admissible.

> The learned author of *Hidaya* has quoted in Chapter on *Hudood* that "Imam Muhammad wrote in *'Asaf* (his book) that Qadi should detain that person in jail against whom evidence has been recorded till the time that purgation about witnesses is made because there is allegation of commission of offence against him and

> The Holy Prophet (peace be upon him) had confined a person on the basis of allegation of offence" (Abu Daud).

From above situations, the following conclusions can be deducted:

> First, that every aggrieved person or complainant should present his grievances and complaint before Judge and not before police. In the existing system of administration of criminal justice, practically the F.I.R. plays the role of complaint for all intents and purposes. It is deemed to be foundation of entire case and its contents are treated to be binding on the complainant. As such the present procedure of lodging F.I.R. with police is wrong and should be done away with and every complainant should file his complaint directly before judge instead of lodging F.I.R. at police station;

Secondly, the statements appear to be unnecessary documents. The present procedural law and law of evidence also do not recognize them as evidence *per se* but in spite of that it is height of anomaly that contents of these so-called statements are deemed sufficient to nullify the evidence of witnesses in Court. Meaning thereby that statements prepared by police and mostly without consulting the witnesses are so important that they can render the evidence given by witnesses in open Court and recorded by Judge himself, ineffective. The law enjoins upon the judge to disbelieve the evidence recorded by himself in open Court *vis-a-vis* the statement prepared by police if the evidence in Court is not in conformity with police statement. Thus, theory and practice on this point are diametrically opposite to each other and indirectly though not directly the police statements are given the status of evidence which is absolutely wrong;

Thirdly, the confessions of accused persons recorded are an exercise in futility because admission of guilt before such

Magistrate who has no authority to enforce punishment is a useless thing; and Fourthly, no person should be kept in confinement without evidence before judge.

Now the question arises as to what procedure should be adopted for the initiation of criminal cases and proceedings in *Hudood* and *Tazirat*. We propose the following procedure:

> If complainant is able to produce the accused before judge then he should produce the accused himself before judge and give him in the custody of Court. The complainant should take his witnesses also with himself at the time of producing accused in Court. After producing the accused before judge, the complainant should present his complaint orally before judge in presence of accused. The judge should record the complaint in the form of examination-in-chief as in vogue in the present system, in triplicate and after recording the same should read it himself or may direct his reader to read the same loudly in presence of complainant and the accused and the complainant would be allowed to make any addition, alteration or subtraction in his statement which would be recorded with such note by the judge. Thereafter, judge will obtain signature of complainant on all the three copies of his statement. The original shall be placed in Court file and a copy thereof shall be supplied to complainant and accused, there and then.

After recording of complaint, the judge shall record plea of accused and framing of formal charge would not be necessary. In the plea form it would be sufficient to mention the name of offence alleged against the accused and it would not be necessary to specify the Section of relevant substantive penal law under which the offence is punishable. After recording of plea, the judge would obtain signature of accused on the plea form in open Court. The judge shall append a certificate on the complaint and plea form in token of having recorded the same and shall make endorsement that signature of complainant and accused as the case may be was obtained in his presence in open court.

If accused pleads guilty, the judge shall convict him on his plea of guilt. If the accused does not plead guilty and claim to be tried, the judge shall adjourn the proceeding for two hours and give opportunity to accused for engaging any advocate of his choice available within that time. The proceedings shall be resumed after two hours and trial shall start with cross-examination of complainant. After cross-examination of complainant, his witnesses shall be examined and cross-examined and thereafter statement of accused shall be recorded. The accused may cite witnesses in his defence and the case shall be adjourned for few days keeping in view the place of residence of the defence witnesses and distance from the court. In the intervening period, the judge shall try to complete purgation of complainant and his witnesses. The Public Prosecutor shall conduct cases on behalf of complainant and remain present to assist the judge.

If after completion of prosecution evidence, the judge is of the view that no case is made out for the enforcement of *Hadd,* he may dispense with *Tazkiat-ul-Shahood* (Purgation Proceedings) and in doing so, he may hear the arguments of both the parties then and there or may adjourn the case according to his convenience to an early date and fix the same for arguments.

If the complainant is not able to express himself properly by oral submission then he may present his complaint in writing as well before judge in triplicate in Urdu duly signed by him. The complaint so presented shall be read over by the reader in open court loudly in presence of the complainant and the accused and after hearing the same the complainant shall state on oath that whatever is written in his complaint is true to the best of his knowledge and belief. The judge shall make such endorsement on all the three copies and shall return a copy thereof to the complainant and supply another copy to the accused. This complaint shall be treated as an examination-in-chief and further proceedings shall be the same as narrated above. If the judge feels that complainant is able to express himself properly then he will not accept the written complaint and shall record the oral complaint in Court as suggested above. Receiving of written complaint shall be in exceptional cases. Any person who has personal knowledge about commission of any offence can be treated as complainant in Court.

If the complainant or aggrieved or affected person feels that taking of accused from the place of incident to the Court would be difficult or risky or cumbersome for him or if the offence takes place at such odd hours that it is not possible to produce the accused in Court on that day in working hours, then the accused may be handed over to police and police shall be bound to take that person in custody and shall produce the accused in concerned court at the earliest opportunity. At the time of taking accused in custody, the police shall issue a receipt to person handing over accused to police in which, name, address and other particulars of accused, name, address and other particulars of the person handing over accused to police, the time of handing over accused to police, shall be written briefly.

The receipt shall be produced and exhibited by the concerned person at the time of his statement in Court. No evidentiary value for or against shall be attached to the facts if mentioned in the said receipt, either for the complainant or the accused. The only importance of this receipt would be to ensure that no person is kept in confinement or detention by police without any reasonable cause so that the accused persons are produced in Court at the earliest opportunity and without any delay.

Production of witnesses shall be primary responsibility of the complainant. However, in exceptional situation and conditions the assistance of Court may be sought. The court shall have full authority to summon the witnesses and compel their attendance by issuance of coercive process also if so deemed necessary.

If in any incident the medical aid is required, or hurt has been caused or murder has been committed then every person who has been assaulted or injured may go or any other person may take the injured or dead body to the nearest Medical Officer without any reference from court or police and the Medical Officer shall be bound to attend, examine and provide necessary medical aid to him. The Medical Officer shall prepare the certificate of his examination and findings for production in Court. If immediate medical aid or first aid is required then every nearest qualified doctor shall be bound to examine such person and provide necessary medical aid to him.

After doing the needful such doctor shall refer the person concerned at the earliest opportunity to the nearest Medical Officer along with the prescription and other documents if any prepared by him. Normally, the unofficial doctor shall not be called in evidence as witness and the documents prepared by him along with his letter of reference, shall be produced in Court by the Medical Officer concerned. However, in special or exceptional circumstances, the court may summon unofficial doctor also. In this connection police and court shall also have power to refer any injured to Medical Officer if he has appeared before police or court without getting himself examined by the doctor.

If complainant is not able to produce accused in court or accused has absconded after the incident or he has not been identified even then the complainant should appear in Court and file his oral complaint before judge and judge shall record statement of his witnesses as well Thereafter, judge may issue such directions to police as deemed fit. As soon as the accused persons are arrested they should be produced before court at the earliest opportunity without loss of any time and the judge shall cause the attendance of complainant and witnesses procured and shall start the trial as suggested above, with a difference that complainant and witnesses shall be read over their statements and they will be allowed to resile from any part of their statement but they will not be permitted to add anything to their previous statement.

If such accused persons are arrested by police who were not identified at the time of incident then after their arrest they will be brought directly to the judge and identification proceedings shall be held in the presence and personal superintendence of the judge and such proceedings shall be treated as evidence in the Court and no further recording of evidence in proof of identification proceedings would be required.

If there are such circumstances when immediate aid or assistance of police is required and it is not possible to reach up to court in working hours or there is apprehension of accused running away from the reach of the law and police or any other compelling circumstances are existing then complainant can lodge report at police station to the extent only that at such and such place, at such and such time, such and such persons identified or un-identified have committed such report and take immediate action. On the basis of such report, the police shall be bound to arrest the persons accused and produce them immediately before court. The police shall supply one copy of such report to the complainant and other copy thereof shall be forwarded to the court concerned.

The complainant shall produce copy of such report supplied to him by police at the time of filing his complaint in Court. If police refuses or neglects to record such report, the complainant shall bring this fact to the knowledge of court at the time of lodging complaint in court and the Court may take action against police after such enquiry as deemed fit. However, the complainant shall not give entire details of the incident in his police report and shall appear before court without loss of any time at the earliest opportunity along with his witnesses and file his oral complaint in Court. If police succeeds in arresting accused persons, they shall also be produced in court and the trial shall start according to procedure suggested above.

The police report shall have no evidentiary value and it shall be deemed to be a source of seeking police aid only. The police should submit entire report of progress in the investigation immediately and day to day before judge.

The entire proceedings of police investigation, concerned with the cases before court shall be brought to the knowledge of court and judge shall have complete control over such matters. If in any case two or more accused persons are required and out of them one or more than one have been arrested and other are absconding then the accused person or persons as the case may be who are arrested shall be produced before court and trial shall commence without waiting for absconding accused persons, and proceedings shall be completed. When absconding accused persons are arrested then the complainant and witnesses shall be called again and the absconding accused shall be tried afresh.

In the existing system, the arrested accused and witnesses attend court hearings unnecessarily in such situations and warrants of arrests are issued, and repeated time and again against the absconding accused persons. After issuance of warrants for several times, the statement of process server is recorded. Thereafter, the absconding accused is declared as proclaimed offender and proclamation for his arrest and attachment of his property is issued. Thereafter, it is ordered that the case may proceed in the absence of absconding accused. This entire procedure causes delay and the waste of time. It is a sort of harassment also to the arrested accused persons and the prosecution witnesses. This procedure should therefore be done away with and court shall issue proclamation for arrest and attachment of the property of absconding accused on the very first date of hearing and shall complete trial against the arrested accused so that the delay and its consequences be avoided.

In the cases of *Hudood* particularly, and *Tazirat* generally, the procedure of, obtaining opinion from Chemical Analyser and Serologist and Ballistic expert should be discontinued and as far as possible the prosecution should depend on the ocular testimony or such circumstantial evidence which can be proved by the evidence of witnesses at the spot or conversant with the facts of the case and in any case other than the so-called expert witnesses.

The trial of cases shall start immediately on the production of accused before court as suggested above and there shall be no adjournment at all. If any trial is not concluded in one day then it shall be compulsorily posted and fixed to the next working day and the cases shall proceed day to day till the conclusion of trial without any adjournment. In the proposed procedure, the prosecution evidence would normally be completed on the very first day of trial and if accused is arrested on the spot, pratically the actual trial would concluded on the very day and thereafter only formalities shall remain to be completed.

If the judge thinks fit and proper to inspect the site, he can visit the place of incidence before or after the evidence of prosecution witnesses or at any stage according to the circumstances of each case. If accused is also present at the time of site inspection, it would be more better. For this purpose the judge should be provided official facilities. The judge can appoint Commissioner also in his behalf who will normally visit the site in presence of both the parties and shall obtain their signature on his report which he will prepare at the spot. However, presence of both the parties would not be necessary always.

If any witness being injured is not feeling well and the Medical Officer issues certificate to the effect that the witness is not able to attend the Court, but he is able to depose, then the judge shall appoint Commissioner at the earliest opportunity to record his statement in the hospital or wherever such witness may be. If accused is not arrested then examination-in-chief shall be recorded only and after his arrest. The cross-examination-in-chief shall be conducted in his presence. If the accused is before court then he shall be sent with the Commissioner so that evidence of such witness shall be recorded in the presence of accused and his advocate, if any. Doing so shall be in consonance with the entire scheme which aims at getting the original version of witnesses recorded at the earliest opportunity in order to avoid the concocted versions.

In our present society there is general tendency of falsely implicating innocent persons, due to enmity, taking of vengeance or for deriving some other benefits. There is another tendency of roping in a large number of innocent persons with the actual culprits. This tendency needs to be checked and curbed strictly. The existing laws and the procedure in this behlaf are so complicated that the false complainant and witnesses are not punished at all. In spite of committing perjury at trial they have sense of security and their respect and status in the society remain unaffected.

There is the saying of Imam Abu Hanifa about the false witnesses that "I will make public announcement in Bazar about the falsehood of a witness who has given false evidence intentionally, but I will not punish him by way of *Tazeer*". On the other hand there is saying of Sahibain (Imam Muhammad and Imam Abu Yousuf) that we will beat him and keep him under imprisonment. Imam Shafaii, Imam Malik and Imam

Ahmed bin Hambal are also of the same view. Hadrat Umar imposed punishment of 40 stripes on a false witness and blackened his face. He issued directions to the Administrator of Syria in connection with false witnesses that they shall be given punishment of 40 stripes, their faces should be blackened, their head shall be shaved and they shall be awarded sentence of imprisonment for long period.

Thus it is proved that punishment can be inflicted on a false complainant and a false witness by way of *Tazir*. Therefore, if at the time of delivering judgement, the judge is satisfied that the complainant has filed false complaint against one or more of the accused persons then by the same judgement he shall suitably punish such complainant. For this purpose the procedure of issuing show cause notice, should be done away with. Likewise, if the judge is satisfied that any witness has intentionally deposed falsely he should also be punished adequately in the same manner.

The minimum punishment should be the making of publicity by the bailiff of court of the complainant or witness being held and declared false by the court with his showing to public in Bazar or at a place where he is generally known, with the message of judge that everybody should be aware of him. The maximum punishment shall be 40 stripes or imprisonment which may extend to 5 years or both. The judge may impose fine only also according to the circumstances of the case, complainant and witnesses.

If any party to the case is not willing for trial in certain court then that party may inform the trial court immediately after the filing of complaint by the complainant and before recording of plea of the accused that he intends to file transfer application. On receiving such intimation, the trial court shall postpone further proceedings and shall take bond of suitable amount from the applicant to the effect that he will file transfer application within two days before the competent authority. If transfer application is not filed within two days then the bond shall be forfeited and trial shall start. If the transfer application is filed, the applicant shall simultaneously supply a copy of the said application to the trial court. He shall send a copy of transfer application to his adversary also before filing of same in the competent court. The applicant shall produce receipt from the Reader or C. O. C. of the trial court and postal receipt along with the transfer application, otherwise the transfer application shall not be accepted. The trial judge shall submit his remarks to the Court competent to hear the transfer application within two days of receiving the copy of transfer application.

The transfer application shall be heard invariably on the 5th day of filing of application and the other side shall be bound to appear on the 5th day of filing of transfer application without any further notice from the said court. Receiving of copy of application by him shall be deemed to be sufficient notice. If he fails to appear the application shall be heard in his absence. There would be no necessity of the filing of counter-affidavit and rejoinder. The final arguments shall be heard on the application and the parties shall be allowed to submit their respective point of view without formal written objections on record. The court competent to hear the transfer application shall be bound to decide the same within a week of the filing of same.

If none of the parties have given any intimation as above then the proceeding shall not be postponed or adjourned at all till the conclusion of prosecution evidence, on the ground that any party wants to move transfer application. However, after the conclusion of prosecution evidence any party to case may intimate to the court that he intends to move transfer application and on receiving such intimation at this stage, the trial court shall not deliver the final judgement within 12 days of receiving such information, but purgation of complainant and witnesses shall be completed. If the case is transferred then the transferee judge may rely on the same purgation or hold fresh purgation according to his satisfaction.

If the competent judge (who would be Sessions Judge) to hear transfer application rejects the application and feels that there were no reasons at all for the transfer application or feels that it was moved for gaining time or causing delay in the trial then he may impose suitable fine on the applicant which will be recovered as arrears of land revenue.

In the existing system of procedural law all the punishments of *Hadd* become barred by time. If the proposed procedure is adopted then the cases shall be decided within few days and punishment shall not become barred by time. The period allowed for transfer application has been fixed keeping the period of limitation in view.

The requirement of recording of evidence in cases of *Hudood* within one month and in the event of failure punishments becoming barred by time is peculiar to the Islamic system of criminal administration of justice. This practice is alien to all other judicial systems and it is pertinent to keep this provision in view at the time of framing of criminal procedural law for carrying into effect the penal law of *Hudood*.

In addition to adoption of proposed procedure at trial stage, it is also necessary to annul the present provision of appeals and confirmation of sentences. In order to reduce the percentage of wrong judgements it is necessary to appoint such persons as judges whose integrity, honesty and efficiency is above Board. However, it is not possible to get cent per cent right judgements from human beings in any system, under any procedure and by any number of appeals, as such reliance should be made on the understanding, knowledge, efficiency, honesty, impartiality and integrity of judges.

However, if the provision of appeal is deemed necessary

as a matter of precaution then the right of one appeal only should be given. For this purpose, the procedure should be like this, that in the cases other than involving death sentence the appeal should be filed within 7 days of the judgement and appeal should be decided within 15 days without fail. In the cases involving death sentences the appeal should be filed within one week of the judgement of trial court and the appeal should be decided within one month without fail.

If any accused is convicted, the trial court shall supply a certified copy of the judgement to him at the time of announcing judgement. After announcement of judgement the file shall be immediately sent to the Appellate Court so that when the appeal is preferred the case file is already available in the Appellate Court. The trial court should send a copy of judgement of conviction to D.P.P. or Advocate-General also as the case may be and inform him about the sending of case file to the Appellate Court.

The system of preparation of paper book in the Appellate Court, in the appeals relating to *Hudood* and *Tazeerat* should be discarded instead of doing so, three photostat copies of entire file (which will not be very bulky in the proposed procedure) should be prepared at the expense of Appellant. The approximate expenses of photostating should be deposited by Appellant at the time of filing appeal. The Appellate Court should arrange for supply of photostat copies of entire file to the advocate for appellant and Government Advocate both within 3 days of filing of appeal. The appeal in *Hudood* and *Tazeerat* should normally be heard in the cases involving sentences other than death penalty on the 10th day of filing of appeal and the appeal involving death sentences should normally be heard on 20th day of filing of appeal However, the Appellate Court and Advocates may make adjustment in this behalf in such a manner that the time schedule for disposal of appeal is not disturbed.

The trial court and the Appellate court may release any accused in custody, on bail, if the court is satisfied that there are sufficient reasons and grounds for doing so. Both the courts shall have authority for granting bail before arrest also.

The courts which will try *Hudood* and *Tazeerat* cases shall not deal with the pending cases under the laws other than *Hudood* and *Tazeerat*. Such other cases shall be tried, heard and adjudicated upon by other courts.

Different Aspects

The Methodology : The belief in Islam as an evolved culmination of the process of divine revelation finds authentication from the Islamic Scripture. Therefore, as an article of Faith, the authenticity of other revealed religions is upheld in Islam." This affirmation of the multiplicity of religious revelations allows an important inference of revealed law or Shariah to be common to all divine religions, irrespective of its extensiveness in any instance. To avail the other revelations as a source of law will become a means of legal development, besides adding a dimension to law in making it commensurate with the universality of Islam. The criteria for such adoption from other revelations will be the need for revealed law not being fulfilled from the Islamic sources, and that such an adopted law is in uniformity with Islamic precepts of legal value as confirmed by its validation with the application of the Legal Method.

The specific reiteration of this latter criterion will be that the provisions of such an adopted law are not in contravention of the general legal implications of the Supreme Principles. In this perspective, as Islam is held to be the consummation of all the antedating revealed religions, therefore, the adoption of revealed law from other divine sources merely becomes the practical manifestation of this prominent religious tenet. Due relevance is accordable to the fact that no other revealed religion maintains its completion, in terms of a culmination of religious evolution, and its universality, in the sense of a source for guidance in all stages of social change and advancement. This utilization of the other revealed religions as a source of Islamic Law has dual legal justifiability.

One, as a form of analogous reasoning in the event that the primary sources of Muslim Law are discovered not to afford applicable analogy. And, secondly, in the event of Shariah's "silence" in the instances where no immediate cause for issuing a command is ascertainable and, as a result, the Scripture remained silent, the acceptance of relevant explicit proclamations in the revealed laws prior to Islam is justifiable. This juristic measure is called as "*Istishab*" and it is to be differentiated from a situation where the cause for issuing a proclamation existed with the coexistence of Scriptural silence, for then it connotes prohibition. Ibn Khaldun described Istishab in these words: "It is the attempt to associate the present legal situation with the past by judging the present in the same way as the past is judged with the result that the legal situation is left as it had been, because no evidence to change it has been found.

Method of Selection : A closely allied and invaluable Islamic juridical approach will be the selection of rules, or even parts of rules, from different Islamic schools of law in order to frame a superior statute. In general, as a part of the juristic principle of Ijtihad, that is, in the nature of further juristic exposition and development of Islamic Law, the principle of selection, designated as "takhayyar," has been adopted in some Islamic nations such as Saudi Arabia. This composite formulation of a statute is explainable on the premise that the legal validity of two or more rules itself validates the combination of their provisions. Now a systematic application of these invaluable principles can open new vistas of legal development due to the eradication of legal "sectarianism" in Islam, the tangible enhancement of the sources of law, and the reinterpretation of the Islamic Law or Fiqh with the methodical application of the juristic principle of Ijtihad, considered dormant in Islam.

Method of Induction : An abbreviated view of a beneficial subject would allow the identification of the common denominator, among the real basis of Faith and the spirit of the Quran, analogous reasoning and scientific method, to be the principle of induction. The comprehensiveness of the source of law that encompasses the inclusive view of revealed law, and the composite structure of legal statutes on the basis of "selection" from different Islamic schools of law, as a part of the legal formulation for the Islamic legal system in the envisaged new era, is remarkably complemented with the adoption of inductive approach. The principles that become ascertainable from the generalization of the particular instances in revealed laws, and the rules or even juristic elements from various schools of law, have the potential of becoming an inestimable source of law *per se*.

Other Methods : The consideration for conscientious interpretation is of pivotal significance in the evolution of law, in general, and this observation is obviously in demand of further emphasis in the instance of religious law. Avoidance of a few evident drawbacks in the interpretation of law is facilitative in the attainment of that purpose. In Shatibi's view, the appreciation of the demand for the right understanding of the purpose of Shariah should bring to notice the relationship between intention and act.

According to the conformity of intention and act with that purpose, four situations are identified. In addition to the two concordant situations of intention and act, the discordant situations are described as "bida" and "hypocrisy" in the presence of sole conformity of intention with the purpose of Shariah without the association of act, and the conformity of act without the correspondence of intention, respectively. Another classification is established on the basis of rational understanding of the meanings as to the usefulness or unwholesomeness from the act itself. "Taabudi," or that pertaining to religious worships, are those acts whose meanings are not rationally understandable, and this is in diametric contrast with "adi," for instance, the penal prescription for crimes and other laws related to the regulation of human conduct.

Now, against this perspective, the tendency of the mechanical observance of the incidents of a legal rule, that neglects completely the purpose which the rule was designed to serve, requires justification. And, thus, the consideration of the relation between the reasons which gave rise to a rule, and the rule itself, acquires legal relevance. A simple reason for this is the continuation in force of a legal rule, long past the original reasons for the rule have ceased to exist. The illustration of the legal value of these distinctions is affordable with the example of the levying of new wealth and property taxes in a specific proportion, that resembles the Islamic tithe, in addition to those prescribed in the original sources of Muslim Law. The act of levying the taxes alongwith the corresponding intention are construed to be in conformity with the purpose of Shariah and, hence, it retains the legal validity. This legal conclusion is further fortified with the instance of the performance of religious observances, in excess of the obligatory demands laid by Shariah, as perfectly falling within the ambit of law, and it cannot be called "bida" because the act of maintaining the excessive religious observances and the underlying intention are in full accord with the purpose of Shariah.

From the practical standpoint, the legal principles inferred from the preceding discourse can find rewarding application, particularly, in relation to Islamic laws of inheritance of property and family laws.

The word conscience connotes the perceptions of, and compulsion to, doing right. A necessary identifying characteristic of the conscientious interpretation will be the discovery of the intention of the Law-giver in relation to law and the ascertainment of the sufficiency of law, according to the well-established juridical principles, with scrupulous application. The Supreme Principles are essentially the fundamentals of Shariah law, and no law, in its legal application, can concurrently circumvent the jurisdiction subtended by the principles and retain its legal validity. These fundamentals also necessarily incorporate the intention of the Lawgiver concerning the Shariah law. In addition, specific intention in relation to a particular law is to be identified. It is obviously inferable that the legal methodology is the judicial province, and the onerous responsibility for the interpretation of law mainly devolves upon the Muslim jurists. And the aspiring enterprise for the constitution of a new legal system lies within their domain of expertise.

The fact of indispensable interrelationship that exists between law and religion, as well as society, transforms the last two entities as an unimpeachable Islamic Judicial concern equal to that of any other social group. The consciousness that the comparability of the envisioned legal system will depend upon the juridical excellence, such as is identifiable with originality, forms an integral part of the juristic approach. As its antecedents, a breadth of knowledge about the legal history concerning the development of legal systems in general, profound insight into the nature of Islamic law-making and an abiding belief in the inspiring instance of an original legal system will be necessitated. In this perspective, the combined genius of Muslim jurists will reflect from the conscientious interpretation of the wide-based sources of law. This requirement is contingent upon the subscription to the legal value of the Supreme Principles to impart universality and permanence to Islamic Law.

The issue of more than one injunctions concerning a particular subject is resolvable through a legal measure that can lay claim to unanimity. In the case of incompatibility of two injunctions, the later injunction will abrogate the earlier one.

The injunctions concerning the subject of polygamy are citable as an instance. The later injunction is a legislative denial of polygamy, which becomes manifest upon conscientious interpretation alone, despite the fact that it is framed in a subtle language for understandable social reasons then current. Similarly, the general subject of the status of women in society, in particular, the married women, comprises an important area of the revealed legislation. Without the complete realization of the fact that injunctions concerning marriage and divorce are multiple and do not preclude mutual variations, hence, any superficial treatment of these subjects in law-making can result in the fostering of imbalance in the social status of women.

This outcome is compounded in case the piecemeal nature of the revealed legislation due to the special circumstances involved, and the general objectives of the legislation for the improvement in the status of women, in divergence from the pre-Islamic customary law, are not allowed to register their proper influence during interpretation. Legal history is a testimonial to the fact that the social ethos left its imprint upon the early Islamic jurisprudence. This particular situation is illustrative of the vital correlation between the intentions underlying the revealed legislation and the law prevalent antedating it.

The importance of this observation is enhanced due to the well-recognized fact of the revealed legislation not being a complete code of law. But, perhaps, a single instance that can epitomize the necessity for conscientious interpretation is the revealed legal concept of "waiting period" or "idda." Its rationale is none other than the improvement of the chances for reconciliation between the spouses, before the divorce is finalized at the end of stipulated period. By taking this into legal consideration, and contrary to the general misconception prevalent concerning revealed Islamic laws, the repudiation of marriage in Islam is anything but an instantaneous act. These legal instances adequately emphasize the juridical necessity for the conscientious interpretation of law, which is to be contrasted with the construction of law according to subjectively determined standards, such as the consideration for legal tradition or social approval.

Delegation of Power

The revealed dictum of the human vicegerency, with its implications ranging throughout the Scripture, is a Supreme Principle and, in Kelsen's term, adoptable as a "grundnorm" to "derive the whole legal system!" However, the definition and legislation of the vital concept of vicegerency, especially, pertaining to the realm of jurisprudence, have not been painstakingly ascertained. The observation that no legislation independent of the original sources of law is feasible, however, the people as the delegates of divine sovereignty are entitled to formulate required laws, has not been translated into a legal formulation, owning the lawful authority of consensus (lima). The present treatise endeavours to compensate for this legal lapse.

A functional analogy for the Supreme Principle of human vicegerency, or people as the delegates of the divine sovereignty, in its legal expression, is inclusive of the latter-day juristic principle of "residual jurisdiction. In a federal-type constitution, the federal legislative power is not altogether exclusive of the legislative jurisdiction of the component political entities. The entitlement to residual jurisdiction allows the latter to legislate in areas related to federal legislative power. However, the prohibition from enacting measures which would "conflict" with the provisions of federal law, exists. On the contrary, the jurisdiction of passing such measures as would complete the lacuna left by federal legislation, or serve as addition thereto, is available. The important limitation upon the residual jurisdiction is imposed by the legal requirement of not permitting the constituent political units to legislate against the spirit of the constitution in an allowable legislative situation, in the absence of relevant federal legislation. The consideration for already existing sufficiency of federal law also has important bearing upon the area of residual jurisdiction. In summation, then, the constitutional measure of residual jurisdiction allows adequate legislative opportunity to the constituents to enact additions to federal legislation.

The engaging subject of the Quran and the authority of human legislation can be dealt with along the conceptual lines of the vicegerency in the perspective of present-day jurisprudential knowledge. In consonance with the legal formulation, the vital legal considerations for the "spirit of the constitution" and the "sufficiency of the law" discover their legal effectiveness. The intention and the direction of legislation have similar, but not the same, jurisdiction, hence, the legal identities of the intention and direction of legislation retain their differentiating features. The legal implications of these particular concepts have the potential for the legal expression of the principle of vicegerency.

The legal analogy of the levying of taxes upon personal wealth and property, in excess of the originally prescribed proportions in Islamic Law, supplemented by the religious instance of the maintenance of observances in addition to the obligatory requirements, is a prototypical illustration of the legal concept of vicegerency in the areas of already existing revealed legislation. The explanation for an historic avoidance in the extrapolation of this legal analogy upon the Islamic laws in relation to those of the inheritance of property concerning women is inconceivable. And not too dissimilar is the revealed issue of equality in relation to polygamy, which has been accorded a moral value in the traditional Islamic Law, whose conversion into legal terms is in conformity with the definition of law, as well as within the legal jurisdiction of vicegerency. The Muslim laws dealing with the inheritance of property are in obvious want of the extension of the same legal jurisdiction by not allowing the bequeathing of property to remain a matter of mere conscience. An inducement to moral degeneracy, casting of a slur upon the faith of Islam, and paving a way for the unsuccess of the Islamic Law-a view that finds substantiation from Fuller's observations are the drawbacks in the relevant law, which will be rectified by the use of legal jurisdiction pertaining to the Supreme Principle of vicegerency, as proposed in the Legal Method.

Law of Evidence

Shahadah : The law of evidence is very clearly laid down in all books of Islamic Law, especially in the *Hidaya* and the *Dur-rul-Mukhtar*.

It is the duty of witnesses to bear testimony, and it is not lawful for them to conceal it, when the party concerned demands it from them. The Holy Quran says :

> "Let not witnesses withhold their evidence when it is demanded of them." (2 : 282)

And again :

> "And never conceal evidence for he who conceals it, has a sinful heart." (2 : 283)

In cases likely to result in corporal punishment, witnesses are at liberty either to give or withhold their testimony as they please ; because in such case they are distracted between two laudable actions ; namely the establishment of the punishment, and the preservation of the criminal's character. Concealment of an offence of others is moreover, preferable because the Holy Prophet (peace and blessings of Allah be upon him) said to a person that had borne testimony, "Verily, it would have been better for you if you had concealed it"; and also because he elsewhere said, "Whoever conceals the vices of his brother Muslim, shall have a veil drawn over his own crimes in both the worlds by Allah." Besides, it has been inculcated both by the Holy Prophet (peace and blessings of Allah be upon him) and his Companions as commendable to assist in the prevention of corporal punishment; and this is an evident argument for the concealment of such evidence as tends to establish it. It is incumbent, however, in the case of theft, to bear evidence to the property by testifying that "a certain person took such property," in order to preserve the right of the proprietor. However the word "taken" must be used instead of "stolen", to the end that the crime must be kept concealed. Besides, if the word "stolen" were used, the thief would be rendered liable to amputation ; and as where amputation is incurred, there is no responsibility for the property, the proprietor's right would be destroyed.

The evidence required in a case of adultery is that of four men, as has been ordained in the Holy Quran (24 : 4) and the testimony of a woman in such a case is not admitted. Al-Zubri says, "During the time of the Holy Prophet (peace and blessings of Allah be upon him) and his two immediate successors, it was an invariable rule to exclude the evidence of women in all cases inducing punishment or retaliation," and also because the testimony of women involves a degree of doubt, as it is merely a substitute for evidence, being accepted only where the testimony of men cannot be had. It is, therefore, not admitted in any matter liable to drop from the evidence of doubt.

The evidence required in other criminal cases is that of two men, according to the text of the Holy Quran; and the testimony of women is not admitted, on the strength of the tradition of Al-Zubri above quoted. In all other cases the evidence required is that of men, or of one man and two women, whether the case relates to property or to other rights, such as marriage, divorce, agency, executorship or the like.

The Imam al-Shafii has said that the evidence of one man and two women cannot be admitted, excepting in cases that relate to property, or its dependencies, such as hire, bail, and so forth; because the evidence of woman is originally inadmissible on account of their weakness of understanding, their want of memory and incapacity of governing, whence it is that their evidence is not admitted in criminal cases.

In all rights whether of property or otherwise, the probity of the witness, and the use of the word "*ashhadu*" (I bear witness) is absolutely requisite, even in the case of the evidence of women. If, therefore, a witness should say, "I know" or "I know with certainty" without making use of the word "ashhadu", in that case his evidence cannot be admitted. With respect to the probity of the witness, it is indispensable because it is written in the Holy *Quran* :

"Take the evidence of two just men." (65 : 2)

It is also because the probity of the witnesses induces a probability of the truth.

If the defendant throws a reproach on the witnesses, it is in that case incumbent on the Qadi to institute an enquiry into their character, because, in the same manner as it is probable that a Muslim abstain from falsehood as being a thing prohibited in the religion he professes, so also is it probable that a Muslim will not unjustly reproach another.

It is not lawful for a person to give evidence on such matters as he has not actually seen personally.

The evidence of any person who is property that is to say, a slave, male or female, is not admissible, because testimony is of an authoritative nature ; and as a slave has no authority over his own person, it follows that he can have no authority over others, a fortiori.

The testimony of a person that has been punished for false accusation (*qadhf*) is inadmissible.

The Holy *Quran* says :

"But as to those who accuse married persons of adultery and produce not four witnesses of the fact, scourge them with eighty stripes, and receive not their testimony for ever ; for such men are wicked transgressors,—excepting those who shall afterwards repent and make amends." (24 :4, 5)

Evidence by Non-Muslims

If an infidel who has suffered punishment for qadhf (false accusation) should afterwards become a Muslim, his evidence is then admissible ; for although, on account of the said punishment he had lost the degree in which he was qualified to give evidence (that is, in all matters that related to his own sect), yet by his conversion to the Islamic faith he acquires a new competency in regard to evidence (namely, competency to give evidence relative to Muslims), and which is not affected by any matter that happened prior to the circumstances which gave birth to it.

Testimony in favour of a son or grandson, or in favour of a father or grandfather, is not admissible, because the Holy Prophet (peace and blessings of Allah be upon him) has so ordained. Besides, as there is a kind of communion of benefits between these degrees of kindred, it follows that their testimony in matters relative to each other is in some degree a testimony in favour of themselves, and is, therefore, liable to suspicion.

So also the Holy Prophet (peace and blessings of Allah be upon him) said, "We are not to credit (in civil cases) the evidence of a wife concerning her husband, or of a husband concerning his wife ; or of a slave concerning his master ; or of a master concerning his slave ; or, lastly, of a hirer concerning his hireling."

The testimony of a convict or a person who has committed a great crime, such as induces punishment, is not admissible, because in consequence of such crime he is unjust. The testimony of a person who receives usury is inadmissible ; and so, also, of one who plays for a stake at dice or chess.

The evidence of a person who openly inveighs against the Companions of the Holy Prophet (peace and blessings of Allah be upon him) and their disciples is not admissible, because of his apparent want of integrity. It is otherwise, however, where a person conceals his sentiments in regard to them, because in such case the want of integrity is not apparent.

The testimony of a *Dhimmi* (Zimmi) with respect to each other is admissible, notwithstanding they be of different religions.

Imam Abu Hanifa is of the opinion that a false witness must be stigmatised, but not chastised with blows. The two disciples are of the opinion that he must be scourged and confined; and this also is the opinion of the Imam al-Shafii.

The mode of stigmatising a false witness is this : If the witness be a sojourner in any public street or market-place, let him be sent to that street or market-place ; or if otherwise, let him be sent to his own tribe or kindred, after the evening Prayers (as they are generally assembled in greater number at that time than any other); and let the stigmatiser inform the people that the Qadi salutes them, and informs them that he has detected this person in giving false evidence ; that they themselves, most therefore, beware of him and likewise desire others to beware of him.

If witnesses retract their testimony prior to the Qadi passing any decree, it becomes void; if, on the contrary, the Qadi passes a decree, and the witnesses afterwards retract their testimony, the decree is not thereby rendered void.

The retraction of evidence is not valid, unless it be made in the presence of the Qadi.

Holy Quran, the Basis

The Holy Quran is a complete code of life for a believer. For adjudicating disputes and regulating social life, it provides substantive and procedural law. It says :

> We have prescribed for each of you the substantive law and the procedural methods (traced out way).
> (5:48).

Substantive law defines what facts constitute a right or liability while the set of rules and principles regulating the inquiry into such facts is termed as "Law of Evidence".

A fact can be proved before a Court of Law in three ways:

(1) Admission;

(2) Oath; and

(3) Testimony, which may be oral, documentary or circumstantial.

The admission before a court of a charge of commission of offence is technically known as confession. Great importance has been attached to confession in the Quran and *Sunnah.* An accused person can be convicted and sentenced under the law on the basis of his confession, provided the judge is satisfied that the confession has not been extorted in any manner and that it is voluntarily made by the accused. However, in crimes punishable under *Hudood* a retracted confession cannot be acted upon and sentence awarded to the accused has to be suspended. In Civil cases, on the other hand, if a person admits the right of another person, then no proof is required for decreeing the claim. The admission will be bending upon the person admitting the claim and effective decree can be passed against him.

In the absence of admission and evidence, claims in the civil matters can be settled on oath taken by either party to the case, but no criminal matter, except the accusation of *Zina* by a husband to his wife before a court (technically known as *'Lian'),* can be decided on the Oath of a party to the case.

Oral testimony is an account of facts before a court of law by a person, concerning any matter, which he has personally seen, observed and perceived. Two words frequently appearing in the Holy Quran are of particular significance in connection with oral testimony. These are *'Baiyanah'* and *'Shahadah Baiyanah* is from *Bayan*. It means clear expression or irrebuttable and clear proof which cannot be denied. *Sahahdah* is a derivative of the word *Shaheed.* Literally it means to watch, to be present and to inspect. Technically it means conveying true information to a court of law in connection with a matter pending adjudication before it. *Shahadah* has been used in the Holy Quran in literal as well as technical meaning and sometimes *Baiyanah* and *Shahadah* have been used in it in the identical sense.

> "And We have revealed unto thee the Remembrance that you mayest explain to mankind that which has been revealed for them" (16:44).
>
> "And let a party of believers witness their punishment." (24:2).
>
> "Were you present when death came to Jacob." (2: 133).
>
> "And whosoever of you is present, let him fast the month." (2:185).

The Holy Quran attaches great importance to the testimony of a witness. Receiving the evidence and then giving it before a court is the collective duty of those who have the information or the knowledge of the facts of an incident. Not discharging this duty and concealing the evidence is a sin, and the entire community will be held responsible for it. When there is only one witness, evidence becomes individual duty. The Holy Quran says:

> "Who will be more transgressing than he who conceals evidence, which he has from God."
>
> "And do not conceal testimony, for he who conceals it, surely his heart is sinful; Allah knows well what you do."

Generally a witness cannot refuse to give evidence when

he is called upon to do so, but he should go to the court when he is called by the party that wants to produce him as a witness. If it is apprehended that due to absence of a witness right of a party will be destroyed, then it is obligatory for him to go to the court voluntarily and give evidence to indicate the right of the aggrieved party.

The object of evidence should be to bear witness or give evidence for the sake of Allah alone, hence in the Holy Quran the following words have been used:

"And keep your testimony upright for Allah."

(45:2).

Allah enjoins upon the believers in *Surah An-Nisa, verse 135* to be witnesses for His sake even if the testimony is against themselves or their close relatives:

> "O, you who believe! Be staunch in Justice (and be) witnesses for Allah, even though (it be) against yourselves, or against your parents or near relatives; whether they be rich or poor. Allah is more near to both than you are. Therefore, do not follow your low desires, lest you deviate from justice, and if you conceal (the truth) or evade it, surely, Allah is well aware of what you do."

Evidence should be accordingly to the best knowledge and belief of a witness, and one should not follow a thing for which he has no information or knowledge. These principles are enunciated in the following verses of the Holy Quran "O, true believers! If a wicked man comes to you with a tale (about other people), inquire strictly, lest you hurt people through ignorance, and afterwards repent of what you have done, and know that Apostle of Allah is among you." (49:6)

"And do not follow that whereof you have no knowledge."

Perjury is strongly condemned by Islam. Quran approves

of the behaviour of those who do not give false evidence. It says:

"And those who do not bear false witness, and when they pass by vain discourse, they pass with dignity."

"And who are upright in their testimonies."

The Holy Prophet said:

> "The false witness will not move from his place on the day of judgement. He will acquire his place in the hell" (Ibne Maja and Bahaqi).

In another *Hadith,* the Holy Prophet was reported to have said:

> "Shall I tell you the most major of all major sins is to associate false gods with Allah, to disobey the parents and false evidence."
>
> The Holy Prophet laid stress on the words false evidence, which led the Companions to consider it to be a crime. (Bukhari, Muslim and Baihaqi).

Hadrat Umar awarded the punishment of forty stripes to a false witness and also got his face blackened with soot. *Imam Abu Hanifa* was of the opinion that a false witness must be stigmatised, but his disciples and *Imam Shafi* followed the action of Hadrat Umar.

On the authority of the traditions mentioned above Qadi Shureh and other Companions of the Prophet ordered different kinds of *Tazirs* to false witnesses. False witnesses were publicly denounced and perjury was made a crime liable to *Tazir.*

In the Islamic Law of Evidence great emphasis has been laid on the character of a witness. A witness must be *Aadil* Gust), which means that he should not have been indulging in major sins and must not be used to minor sins. Moreover, he should not have been punished for *Qazf.* The cardinal and basic principle is that every Muslim is to be taken to be an *Aadil* unless proved otherwise.

> "Muslims will be considered competent witnesses amongst themselves, except the one who has been striped in a crime of moral turpitude."

The same principle has been explained by Hadrat Umar in his letter to Abu Musa Ashari. The first sentence of that letter is almost the same as that of the *Hadith* mentioned above.

Various Conditions

In the authoritative books on Islamic Law of Evidence a number of conditions have been laid down under three heads for giving evidence by a witness:

(a) Conditions for receiving evidence :

(1) Except in case of hearsay evidence universally accepted, a witness must have good eye-sight;

(2) He must be sane;

(3) He must have seen the facts to be proved, but this is not necessary in a universally accepted hearsay evidence;

(4) He should be a freeman; and

(5) He should not be a *Fasiq*.

(b) Conditions for being a witness:

(1) A witness must be sane;

(2) He must be adult;

(3) He must have good eye-sight, but this condition is not necessary if eye-sight is lost after receiving the evidence and also in case of a hearsay evidence of universal import;

(4) In *Hudood* cases, a witness must be able to speak as evidence of dumb man in such cases is not acceptable;

(5) He must be *Aadil;*

(6) He must be male (in *Hudood* cases);

(7) He must not have been punished for *Qazaf;*

(8) He should not give evidence for acquiring benefit or to avoid any harm; and

(9) He should be of the same faith or *Deen* as that of the person against whom he gives evidence.

(c) Conditions for giving Evidence:

(1) Claim or cause must exist at the time of giving the evidence by a witness about it.

(2) Evidence must be given in the court.

(3) Except in cases where hearsay evidence is universally accepted, a witness must have personal knowledge about the person against whom he gives the evidence;

(4) Facts of the case must be in his mind;

(5) At the time of giving evidence he should say I bear witness to such and such facts;

(6) He should be able to identify and recognise the parties to the case by their voice and faces;

(7) The testimony must agree with the claim;

(8) The statements of the witnesses of a party should corroborate one another;

(9) Except *Qazf,* in other *Hudood* cases there should be no delay in giving evidence; and

(10) In *Hudood* cases witness has to appear in person before the court to give evidence.

Evidence of a witness must also be free from bias and prejudice. Enunciating this principle, Muslim jurists have held that testimony is not admitted of a slave in favour of his master, of a person who bears grudge against the opposite party, of the father in favour of his son and *vice versa,* of parties in support of their own case, of a non-Muslim (except under exceptional circumstances) against a Muslim and so on.

Having regard to reliability of character, the evidence is not accepted of persons carrying on certain professions of degrading nature, such as dancers, singers and actors, of gamblers, drunkards and public mourners, of corrupt public officials, of persons who are not of virtuous character, but, according to Abu Yusuf, a man may not be of virtuous character yet his evidence ought to be admitted if he is of such a position in life that he is unlikely to depose a falsehood.

The evidence of *Fast* (those who indulge in the breach of religious injunctions) *Murtad* (apostate), *Khain* (who indulges in breach of trust) habitual liars, eunuchs and person convicted in *Hudood* cases is not accepted. On the grounds of maturity of understanding and power of perception, the evidence of a small child, a lunatic and a blindman is also not accepted in matters, which have to be proved by ocular testimony. In such cases they are declared unfit for giving testimony.

The evidence of a blindman is admissible if he had seen the incident before he became blind. His evidence will also be admitted in cases wherein facts have been perceived through his ears. The evidence of a child pertaining to any facts arising out of a play with others is acceptable. On attaining puberty he will be a competent witness, to depose about the facts perceived by him during his childhood.

As to the number of witnesses, for proving a right, the evidence of two men or one man and two women is sufficient. In case of *Tazir* the evidence of two men or one man and two women is required. The reasons for the evidence of two women instead of one man are that women are brought up in such circumstances that they cannot draw correct conclusions about the hard facts of outer world. Secondly, women do not express their conscience in clear words. Thirdly, women do not remember all the details of an incident. Moreover, women tend to forget things easily *Verse No. 282 of Surah Al Baqr* directs a woman to remind another if she forgets.

The evidence of one woman is sufficient in a case in which men generally have no information. For instance, only a woman can see the private parts of the body of another woman. Similarly, in matters which are generally in the knowledge of men, the evidence of women alone will not be acceptable, but in the exceptional circumstances i.e. when all the witnesses to the incident are women and no male witnesses are available, the evidence of women alone will, as per necessity, be acceptable in all matters, including *Qisas* and *Hudood.* Such view is held by Ibnul Qaiyem, the great Muslim jurist. (Reference can be made to page 44 of his book *Al Muqaeen.)*

In case of *Zina* the evidence of four eye-witnesses is required while in other *Hudood* cases, evidence of two witnesses is sufficient. Generally, the evidence of women is not valid in cases of *Hudood* and *Qisas,* but for the sake of convenience and in case of when it is necessary, the evidence of women in such cases be accepted with care and caution. The *Shias* admit the evidence of women along with men, with a ratio of two women for one man even in a case of *Zina,* but for lapidation the evidence of four male witnesses is required.

The verses of the Holy Quran dealing with the number of witnesses are asunder:

> "And those who accuse chaste women of adultery and produce not four witnesses, flog them with eighty stripes." (Surah Noor - 4)
>
> "And call two witnesses from among you men, two witnesses. And if two be not (at hand) then a man and two women, of such as ye approve as witnesses, so that if one erreth (through forgetfulness) the other will remember." (2:282).

'O ye who believe! Let there be witnesses between you where death draweth nigh unto one of you, at the time of bequest, two witnesses, just men from among you, or for others four another tribe in case you are campaigning in the land and the calamity of death befall you.'

The acceptance and admissibility of the evidence ultimately rests on the satisfaction of a judge about it. In *verse No. 282 of Surah Al-Bazr* this principle has been enunciated. A judge may, therefore, make inquiry into the competency of witness privately or in court (preferably after evidence of the witness) through reliable persons acquainted with the life and character of such a witness. This sort of purgation of witness is known as *Tazkia tush Shahood* and it is undertaken in cases punishable with *Hudood.* Imam Abu Hanifa did not consider *Tazkia tush Shahood* necessary if the witness otherwise appeared to be or is known to be *'Aadil'* (a man of rectitude).

The evidence of a non-Muslim against a non-Muslim is valid, but the evidence of a non-Muslim against a Muslim is ordinarily not accepted. However, in verses 106 and 108 of *Surah Al Malda* the Holy Quran has permitted evidence of a non-Muslim against a Muslim in case of journey when Muslim witnesses are not available. This shows that the evidence of a non-Muslim is not *ipso facto* inadmissible and in case of necessity the evidence of a non-Muslim against a Muslim can be accepted.

The highest kind of oral testimony in Islamic Law of Evidence is known as *Tawatar* or universal testimony. It consists of the evidence of such a large body of men that our reason cannot conceive that they would join one another in falsehood, or they would agree in an error. When any fact is proved by *Tawatar,* no evidence against it would be admissible. The witnesses of *Tawatar* are not subjected to cross-examination. There is also no need of holding an inquiry into their rectitude.

Hearsay evidence is generally not accepted, but in the Islamic Law of Evidence it is admissible for proving the facts of death, paternity, marriage, *waqf* and appointment of a Qadi.

Another kind of oral evidence in the Islamic Law of Evidence is *Shahadat Alas Shahadah.* When a witness is not able to give evidence due to any disability, another person can give evidence in court on his evidence. This is permissible only in case of death and illness, or in case of a *Purdah Nashin* lady who does not move out. It is also permissible where the court is at a distance of three days journey from the residence of the witness. It is however, not permissible in *Hudood* cases. The. procedure, for giving such evidence is that the real witness (may be man or woman) should ask one or two adult male person or persons to bear witness that he gives such and such evidence. Then the said person or persons will give evidence before the court that the real witness has appointed him as a witness on his such and such evidence. The appointed witness is liable to cross-examination and evidence in connection with rectitude of the real witness will also be taken.

Documentary evidence is considered in Islamic Law of Evidence as reliable proof of facts, provided the document tendered in evidence is not disputed and it has been written in accordance with the custom prevalent in a country. Forged and suspicious documents cannot be acted upon by a court, but official documents record of courts of justice and books of accounts can be accepted in evidence. Similarly, document executed in presence of two witnesses can also be admitted in evidence. Verses 282 and 283 of *Surah Al Baqr* of the Holy Quran contains considerable details about drawing deed of debt in presence of two male or one male and two female witnesses.

In addition to oral testimony, evidence based on facts and circumstances known as circumstantial evidence can also be relied upon as a proof, if it is of a conclusive nature. For instance, if a person is seen running out of a house with blood-stained dagger and a dead body with its throat cut, is found in that house, these facts will be taken to be proof of murder by the person who was seen running out of that house. Pregnancy of a virgin and delivery of a child by a woman within six month after her marriage are strong pieces of circumstantial evidence of *Zina*.

Similarly, foul smell coming out of the mouth of a person together with an unsteady staggering gait is circumstantial evidence of drinking. Verses 24 to 29 of *Surah-e-Yusuf* show that the tearing of the shirt of Hadrat Yusuf from backside was a proof of his innocence based on circumstantial evidence. The scope of circumstantial evidence has been widened and made more reliable by modern scientific technique, especially in the medical field wherein age, virginity and pregnancy can be determined with considerable accuracy and certainty. Thus, virginity proved by medical evidence can believe the witnesses of *Zina*.

Unlike other systems of law which have been developed by men through ages, the Islamic system of law is based on Quran and *Sunnah* and developed by the great Muslim jurists by *Ijma, Qiyas* and *Ijtihad*. The man-made laws keep on changing with changing norms of human society, but the divine laws of Islam are permanent and unchangeable in their nature. These laws tend to preserve life, liberty, honour and property in a better way than other man-made systems of law. These provide substantive justice to mankind and promote a peaceful harmonious social life. No doubt, the *Shariah* laws prescribe extreme penalty in crimes of *Zina*, theft, robbery, dacoity *Qazf* and drinking, but for the proof of such crimes, evidence of a very high standard is required.

Evidence falling short of the prescribed standard would be sufficient to change the punishment of *Hadd* into *Tazir*. Similarly, evidence creating slightest doubt, will give benefit of doubt to the accused. On the other hand, false evidence, especially affecting the honour of a woman is severely dealt with and false witnesses are liable to be punished for *Qazf*.

The Holy Quran says :

> "O ye who believe! Retaliation is prescribed for you in the matter of the murdered, the freeman for the freeman, the slave for the slave, and the female for the female. And for him who is forgiven somewhat by his (injured) brother, prosecution according to the usage and payment unto him in kindness. This is an alleviation and a mercy from your Lord. He who transgressed after this will have a painful doom."
>
> (Al Baqara 178).

> "And there is life for you in retaliation, O men of understanding that ye may ward off (evil)".
>
> (Al-Baqara 179).

No system of justice other than Islam has such principles of justice tempered with mercy.

Law under Islam

Allah in His Infinite Wisdom created this universe and unto the Earth He sent the first Prophet and the first man. Allah said to angels: "I am going to place a *Khalifah* in the Earth". They said "Will you place there one who will cause disorder therein and shed blood. God (Almighty), answered; "Verily, I know what you not". Allah then ordered the angels to fall in obeisance before Adam. They all made obeisance except Iblees who refused because of his pride and became one of the disbelievers. This marked the beginning of two opposite directions; first one leading to the path of Allah and the other one misleading man and taking him to the fold of Satan. From this juncture the good and the evil started proceeding in different directions. The divergence so caused gave rise to a number of problems and disputes. Allah, being Most Gracious and Most

Merciful provides guidance to the people. Those who follow the guidance of Allah have no fear nor shall they grieve and those who do not believe His signs shall be thrown into fire and wherein they shall remain for ever.

The idea of the above mentioned reference was to indicate that a conflict started between righteousness and evil with the birth of the human race which continues and will continue till the end of the world. The simultaneous existence of the right and wrong must result in causing disturbance in the community which needs some checks to evolve a balanced society. God has endowed man with sufficient means of understanding. God is also Gracious and Kind to show us the familiar and known path leading to His decisions. This path is called *Shariah,* which constitutes the substantive law of Islam.

The Subjects: *Shariah* deals with the following subjects :

(1) Rituals;

(2) Family Laws;

(3) Worldly Transactions;

(4) Constitutional Law;

(5) *Al-Siyar;* and

(6) Criminal Law.

The Holy Quran says :

> "We have prescribed for each of you the substantive law and the procedural methods."
>
> It becomes evident from the above mentioned Verse of the Holy Quran that Islam has provided the details of substantive law and has also given the details of procedure to be adopted while deciding a cause arising out of the above cited subjects of *Shariah.*

A cause of action or subject matter of a case consists of a bundle of facts which if proved entitle a person to have a favourable decision from a Court of law. The object of the law of evidence is to prescribe rules to prove the facts relevant for the decision of the case. M. Munir explains the Law of Evidence in the following words :

> "The Law of Evidence may be defined as a system of rules for ascertaining controverted questions of fact in judicial inquiries. It bears the same relation to a judicial investigation as logic to reasoning. The object of every judicial proceeding is the enforcement of some right or liability which invariably depends upon certain facts. The substantive Law, whether it be statute law or Common Law, merely defines what facts go to constitute a right or liability. Before a tribunal can pronounce as to the existence of a right or liability it must ascertain the facts which according to the rule of substantive Law, applicable to the case, are the necessary constituents of that right or liability. This duty of ascertaining the facts which are the essential elements of a right or liability is primary and perhaps the most difficult function of a tribunal. The inquiry into these facts is regulated by a set of rules and principles which go by the name of 'Law of Evidence'.

Nature and Significance of the Law of Evidence

The Law of Evidence forms a foundation for every system of Justice. So is the case in Islamic System of Administration of Justice. In systems other than Islam, the development of Law of Evidence is attributable to History of Judicial organisations. The rules of evidence were framed by the people as and when it was considered expedient by them whereas in Islamic System of Justice, the sources of Law of Evidence are the Quran and the *Sunnah* of the Holy Prophet (PBUH).

The principles are set out in Quran and *Sunnah,* while the details of Law of Evidence are worked out by *Ijma* and *Ijtihad* and other methods such as *Qiyas,* etc.

Holy Quran attaches great importance to the evidence and the witnesses for dispensation of Justice. It is the collective duty of the community to give evidence. Sufficient number of the members of the community must execute this duty, otherwise the entire community shall be held responsible. Sometimes it is primary duty of a particular member of the community who has seen the actual occurrence to give evidence. Quran says:

> "And do not conceal testimony, for he who conceals it, surely his heart is sinful; Allah knows well what you do."

A witness as a general rule cannot refuse to give evidence when he is called to do so, but he will come to the court when he is called by the party who wants to produce him as a witness.

The object of testimony should be for the sake of Allah, as He desires that the rights of the people must be vindicated. If a person has information as to the existence of fact and he withholds the information there is every likelihood that the right of the aggrieved party will be destroyed causing injustice to that party. Allah, therefore, enjoins in the Quran to be witnesses for Allah, even if the testimony is against the witness himself or his close relatives. Quran says :

> "Oh you who believe! Be staunch in Justice (and be) witnesses for Allah, even though (it be) against your parents or near relatives; whether he be rich or poor. Allah is more near to both than you are. Therefore, do not follow your low desires, lest you deviate from Justice and if you conceal the (truth) or evade it, surely, Allah is well aware of what you do."

It is again one of the essentials of bearing out testimony that the witness should depose in accordance with best of his knowledge and belief. Declaring this principle of Evidence, Quran says:

> "Oh! true believers! if a wicked man comes to you with a tale (about other people), inquire strictly, lest you hurt people through ignorance, and afterwards repent of what you have done and know that the Apostle of Allah is among you."

Quran also enunciates this principle in Verse 108 of *Sura Al-Maidah:*

> "Thus it is more likely that they will bear true witness according to facts or they shall fear that other oaths will be taken after their oaths. Therefore, fear Allah and hearken for Allah does not guide the transgressors to the right path."

Quran does not approve the practice of following the information for which one has no knowledge. Quran says :

> "And" do not follow that whereof you have no knowledge; for the hearing, and the sight, and the heart, each of them shall be questioned (on the day of judgement).

Islam is the most favourite *Din* of Allah. Allah has made it perfect in every respect. Quran provides extreme moral consideration, and any act involving discredit to such moral consideration is taken as highly obnoxious and severely condemned. It is, therefore, ordained by God that the witnesses should not bear out false evidence. Quran says :

> "And those who do not bear false witness and when they pass by vain discourse they pass by with dignity."

In *Sura Al-Ma-Arij, Verse 33* it is again stressed: "And who are upright in their testimonies".

The cardinal principle given in *Hadiths* is that every Muslim shall be considered *Adal* unless established otherwise. This principle is declared in the following tradition of the Holy Prophet (PBUH).

Following are some of the other instances where Holy Prophet (PBUH) has disapproved the false evidence.

"The false witness will not move from his place on the day of Judgement. He will acquire his place in the Hell". (Abdullah-Bin-Umar in *Ibne Maja; Bahaqi* and *Hakam).*

Hadith reported in *Muslim, Bokhari* and *Behaqi:*

> "The Holy Prophet (peace be upon him) is reported to have said; Shall I tell you the most major of all major sins is to associate false gods with Allah, to disobey the parents and the false evidence. The Holy Prophet (PBUH) repeated the last words thrice. The stress on the words "false evidence" led Companions to term it as a crime."

The act of perjury has been termed as a crime in criminal law of the present day. A person who has perjured himself before a Court of law is liable to a sentence which may extend to seven years under section 193 Pakistan Penal Code. Islamic Law makes no exception to this rule. It, rather goes a further step by providing the sentence of exposing the person in public. It is stated in *Hedaya, Book XXI, Chapter V, page 372* as under:

"Abu Hanifa is of the opinion that a false witness must be stigmatized. The two disciples are of opinion that he must be scourged and confined; and this is also the cpinion of Shafi. The arguments of the two disciples upon this point are two-fold. First, it is related of Umar that he caused a false witness to be scourged with forty stripes and to have his face blackened with the soot of a pot. Secondly, false testimony is a great crime of which the evil results to others, and as no stated punishment has been ordained for it in Law, it must, therefore, be punished by *Tazeer* or discretionary correction."

The arguments of Abu Hanifa are also two-fold. Firstly, *Shureeh* stigmatized a false witness, but did not scourge him. Secondly, prevention of crime in future may be affected by stigmatizing, and it ought, therefore, to be adopted as sufficient, for mere beating or scourging enjoined in such cases, may operate to the concealment of the crime and consequent destruction of the rights of others; in other words, as being a grievous punishment, the fear of it might deter false witnesses from a confession of their falsehood. With regard to the relation concerning Umar, it evidently alludes to the infliction of punishment on a criminal, as appears by the number of stripes (namely forty) and blackening of the countenance.

Islam, not only abhors the tendency of telling lies and upholds the dignity of trustworthiness but also recommends that a person appearing as a witness should be shown utmost respect. Holy Prophet (peace be upon him) says:

> "You should honour and respect the witnesses because God revives the rights of the people through them."

The object of the law of evidence is to formulate principles which are essentials for proving facts relevant for disposal of a case. In Article 77 of the *Mejella* it is provided:

> "The object of evidence is to prove what is contrary to the apparent fact, the object of oath is to insure the continuance of the original state."

A fact can be proved in three ways before a Court of Law:

(1) Admission;

(2) Oath; and

(3) Testimony, which may be oral, documentary or circumstantial.

When a person accused of an offence pleads guilty to the charge before a court of competent jurisdiction, he is said to have admitted the charge. This admission is known as a confession of the accused. A judge can act upon the confessional statement of the accused, who is bound by his confession and may award sentence provided under the law. If the Judge is satisfied that the accused has confessed his guilt with free-will and without any undue influence or duress. An exception is, however, placed in case of *Hadood* Crimes, where a retracted confession cannot be acted upon and the sentence given on a confession has to be suspended. In civil matters, if a person admits the claim of another person, the admission is binding upon him and an effective decree can be passed against him.

Proof of a fact is valid on oath if there is no admission or in case, evidence is not available. An oath is only acceptable in civil cases. Oath is not admissible in criminal matters.

Testimony literally means to watch, inspect or to be present but in its technical sense it means to convey true information to a Court of Law in connection with a matter pending adjudication before it. An account of facts stated in a court of law by a person concerning any matter which he has personally seen, observed or perceived, will constitute oral evidence.

From the provisions of New Islamic Laws it is evident that not only the requisite number of witnesses is essential to prove the accusation but the witnesses should be adult male Muslims who should also stand the test of *Tazkia-al-Shuhood* with further qualification of being the men of high morality. The female testimony, has, specifically been excluded in Penal Matters. The exclusion of female testimony may appear strange to the persons nourishing always the ideas alien to Islamic system. Islam is a complete code of life.

Its various terms, rules, ethical or legal, are to be understood within the fram work of this Code. For efficient, smooth working of a system the different components constituting that system must be allotted definite places and specific functions, otherwise the whole system shall collapse and desired effect cannot be achieved. Woman is supposed to be the mistress of household affairs and remains secluded from public life. Due to her seclusion from public life and her inexperience in worldly affairs, the testimony of a female witness is excluded in criminal cases and in other matters testimony of two women is regarded equal to that of one man.

The following commentary has been given in Hidaya regarding female testimony at page 353, Book XXI, Chapter I.

The evidence required in whoredom is that of four men, as has been ordained in Quran; and the testimony of a woman in such case is not admitted, because *Zihara* says: "In the time of the Prophet and his two immediate successors it was an invariable rule to exclude the evidence of women in all cases inducing punishment or relation; and also because the testimony of women involves a degree of doubt, as it is merely a substitute for evidence, being accepted only where the testimony of men cannot be had and therefore, it is not admitted in any matter liable to drop from the existence of a doubt".

On page 354 of the same book it is said:

> "The evidence of women alone suffices concerning matters which do not admit the inspection of men. The evidence of one woman is admitted in cases of birth. The principle of the law, in these cases is derived from a traditional saying of Holy Prophet "The evidence of women is valid with respect to such things as it is not fitting for man to behold".

In *Hudood* and *Qisas* cases the court must be satisfied as to the requirement of *Tazkia-al-Shuhood. Tazkia* or Purgation of the witnesses is the nature of inquiry to be held by a Judge, either openly or secretly after the evidence of the witnesses has been recorded. The purpose of this inquiry is to judge and ascertain the credibility and rectitude of witnesses by probing into their character, status and their behaviour in private as well as public life. If it is found on the basis of such inquiry that their testimony is not trustworthy their evidence shall be rejected. It was held in PLD 1979 A J and K 74 that purgation is not synonymous with cross-examination. It is a secret or open inquiry to be conducted by a Judge or Qadi as to the competency, character and rectitude of the witnesses. It has been held by various authors on this subject that the question of purgation arises only when the accused throws a reproach on the witnesses. On the other hand, if the accused accepts the testimony of the witnesses or he confesses the guilt, it is not necessary for the Qadi or Judge to conduct the purgation.

When a matter required under law to be reduced to writing is proved by the production of the document, oral evidence to prove fact contained in the document is not allowed. *Shariah* has made it compulsory to reduce to writing the contract of debt for fixed time. Quran says:

> "Oh you who believe when you deal with each other in contracting a debt for a fixed period then write it down."

In the same *Verse of Al-Baqarah* stress is again laid on writing down the contracts of transactions, small or big except those of ready merchandise which can be made on the spot. It is in the Quran:

> The significance and importance of execution of documents and bearing out the testimony are well evident from verses 282 and 283 of *Sura Al-Baqara.*

It has been recorded above that qualification of a witness under Evidence Act is his capacity or capability to depose facts before a Court of Law. The only thing which matters is the truthfulness of the witnesses. The relationship of the witnesses with the litigants, is not of much significance. In Islamic Law of Evidence, the evidence of a slave in favour of his master, of relations within the prohibited degree of paternity, of husband in favour of wife and *vice versa,* of master in favour of slave, of one partner in a firm in favour of another is not admissible. The rigidity of the rule may become clear from the complaint of Hadrat Ali which he brought in the Court of Qadi Shureeh against a jew alleging theft of his mail. The witnesses of the theft were his son Imam Hassan and a slave. Qadi declined to accept the testimony. Thereupon Hadrat Ali brought to the notice of the Qadi that he was not an ordinary man and his son had been declared by the Holy Prophet (peace be upon him) as the Leader of young people in the Heaven Qadi Shureeh replied that he was also following the decision of the Holy Prophet (peace be upon him) who disallowed the evidence of a son in favour of his father.

The evidence of public mourners and singers common drunkards or falconers, atrocious criminals, usurers or gamesters, persons guilty of indecorum, immodest persons and some of the other persons such as freethinkers, bastards and eunuch is not admissible.

The subject of false evidence has already been dealt with at some length. There remains a very important aspect of the Islamic Law of Evidence. Islam takes a great care of the chastity of pious women. If a person accuses another of fornication or adultery, he is required to prove his allegation by four reliable witnesses failing which he is guilty of *Qazf* and liable to punishment of eighty stripes. He also loses the right of being a witness in future. The law relating to *Qazf* has been embodied in offence of *Qazf* (Enforcement of *Hadd* Ordinance, 1979). The Holy Quran makes provision for protection of honour of chaste women in *verse 4 of Sura Al-Noor.*

"And those who accuse chaste women (of adultery) and do not produce four witnesses, flog them with eighty stripes and never (afterwards) accept their testimony and it is they that are the transgressors. Section 6 of the above said ordinance prescribes the mode of proof of *Qazf* liable to *Hadd* namely:

(a) Confession of the accused;
(b) Commission of *Qazf* in the presence of the court; and
(c) Evidence of two Muslim adult male witnesses, satisfying the requirements of *Tazkiah-al-Shuhood* and being truthful persons abstaining from major sins."

Circumstantial evidence is not relied as conclusive proof of existence or non-existence of a fact. This evidence is, however, taken as conclusive presumption, and has a great corroborative value because it can afford the proof of missing links in a case. Hadrat Umar, once imposed *Hadd* of *Zina* on a woman who was pregnant and was not able to satisfy the great Caliph as to the justification of her pregnancy. He imposed *Hadd* on the basis of circumstantial evidence. Medical Jurisprudence and other modern techniques have considerably improved the field of this kind of evidence. The Quranic source of circumstantial evidence is afforded by a well-known story of Hadrat Yousaf. *Verses 24 to 29 of Sura Yousaf* wherein the tearing of the shirt of Hadrat Yousaf from the back was declared as guilt of the wife of the Ruler of Egypt (Aziz) by one of the inmates of house (of Aziz).

To, conclude, we can say that the Rules of Evidence in Islam are very strict, particularly the *Hudood* cases. One of the objects of *Shariah* is to protect property, person and race of all citizens. Islam provides extreme punishments for the violation of these matters. It is, therefore, just to provide strict proof of the allegations. Honour and respect of female members of the society is also a paramount consideration in Islam. In order to stop false accusations against women, it was made imperative for the complainant to bring four adult pious Muslims to prove the accusation. If the accusation turns out to be false, the complainant and the witnesses are liable to the punishment of *Qazf*. Every Judicial system aims at doing justice but Islam desires the administration of substantial justice. With this view of the matter, Islam does not rely only on the preponderance of evidence but real and substantial evidence which may leave no room for entertaining even the slightest doubt in the dispensation of justice.

6

Criminal Law

Islam protects the rights of human beings; it has devised all ways and means to create such an atmosphere wherein the rights of the people are fully safeguarded. Islam stands for the peace of the mankind in this world and the hereafter. The Islamic law of punishment aims at eradication of all sorts of vices which corrupt human beings and human societies. Punishments are effective means to purge human societies of evil and undesirable elements. Islam considers punishment as means of purification from sins and crimes, as an eye opener to the people. The ultimate object of punishment is to establish and to enforce justice, peace, equality, security of life, honour and property. Punishment in Islam derives its moral justification from the simple fact that it constitutes indispensable self-defence of societies against crimes. Punishment subdues the wrong; hence punishments under Islamic Law are indeed very strict and deterrent, but very strict proof is also required to find one guilty. These punishments are not only redressive and retributive but also reformative.

Crime and Punishment

After the migration of the Holy Prophet to Medina, authority was established to settle disputes between people and to award punishment. As more and more people and more territory fell under the sway of the Central Government at Medina, the arm of the law was extended to cover large areas and, in some cases, the function to dispense justice was also delegated according to the needs. It is an admitted fact that the primary source of law in Islam is the Quran supplemented by the injunctions of the Holy Prophet (peace be upon him) who was the first Head of Islamic State. After him, his successors followed the path shown by him.

But as the simple society of Arabs was confronted by new and complex situations presented by fresh contacts and fresh conquests, the original sources were found insufficient. To the primary sources—others were added which were no more than rationalistic application and extension of the principles contained in the Quran and the *Sunnah.* While the principles were basic, the working out of solutions was necessarily influenced and conditioned by environments which could not fail to take into account the habits and traditions of the people for whom the "analogical deductions" were intended. The Quran has made three-fold protection of person, property and honour of the mankind as human life is the most sacred, so sacred that the annihilation of one life for other than man slaughter or corruption in the earth has been considered equivalent to the destruction of life, and the slaying of all mankind *(Al-Quran* Ch. V *verse* 35).

Quranic Law about Manslaughter : The general law in cases of man-slaughter is contained in Ch. II, verse 178-179. The English translation of verse 178 is reproduced as under:

> "O ye who believe, the law of equality is prescribed for you in cases of murder: the free for the free, the slave for the slave, and the woman for the woman. But if one is granted any remission by one's brother, then pursuing the matter for the realisation of the blood-money shall be done with fairness and the murderer shall pay the blood-money in a handsome

> manner. This is an alleviation and mercy from your Lord. He who transgresseth after this, shall have a painful doom."
>
> In this way the gross and inequitable custom of killing a freeman for a slave or killing more for one on the basis of higher status or of superior claim as it existed in pre-Islamic days has been abolished for all times. Verse 179 of Ch. II refers to the principle of retaliation. It says "And there is life for you in retaliation, O men of understanding, that you may ward off (evil)."

The two kinds of man-slaughter are mentioned as under:

(a) Murder by intention.

(b) Murder by mistake.

The penalty for each such offence is mentioned in Quran and prescribed as under :

> "Never should a Believer kill a Believer but (if it so happens) by mistake, compensation is due if one kills a Believer. It is ordained that he should free a believing slave and pay compensation to the deceased's family unless they remit it freely. If the deceased belonged to a people at war with you and he was a Believer, the freeing of a believing slave is enough. If he belonged to a people with whom you have a treaty of mutual alliance, compensation should be paid to his family and a believing slave be freed. For those who find this beyond their means is prescribed a fast for two consecutive months by way of penance from Allah." *Chapter IV, verse 92.*
>
> A Muslim shall not kill a Muslim deliberately; it may be by accident only and, in that case, compensation is the only satisfaction prescribed. But where this is done by intention (in modern legal phraseology called murder), the penalty is extremely serious. "Whoso

slayeth a Believer of set purpose, his reward is Hell for ever and the wrath and the curse of God are upon him, and dreadful penalty is prepared for him"

(Ch, IV, verse 93).

Varying Degrees : The offence of killing may vary in degrees. It may be deliberate killing with the intention to kill it may result in death without the intention to cause it; it may be the consequence of a grave and sudden provocation, etc., and the punishment should be commensurate with the offence. This is for the legislation to fix.

Injuries other than Death : As regards injuries short of death, the general principle is contained in V. 48, XVI 126. The legislature has the right and the power to make laws on the subject. Injuries might be classified as grievous or simple, and some may be compounded with the sanction of the Courts and others without such sanction. There is nothing against Islamic law to cover by legislation the entire gamut of injuries to "person" from the ordinary to the serious, culminating in death. This is wholly within the province of the legislature and is known as what is called *"Tazir"* as distinguished from *"Hadud"*, the limit prescribed in the Quran.

Zina Defined and Punishment Indicated : *Zina,* usually translated as adultery or fornication in *Fiqh,* has a wider meaning than sexual cohabitation with or without consent; it covers all sexual intercourse out of lawful wedlock. It is an offence both against person and honour. The punishment is prescribed in XXIV 2: "The adulterer and the adulteress, scourge ye each one of them (with) a hundred stripes. And let not pity for the twain withhold you from obedience to Allah if ye believe in Allah and the Last Day and let a party of believers witness their punishment".

In IV 15, it is prescribed: "As for those of your women who are guilty of lewdness, call to witness four of you against them. And if they testify (to the truth of the allegation), then confine them to the houses until death takes them or (until) Allah appoint for them a way". In XVII 32, *Zina* is described as a foul thing and an evil way, and the Muslims are prohibited from going near it.

Doctrine of Rajm (Lapidation) : *Surat Al-Noor* (Chapter XXIV) which prescribes punishment for *Zina* was revealed between the 5th and 6th Hijra, and before that no specific punishment for *Zina* was provided in the Quran. In the Old Testament punishment for adultery was known to be "stoning to death". It is no more to be found therein. In *Oxodus, Chapter XXI, Verse 28,* it is said: "If an *ox gore* a man or a woman, that they die, the ox shall be surely stoned, and his flesh shall not be eaten". If an animal could not escape stoning to death for the sin of goring a human being, how could a man be treated differently for adultery. Reference to this aspect of Jewish law may be found in the New Testament. In *St John, Chapter VIII, verses 3 – 11* describe the case of a woman "taken in adultery" and produced before Jesus. "They say unto him, Master, this woman hath been taken in adultery, in the very act. Now in the law Moses commanded us to stone such: what then sayest thou of her? Jesus said: He that is without sin among you, let him first cast a stone at her".

Penalty of Rajm Examined : On the strength of some Traditions, it has been laid down in the Islamic law books that in case of *Zina,* if the parties are unmarried, punishment of one hundred stripes each shall be inflicted, and if they are already married, then they shall be "stoned to death". This distinction is not supported by the Quran. The words used in the Quran are of a general nature and include all kinds of *Zanis* (adulterers), married or unmarried, free or slave. In his *Tafsir-ul-Kabir,* Volume VI, p. 214. Imam Razi records: All are agreed that the punishment of one hundred stripes is applicable to all types of delinquents".

As mentioned above in XXIV 2, the punishment of one hundred stripes alone is prescribed, the word *Rajm* (lapidation) is nowhere mentioned in the Quran as punishment for *Zina.* In this connection, IV. 25 may also be kept in view: "And if when they (the slave-girls) are honourably married, they commit lewdness, they shall incur the half of the punishment (prescribed) for free women in that case." Now "half of the punishment (prescribed) for a free-woman" can be one half of one hundred stripes, that is fifty, by lapidation consummating in death cannot be so divided.

Traditions Scrutinized : The Traditions relied on in support of "lapidation" are discordant and fail to establish that any such punishment was awarded after the revelation of *Surat Al-Noor* (Chapter XXIV). In one Tradition quoted in *Bukhari* and *Muslim,* Hadrat Umar, the Second Caliph, is reported to have said: "In the Book revealed to the Holy Prophet, there was a verse relating to *Rajm* which we read and understood. The Prophet himself acted upon it and gave the punishment of *Rajm.* Ibadat, son of Samit (Muslim) on the authority of the Holy Prophet said: "Unmarried man and woman guilty of adultery should be punished with one hundred stripes and one year's banishment. The married couple should be given one hundred stripes and then stoned to death" *(Muslim).* The only specific instance mentioned in *Bukhari* and *Muslim* is that of Maiz, son of Malik.

Rape : A distinction does exist between an ordinary case of sexual intercourse with mutual consent and one done with a person incapable of giving consent. The punishment must also be more serious in one than in the other. Besides actual cohabitation, there are other lewd or improper acts which, if not checked in time, might eventuate in sexual relations. These too should be made punishable by the State.

Protection of Property : The Quranic injunction is as follows:

> And as for the man who steals and the woman who steals, cut off their hands in retribution of their offences, an exemplary punishment from Allah. And Allah is

> Mighty, Wise. But whosoever repents after his transgression and amends, then will Allah surely turn to him in-mercy: verily Allah is Most Forgiving, Merciful (Ch. V, Verses 41-42).

Suraqah **:** "*Suraqah*" literally means secretly taking away of another's property. In the language of the law, it signifies taking away the property of another in a secret manner, at a time when such property is in custody, that is, when the effects are in supposed security from the hands of other people and where the value is not less than ten dirhams and the effects taken are the undoubted property of some other than of him who takes them.

Cutting of Hand is not the only Punishment **:** It is not correct to say that for every offence of theft, the hand shall be cut. This shall be clear from the following instances:

(1) A slave who had committed theft was brought before the Holy Prophet. He was forgiven. The same leniency was shown to him for the second, third and fourth thefts. When he was brought again for the fifth time for the same offence, the Holy Prophet ordered his hand to be cut. On his subsequent repetition of the offence thrice, his hand and foot were cut.

(2) The slaves of Habit stole away the camel of a person of the tribe of Madia. The culprits were produced before Hadrat Umar, the Second Caliph. He first ordered that the hands be cut but modified the same and directed that, in lieu of cutting of the hands, the offenders should be punished with a penalty which should be felt. The owner was asked about the price of the camel. He said it was 400 dirhams, that is, twice the amount.

(Izalat-ul-Khifa', Volume II, p. 130 ; Sunan Kubra, Volume VIII, p. 278).

Cases where no cutting is to be done *Hidayah* enumerates a long list of cases in which the penalty of cutting of hand or foot cannot be inflicted. The thefts of dry wood, birds of prey, for example, hens or ducks, milk, butter and fresh fruits on trees; the instruments of music; copies of the Holy Quran; the doors of the *Kaaba,* the money from the public treasury, would not entail the cutting of the hand. Similarly, the hand shall not be cut where the thief had committed the theft in the house and made over the property to another outside the house. It cannot be pleaded that they are not cases of theft, but they are relevant for the purposes of showing that the amputation of limbs is not the only punishment in the case of *Suraqah.*

> In Islam, opportunity is always given to a sinner to reform himself. If for a petty theft for the first time, a person is to be permanently deprived of the use of his limbs and made a cripple for the rest of his existence, it is useless for him to repent or to make amends. This would render the Quranic verse: "But whosoever repents after his transgression and amends, then will Allah surely turn to him in mercy. Verily Allah is Most Forgiving, Merciful" (V. 42).
>
> True import of Quranic injunction. In V. 41, the injunction about cutting of hand is described as a retribution and by way of exemplary punishment. The Arabic word used in the verse is *nakal* which means, "to prevent: to deter; to give exemplary punishment". *"Nakal"* means curb for race horses. Qadi Abdul Jabbar has pointed out that a small evil is not called *nakal;* it becomes so when it has increased considerably and become rampant; consequently the cutting of hand for theft is reserved only for the habitual thieves who could not otherwise be prevented from repeating the offence.
>
> (*Tafsir al-Kabir,* Volume I, p. 382).

In the *Tafsir Bayan al-Quran,* Maulana Muhammad Ali has expressed the view that the cutting of hand is the maximum penalty provided for taking away another's property and appropriately for habitual offenders.

Varying Degrees : The offence of the theft is of various degrees. It may be simple, serious or aggravated; it may be removing by stealth, by breaking open a house and may or may not be accompanied by force or threat of force. To suit various forms, the punishment has to be suitably regulated.

Honour Safeguarded

> The Quran makes special provisions for the protection of honour. In the case of chaste women, it is prescribed: "And those who launch a charge against a chaste woman, and produce not four witnesses (to support their allegations), flog them with eighty stripes and reject their evidence ever after: for such men are wicked transgressors" (XXIV 4).

Allama Yusuf Ali, in his Note 2958 of his English translation of the Holy Quran, says:

> The most serious notice is taken of people who put forward slanders or scandalous suggestions about women without adequate evidence. If anything is said against a woman's chastity, it should be supported by evidence twice as strong as would ordinarily be required for business transactions, or even in murder cases. That is, four witnesses would be required instead of two. Failing such prepon-derating evidence, the slanderer should himself be treated as a wicked transgressor and punished with eighty stripes. Not only would he be subjected to this disgraceful form of punishment, but he would be deprived of the citizen's right of giving evidence in all matters all his life, unless he repents and reforms, in which case he can be readmitted to be a competent witness.

Laen (XXIV 6 – 9). Where a husband so charges his wife and cannot produce the required number of witnesses, he shall have to take oath by God four times that he was solemnly telling the truth and the fifth oath involving the curse of Allah on him if he was a liar. The wife can in her turn avert the punishment by similarly taking an oath four times that the charge was false and the fifth time that the wrath of Allah be upon her if he was telling the truth.

The false accusation, in the language of law, is described as *Kazaf* which is defined in the *Hidayah* as follows :

> *Kazaf,* in its primitive sense, simply means accusation. By *Kazaf,* in the language of law, is understood a man insinuating a charge of whoredom against a married man or woman.

Different Provisions for Punishment

Punishments are divided into two classes, one of which is called *Hadd* and the other *Tazir. Hadd* in its primitive sense signifies "obstruction", whence a porter or a gate-keeper is termed the *Haddad* or "obstructer" from his office of prohibiting people from entering. In law it expresses the correction appointed and specified by the law on account of the right of God and hence the extension of the term *Hadd* to retaliation is not approved; since retaliation is due as a right of man and not as a right of God and, in the same manner, the extension of it to *Tazir* (or discriminatory chastisement) is not approved as *Tazir* is a species of correction not specified or determined by any fixed rule of law but committed to the discretion of the Qadi. The original design in the institution of *Hadd* is deterrent, that is, warning people from the commission of offensive actions.

Tazir (Hidayah, Vol II, Chapter VI) : In its primitive sense, *Tazir* means prohibition and also instruction; in law it signifies an infliction undetermined in its degree by the law, on account of the right either of God or of the individual, and the occasion of it is any offence for which *Hadd* or stated punishment has not been appointed whether that offence consists in words or deeds.

Degrees of Chastisement **:** In the *Fatwa-i-Shafii,* it is said that there are four orders or degrees of chastisement. First, the chastisement proper to the most noble of the nobles, for example, princes or men of learning, which consists merely of an admonition; secondly, chastisement proper to the nobles which may be performed either by admonition or by *jirr,* that is, by dragging the offender to the floor and exposing him to scorn; thirdly, the chastisement proper to the middle order, for example, merchants and shopkeepers, which may be performed *jirr* as above and also by imprisonment; and, fourthly, the chastisement proper to the lower orders in the community which may be performed by *jirr* or by imprisonment and also by blows.

Fine **:** It is recorded from Abu Yusuf that the Sultan may inflict chastisement by means of property, that is, by exaction of a small sum in the manner of a fine proportionate to the offence.

Scope and Purpose of Punishment **:** Any misconception regarding the criminal provisions in the Quran might be avoided if their purpose and scope were properly understood. The Quran is not the Penal Code; only a few offences are mentioned. A careful analysis would show that they refer to the preservation of the State and to the categories dealing with the fundamental human rights to person, property and honour. The penalty prescribed for each category is the maximum one and within the maximum and the minimum limits the society is free to frame necessary laws falling in that category and to fix the punishment for each to be enforced with the sanction at its command. The criminal provisions are only ancillary to the grand objective the Quran has in view of creating a society which shali breath and exist in the ever-living presence of the

Almighty and possessed of desire to make sacrifices for the welfare of their fellow-beings and thus realise the purpose of life on this earth. As man is born weak, and is apt to go astray, some correction is needed to reform him or to warn others for their ultimate good.

Particular Laws

The general law of punishment is contained in the Quran, V. 36, which says: "The punishment of those who wage war against Allah and His Apostle and strive with might and main for mischief through the land is only this: that they be slain, or crucified, or their hands and their feet be cut off from opposite sides, or they be exiled from the land. That shall be a disgrace for them in this world and in the Hereafter. They shall have a great punishment".

All conceivable offences against the State, such as treason or public disorder or wilful defiance of the laws of God and of constituted authority, are made punishable with anyone of the four punishments enumerated above, that is (1) killing; (2) crucification, (3) cutting hands and feet, and (4) exile from land. The expression which literally means "elimination from land" may mean banishment or imprisonment in a jail to prevent the commission or repetition of an offence. It should be distinctly noted that the punishments are in the alternative, that is, for one, the other may be substituted in view of the exigencies of the case. It shall, therefore, follow that where the killing or cutting of hands is prescribed, it shall not be un-Islamic to commute it to some other form of punishment. In selecting a particular form of punishment the habits and usages of the people, the facts and circumstances of each case including the status of the offender may be taken into consideration by the Qadi. A wise administrator or legislator would not like to do anything which might shockingly hurt the feelings of the populace or act in a manner which might appear as atrocious or needlessly cruel.

In the verse, the words "waging war against Allah and His Apostle" are of very wide import. It does not mean actual taking up of arms against Allah for that would be meaningless; it means disobedience to His commands.

The offence of drinking wine has been very much condemned in the Holy Quran but no punishment has been prescribed for it. However, the said offence is punishable with 80 lashes as mentioned in *Mishkat Book XV, Chapter IV*. It is sufficient to say in this respect that the punishments by way of imprisonment is not favoured by Islam because the objective of punishment is to deter both the criminals as well as the general public. According to Islam, the most severe offences are the crimes against the societies for example, adultery, drinking, slander and fornication, etc. These crimes are punished strictly according to the injunction of Quran and *Sunnah* as Islam is keen to remove the factors that lead to the commission of crimes as it wants to purify societies of all the social crimes by deterrent punishment.

The Great Source

Ahkam, the religious commands are the fount-head of all Islamic Laws as is evident from the Holy Verse :

> "For each we have appointed a Divine law and traced out way" (V-45 Al-Maida).

The principles laid down by Allah in the Holy Book are expounded by *Sunnah* of the Holy Prophet (Peace be upon him). Holy Prophet did not speak of his own in such matters. Quran has put the words of the Prophet at par with the Quran:

> "Nor doth he speak of his own desire. It is naught save an inspiration that is inspired".
>
> (LIII, 3 &4 Al-Najm).

Muslims are duty-bound to follow *Uswa-i-Hasana* (III, 21 *Al-Ahzab)*. Whenever unanimity is reached among the Muslim Jurists of a time, the consensus has the same validity as a verse of the Quran or the most reliably proved *Sunnah* of the Prophet, the latter con senses may, over-rule the former.

The solution of practical problems are permitted through analogical deduction *(Qiyas)* based on the principle laid down by the Quran, *Sunnah* and *Ijma.*

Four sources, the Quran, *Sunnah, Ijma* and *Qiyas* are the roots *(Usul)* of *Fiqh* i.e. the knowledge of what is for and upon man and are the foundations of religious command and basis of Lawful and forbidden. Thus religious commands regarding practical affairs of life are ascertained on the principles which may be traced to Quran, *Sunnah,* and the rights and obligations of "man and society" and what is permitted and forbidden to him are also determined in accordance with these principles.

Fiqh divides *Ahkam* (religious commands) relating to rights and obligations of man *viz-a-viz* society into following categories:

(a) *Huququllah (Rights of God):*

These relate to "good" of the society as a whole i.e. prohibition of adultery, and *Ahteram* of *Baitullah.* It is on account of reverence that we call them *Huququllah,* otherwise Allah is besought of all (112-12 *Al Akhalas).*

(b) *Huququl Ibad (Right of Man):*

These commands relate to the rights and obligations of an individual e.g. right to own property and obligation not to damage the property of others. Thus with the permission of the owner, the property becomes lawful for others.

(c) Mixture of the above two *Huquq* with predominance of *Huququllah* i.e. punishment of slander.

(d) Mixture with predominance of *Huququl Ibad* e.g. *Qisas* (Retaliation).

It is *Ibadat* in the sense that *Kaffara* is fulfilled through fasting, freeing a slave and feeding the poor and *"Uqubat"* in the sense that this liability comes into existence when a prohibited act is committed.

In *'Fiqh"* offence means an act or omission rendering a person liable to *"Hadd"* or *"Tazeer"*. *Hadd* expresses the correction appointed and specified by Holy Quran, and *Sunnah* on account of right of God. *Tazeer* signifies an infliction determined in its degree by the law on account of right of God or of the individual and the occasion of it is any offence for which *Hadd* has not been appointed. In the language of Law *"Janayat"* is expressive of any prohibited act committed upon the person or property. In the practice of Lawyer *(Fiqh)*, *"Janayat"* means prohibited act committed upon the person which is called Murder or upon a part of the body which is termed wounding or maiming. Thus it is possible to include *"Janayat"* in the term offence. There is provision of *Qisas* for such cases *Qisas* literally means tracking the footsteps of an enemy and is the law of retaliation.

The definition of the offence suggests the following divisions of the offences according to the corrections and chastisements:

(i) Offences where punishment is *Hadd.*

(ii) Offences where correction is *Qisas.*

(iii) Offences where chastisement is *Tazeer.*

Thus punishments in Islam are of three kinds : — *(1) Hadd; (2) Qisas; and* (3) *Tazeer.*

Hadd : *"Hadd"* in its primitive sense signifies, "obstruction", as a gate-keeper is called *"Haddad"* i.e. intercepting people from entering. The word *Hadd* also means definition as term, the essential limits of a certain thing by which it is distinguished. The word *"Hadd"* in the strict legal sense denotes Allah's restrictive ordinances par excellence, the fixed punishments, which have been prescribed by the Holy Quran. Later on it also came to define the punishment proved or established by the *Sunnah* of the Holy Prophet and his Companions on which there is an *"Ijma"* (consensus) of the Holy Prophet's Companions. These punishments are as under :

(1) Theft *(suraqa)* – punishable with cutting of right hand.

(2) Dacoity or highway robbery *(Haraabah)* – without murder punishable with cutting of right hand and left foot and if accompanied with murder punishable with death.

(3) Fornication or adultery *(zina)* – punishable with one hundred stripes when committed by unmarried person and by stoning to death when committed by married person.

(4) Falsely accusing a person of committing unlawful sexual intercourse *(Qasaf)* – punishable with eighty stripes.

(5) Drinking wine *(Shurb al Khamr)* – punishable with eighty stripes.

(6) Apostasy *(irtidad)* – punishable with death.

The aforesaid *Hadud* offences are neither compoundable nor open to settlement, pardon or waiver because in principle it is right of God and no obstruction is permissible in the execution of punishment in the prescribed manner. Theft under Islamic Law signifies surreptitiously taking away the property of another from his *Hirza* (custody) of the value of or above 10 dirham i.e. *"Nisab"* equal to 4.457 grams of gold or other property of equivalent value (at the time of theft) by an adult person (accused).

The word surreptitious means that the victim of theft does not know that his property is being stolen and it is deemed to have been secretly removed during daytime (meaning one hour before sunrise and two hours after sunset), Surreptitious continues till the completion of the offence. If theft is committed at night surreptitious need not continue after the commencement of the offence.

Another Gravamen of the theft is *"Hirza"* which means an arrangement made for the custody of the property by the owner. The custody may be of two kinds; firstly such as house, shop, box, container and secondly by personal guard which means a personal watch over the property. Thus if an adult male or female of sound prudence steals property of or above the value of 4.475 grams of gold or other property of equivalent value or above from the custody of another, the Islamic Law provides the punishment of amputation of hand. The Holy Quran, says:

> "As for thief, both male and female, cut off their hands." (7,38 Al Maida).

The offence is proved by confession of the accused or the evidence in court by at least two truthful adult male eye-witnesses (other than the victim of theft) abstaining from committing major sin to satisfaction of the trial court.

The concept of vicarious responsibility is also available under the Islamic Law, so if theft liable to *Hadd* is committed by more than one person and the total value of the stolen property is such that if the property is equally divided by the thieves, the share of each amounts to or exceeds, the *"Nisab" Hadd* shall be imposed on all of them as have entered the *Hirz,* even if each one of them has not removed the stolen property or any part thereof.

In addition to the aforesaid conclusive proof with regard to the ingredients of the offence and high standard of evidence the following categories of persons and article are immuned from *Hadd* punishment :

(a) When the offender and victim of the theft are related to each other i.e.

  (i) spouse;

  (ii) ascendants : paternal or maternal;

  (iii) descendant: paternal or maternal;

  (iv) brother, sister, father or mother;

  (v) brother, sister or their children.

(b) Guest committing theft from the house of his host.

(c) Servant or employee having authorised access to the Master's *hirz.*

(d) Property such as wild grass, fish, bird, dog, pig, intoxicant, musical instruments or perishable foodstuff for the preservation of which provision does not exist.

(e) When the offender has a share in the stolen property the value of which after deduction of his share is less than the *Nisab.*

(f) When the offender commits theft under *"Ikrah"* or *"Iztrar"* i.e. duress or compulsion arising out of situation of fear of injury to his property or honour or of any other person or the apprehension of death due to extreme hunger or thirst.

(g) When a creditor steals his debtor's property, the value of which after deduction of the amount due to him, is less than the *Nisab.*

(h) When the offender before his apprehension has, on account of repentance, returned the stolen property to the victim and surrendered himself to the authority.

The *Hadd* punishment abates if confession is retracted by convict or in case of witnesses, any, witness resoles from his testimony so as to reduce the number of witnesses less than two.

The previous conviction also applies on the first conviction the right hand of the convict is cut at the joint of the wrist and stump, thereafter cauterised, for the second theft the left foot is cut and for subsequent offence the convict is imprisoned.

It will thus be seen that theft contemplated by Islamic Law excludes petty theft of daily necessity of life or for subsistence and also exempts near and dear ones of a person who believe to have some right or share in the property of the other. The Islamic Law penalises theft by professionals.

Haraabah (dacoity, highway robbery, bloodshed and high-treason) : The provision for this category of crime is derived from the following verse of Holy Quran :

> "The only reward of those who make war upon Allah and his Messenger and strive after corruption in the land will be that they will be killed or crucified or have their hands and feet on alternate side cut off or will be expelled out of the land. Such will be their degradation in the world and hereafter, there will be an awful doom."
>
> The provisions relating to *Haraabah* are based on Chapter V., V. 33 of Holy Quran, which refers to those who wage war against an Islamic order either on a full scale revolt or through such acts as highway robbery, disruption of public order or the commission of murder. These acts even if devoid of the intention to overthrow an Islamic order, are deemed liable to prescribed punishment because such acts undermine, "The Nizam-e-Salih".

A dacoit or robber in this sense is one who overpowers the traveller and commits theft. If the offender did not carry out theft but in the process commits murder, the punishment is death. If the offender in the course of dacoity or robbery has stolen the property equivalent to *Nisab* of theft, the offender's right hand and left foot shall be cut off. However if the offender has no right hand or left foot or if these are paralyzed, the same are not to be amputated and instead he is liable to *Tazir.*

If the offenders have committed robbery as well as murder, their right hand and left foot are to be first amputated and then they are executed." If the culprits are arrested in an attempt to commit the offence, they will be exiled but some jurists say that they be jailed. In few Muslim countries such are liable to imprisonment and whipping.

Murder committed in the course of dacoity or robbery is not compoundable like ordinary murder. The accused conjointly committing the offence owe vicarious liability and each one of them is punished. The punishment of dacoity during famine may be dealt with leniently and may vary if it is committed on *Harbis* (non-Muslim from an Islamic Jurisdiction) and *Mustamilis* (non-Muslim from in Islamic Jurisdiction coming to an Islamic Jurisdiction seeking peace).

The mode of proof is the same as required in case of theft liable to *Hadd.*

***Zina* (adultery) :** It means either adultery or fornication and signifies carnal conjunction of a man with a woman, not validly married or neither suspecting themselves to be married. As to whoredom of a woman, it means her submission to the man to commit that act. In such cases man and woman are equally guilty as ordained by the Holy Quran:

> The adulterer and adulteress scourge ye each one of them with a hundred stripes. And let not pity for them twain withhold you from obedience to Allah, if ye believe in Allah and the last day. And let a party of believers witness their punishment,
>
> (XXIV, 2 Al Noor).
>
> In Islamic law, if the adulterer and adulteress are not married, each of them shall suffer the *Hadd* punishment of hundred stripes as per Holy verse. In case they are married, each one of them shall be stoned to death according to the *Sunnah* of the Holy Prophet(peace be upon him).

The offence is proved by confession of the accused before court of competent jurisdiction or direct evidence of at least 4 Muslim adult male eye-witnesses about whom the court is satisfied, having regard to the requirement, of *"Tazkiyah-al-shuhood"* that they are truthful and abstain from major sin

(Kabir) give evidence as eye-witnesses to the act of penetration necessary for the offence. The "Qadi" or the judge is required to satisfy himself that the confession is voluntary and not on account of some infirmity such as insanity or inducement, threat or promise. Similarly the four eye-witnesses require clearance of the "Qadi" that they are persons of unimpeachable character, just and righteous. Again the witnesses have to stand test of cross-examination with regard to nature of offence, the time of occurrence, before their evidence is acted upon:

> The circumstantial evidence such as birth of child to an unmarried female is admissible but emphasis lies on conclusive proof. Hadrat Ali punished *"Shurah"* on the basis of pregnancy. She was first flogged on Thursday and then stoned to death.
>
> (Bukhari, Vol. III, Hadith 1716, p. 631).

"Another case cited by Maulana Maududi in his *Tafheem ul Quran* (Vol. III under verse 2 *"Surah Noor"* is reproduced as under :

> "It is reported by Tabir, son of Abdullah *(See* Abu Daud and Nisei) that a person who committed adultery was punished whipping oniy but when it was found that he was married, he was stoned to death"(Abu Daud, Vol. HI, Hadith 1029).

The study of these two cases also indicates that dual punishment is permissible for the same offence.

On the face of conclusive evidence, still there are some more legal exceptions in the way of imposition of *Hadd* punishment such as (1) cohabitation due to some doubt or semblance of validity recognised by the *Shariah;* (2) Sexual intercourse under duress or coercion; (3) case proved solely by confession if the same is retracted by convict before or during the imposition of the *Hadd* punishment or part thereof; and (4) in case the offence is proved by the testimony of witnesses, any witness resile so as to reduce the number of witnesses less than four before or in the course of imposition of *Hadd.*

Adultery or fornication is the root evil in human society. It damages the social health and moral order of the human society which Islam wants to preserve for its dignity. It gives rise to heinous crime like murder, attempted murder and lays ground for future bickering and blood feuds in the society. All over Islamic nations, the fornication plays vital part in crime contribution. In few countries the couple involved in adultery are killed by their own relatives as *"Kala Kali"* and there is hardly any report to the authorities. This shows that penalty of death for this sin is in complete conformity and consonance with human nature.

The punishment of stoning to death does not mean to kill the offender with stones. He is to be killed by some other weapon after initial stoning such as shooting, also provided by *Zina* Ordinance. The condition of stoning provides the chance of survival to convict till last because he may retract his confession or any out of 4 witnesses, may resile or any witness may refuse to stone the convict and in such eventuality, the convict will escape capital punishment.

Qazf (false accusation of adultery) : The literal meaning of the word *"Qazf"* is to throw. The theological meaning is false accusation of adultery.

The Holy Quran provides two categories of this crime. The first relates to the accusation of unchastity levelled by husband against his wife technically known as *"Lian"* and it is outside the scope of *Hadd* punishment. The second relates to a person other than the husband who accuses a woman of adultery. As to the *"Lian"*, the Holy Quran lays down the following procedure to be followed by the court of Law :

> "And for those who launch a charge of unchastity against their spouses and have in support no evidence

> but their own, their solitary evidence can be received, if they bear witness four times with oath by Allah that they are solemnly telling the truth and the fifty oath should be that they solemnly invoke the curse of Allah on themselves, if they tell lie. But it would avert the punishment from the wife, if she bears witness four times with an oath. Allah! that her husband is telling a lie and the wrath of Allah on herself if her accuser is telling the truth" (XXIV-6-11).

The situation for *'Lian'* may arise if husband spots his wife in act of adultery but is unable to produce four witnesses to substantiate the charge of *zina* and at the same time is unable to lead a normal married life. The matter is then left to the honour of both the spouses. If the husband so chooses he may solemnly swear four times to the fact, invoking also a curse on himself, if he lies which is *prima facie* evidence of the wife's guilt. But if the wife swears similarly four times and also invokes a curse on herself, she is in law acquitted of the guilt. If she does not take this step, the charge stands proved and she will be punished for *zina*. In either case the marriage is dissolved as it is against human nature that the parties can live together after such an incident.

As regards accusation of unlawful intercourse against chaste woman by an outsider, the Holy Quran provides *Hadd* punishment as under :

> "And those who accuse chaste woman of unchastity and produce not four witnesses to support their allegation, flog them with eighty stripes and reject their evidence ever after for such men are wicked transgressors, unless they repent thereafter and mend their conduct, for Allah is oft-forgiving most merciful"
> (XXIV-4-5) (Al-Noor).

The *Hadd* punishment for slandering a chaste woman of adultery is flogging of the offender with eighty stripes and depriving him from the right of giving evidence in court for good.

Drinking Wine (shurb-al-khamr) : Drinking wine is forbidden in the following verses of Holy Quran :

> "They ask thee about wine and games of chance, say: in both is great sin, and advantage also, to men: but their sin is greater than advantage"
>
> (Chap. 11:26).

> "O believers: surely wine and games of chance and idols and the divining arrows are an abomination of Satan's work: Avoid them, that we prosper. Only would satan sow hatred and enmity among you, by wine and games of chance and turn you aside from the remembrance of God and from prayer: will you not therefore, abstain from them? Obey God and obey the Apostle, and be on your guard: but if you turn back, know that our Apostle is only bound to deliver a pain announcement." (Chap. V. 92).

Neither the Holy Quran, nor the tradition of Holy Prophet ordained *Hadd* punishment for drinking wine or any other toxicant substance. However Holy Prophet gave 40 shoe-beating to a drunkard and at another occasion 40 lashes with two branches of date tree. Forty lashes were prescribed by First Caliph Abu Bakr. Eighty stripes for a freeman and Forty stripes for a slave is the *Hadd* punishment for drinking from the time of Caliph "Umar" on the sanction of *Ijma* (Consensus) of the Companions of Holy Prophet. If an adult Muslim takes intoxicating liquor by mouth and is seized whilst his breath yet smells of wine he is brought before the 'Qadi' whilst he is intoxicated and two Muslim adult male witnesses give evidence of his having committed the offence of drinking, the punishment would be eighty lashes provided the drinking was voluntary. Offence can also be proved by the confession of the accused. As to the confession after the smell disappears Imam Hanifa and Imam Yusuf differ with Imam Muhammad, the latter holds the confession sufficient for conviction but formers do not.

Apostasy from Islam (Irtidad) : A Muslim male who renegates from Islam after having professed the faith in Dar-al-Islam is liable to death if he persists and does not recant in spite of opportunity granted to him and his doubts removed. A female apostate, is not to be killed but kept in confinement until she recants. If a boy under age turns an apostate, he is to be imprisoned until he attains majority and offered the faith, if he does not return to Islam, he will be killed. The lunatics and drunkards are not responsible for apostasy from Islam. Similarly persons converted to Islam under compulsion are not liable to capital punishment.

This rule is derived from Quranic verses :

(1) "And who so becometh a re-negate and dieth in his disbelief such are those whose work have fallen both in this world and hereafter." (II, 217 Al-Baqra).

(2) "And remember Moses said to his people: O My people: You have, indeed wronged yourselves by your worship of calf so turn in repentance to your Maker and slay yourselves, the wrongdoers, that will be better for you in the sight of your Maker. Then He turns towards you in forgiveness, for He is oft-returning most merciful. (Chap. II, Verse 54).

The death penalty for Apostasy is also proved from a Member of *Ahadith* of the Holy Prophet and his four Caliphs. The Holy Prophet said, "whoever changes his religion, kill him".

The *Hadood* punishments are misconceived as harsh is due to lack of knowledge. The *Hadd* is applied only if the guilt is conclusively proved and for that purpose *"Nisab-e-Shahadat"* is prescribed. Four male eye-witnesses are required to prove *zina* and in other cases two such witnesses. The voluntary confession is also acted upon. *Hadd* is called of, if there is any doubt. Holy Prophet said, "Do away with *Hadd* punishment in case of doubt". At another occasion the Holy Prophet observed that it is better to let off ten offenders than to convict one innocent person. The judge cannot base his decision only on his knowledge. There is thus no possibility of execution of *Hadd* on an innocent person.

The lapidation and amputation of hand to the Westerners appear barbaric. Under Islamic Law, a Muslim can go through polygamous marriage to the extent of 4 wives at a time. The divorces and re-marriage by widow is permissible as such legal facilities exist for this biological need. Therefore capital punishment is quite justified. The stoning to death is just a condition providing the escape valves to the convict till last, otherwise he has to be executed with some other weapon such as shooting as under *Hadood* Ordinance.

The amputation is inflicted on a professional thief who resorts to theft or robbery not for the necessity of life but richness without work. If a thief puts the life and property of an innocent person at stake and the charge is proved he deserves amputation of hand as prescribed.

The punishments of flogging under Islamic Law are quite different than under the Roman Law. The flogging is intended to put the convict to public shame in order to avert the repetition of crime. The floggings are of moderate force without causing death or laceration on the body or the convict. The clothes are left on the person of the convict. The flogging can be postponed or inflicted in installments on grounds such as sickness, old age, infirmity or pregnancy. Maulana Maudoodi in his *Tafhemm-ul-Quran,* Vol. III, page 341 writes that the floggings are to be struck in such a way that armpit should not open. Mostly there used to be a book kept under arms. Further flogging used to be done at a cool hour during summer, at a hot hour during winter and by 'Qadi' who knew that it was being administered not to cause much pain as to create notoriety for the dark deed. If the offender was weak or infirm, a broom with 100 sticks was considered sufficient so that one blow would meet the ends of justice.

The criticism of *Hadd* punishment is improperly judged inasmuch as the mitigating circumstances are overlooked. The Islamic law does not approve long term punishment which do no good to the society rather produce hardened criminals at state expense beside causing starvation to the dependents of the convicts.

Tazir : It is discretionary correction which is administered for offences for which *'Hadd'* has not been appointed. It may be applied to enforce and protect the rights of individual and Allah. It may be used to prevent the commission of offence for which *Hadd* is appointed. The following punishments are included in *Tazir:*

(1) Slapping

(2) Lashing or flogging (not more than 39, i.e. less than the lowest number prescribed as *Hadd* for slave).

(3) Externment, exilement.

(4) Imprisonment which in Islamic Law is a coercive measure aiming at producing repentance *(Tauba).*

(5) Public proclamation of the convict on a donkey's back *(Tashhir).*

(6) Amonition or reprimand, slapping, beating, etc.

(7) Punishment of abandonment.

(8) *Zaman* (compensation) payable to the aggrieved person in case of loss of property.

(9) *Diyat* (money compensation against injury).

(10) Suspension or dismissal.

One or more punishments can be awarded by the Qadi regard being had to circumstance of each case and the gravity of the crime. Islam does not approve of long term imprisonment. As regards fine the *Hanafis* do not approve but Imam ibn Taymiyyah strongly favours.

***Qisas (Retaliation)*:** The punishment for intentional murder as prescribed in the Holy Quran, is the *Qisas,* i.e. life for life as the Holy Quran, says:

> "O, ye who believe retaliation is prescribed for you in the matter of murder; the freeman for the freeman and the slave for the slave and the female for the female. And for him who is forgiven somewhat by his (injured) brother prosecution according to usage and payment unto him in kindness. This is an alleviation and a mercy from your Lord. He who transgressed after this will have a painful doom. And there is life for you in retaliation. 'O'! man of understanding that ye may ward off evil." (II, 178 and 179 Al-Baqr)
>
> And we have prescribed for them therein: The life for the life, and the eye for the eye, and the nose for the nose, and the ear for the ear, and tooth for the tooth, and for wounds retaliation. But whoso for giveth if (in the way of charity), it shall be expiation for him whoso judgeth not by that which Allah has revealed such are wrong doers". (V 45, Al-Maida).
>
> "And slay not the life which Allah hath forbidden save with right. Who is slain wrongfully, We have given power unto his heir, but let him not commit excess in slaying. Lo; he will be helped."
>
> (XVII, 33 Bani Israel).
>
> "*Shariat* has attached great sanctity to the life of a man: And that you slay not the life which Allah hath made sacred, save in the course of Justice."
>
> (VI 152 Al-Anaam)

"*Janayat*" as already described as unlawful act committed upon the person or upon a part of the body is offence against person where death is caused, is called homicide *(Qatal)* and that against a part of the body is called causing wound or dismemberment. In offences affecting life, retaliation is incurred by wilfully killing a person whose blood is under continual protection such as a Muslim or a *Dhimmi,* in opposition to aliens who have only an occasional temporary protection. A freeman is to be slain for a freeman and a slave for a slave but according to Abu Hanifa a freeman is to be slain for the murder of slave if he be of a *Dhimmi.* A man is slain for the murder of slave if he be the property of a Muslim. A Muslim is also slain for murder of a *Dhimmi,* according to Abu Hanifa but Al-Shafii disputes on the plea that Holy Prophet said that a Muslim is not to be put to death for an infidel. A man is slain for a woman and a sound person for one who is blind, infirm, dismembered, lame or insane.

A father is not to be slain for his child because the Holy Prophet said "Retaliation must not be executed upon the parents of his offsprings".

But a child is slain for the murder of his parents. Retaliation to be executed by the next kin with some mortal wound. If a person wilfully strikes off the hand of another, his hand is to be struck off in return and similarly foot in return of foot. Retaliation is allowed where perfect equality in causing wound may be preserved. Hence if the eye is forced out of the socket, there will be no retaliation but if eye-sight only is destroyed, the eye-sight of the offender may also be destroyed. Similarly, retaliation is not allowed in the case of breaking any bone except tooth.

It is lawful for the heirs of the deceased or the injured person to compound the murder for a certain sum and then retaliation is remitted and sum agreed is due to the heirs by the accused. Next of kin may also remit *Qaisas* by pardon. In the absence of intentional murder there is provision for compensating the heirs of the murdered or the injured. Such compensation in economic units for life is called *"Deet'* and for loss of limb, *"Arsh"*. For compensation in these circumstances *Aqla (Baradri)* of the accused are liable. By *"Aqla"* is meant relatives who have to pay expiation or legal fine.

"Nisab Shahda" for *Qisas* is the same as for the *Hadd* punishments. If there is any doubt for any reason, *Qisas* is remitted. In such cases compensation may be made payable by the accused. If the prescribed evidence is not available to support claim for *Qisas,* oath may be offered to the support and his refusal will prove his liability to pay compensation. The judge may determine liability of compensation on his own knowledge.

In case where liability for murder cannot be fixed on an individual or tribe *(Baradri),* there are elaborate provisions for compensation *(Deet)* Blood Money to the heirs of the murdered. Thus if a dead body is found in a *"Mohallah",* oath will be offered to 50 men of the *Mohallah* by the heirs of the murdered if they take oath, *Qisas* will be remitted and the *Mohallah* people will be liable to pay *Deet,* such liability arrays people against crime. Where the liability cannot be fixed on anyone the state is liable to pay compensation from *Baitul-Mal.* Thus justice is meted out to the injured in every case.

The Islamic Law of Punishment is summed up as under:

(1) The Islamic Law of Punishment has root in Quran and *Sunnah,* and ensure the preservation of human values.

(2) *Hadd* is administered only when the offence is proved conclusively and there is not even a remote chance of an innocent person suffering punishment.

(3) In offence where right of an individual is involved every attempt is made to see that he gets his due.

(4) It is left to the aggrieved to claim *Qisas* if that satisfy his feelings or compound the matter on just suitable and lawful terms.

(5) In cases where the liability of the crime cannot be fixed on an individual, the aggrieved is compensated by the people of the locality. The people are arrayed against crime.

(6) Islamic punishment also imply the spiritual purification of human soul and expiation for the world hereafter, this is an addition to obtaining human good in this world through implementation of its penal law. A lapidated person is entitled to burial, as is a Muslim with a *Namaz-i-Janaza* and benediction.

(Fathe-ul-Qadir 4.125).

(7) The Islamic punishment does not approve of long term imprisonment to provide centres for producing harden criminal, who on release from jails operate as organized gangs of criminals.

(8) The statistics show that in countries where the Islamic Laws are in practice the crime rate is the lowest or negligible such as in Saudi Arabia.

(9) Islamic Laws *suo moto* safeguard the rights of minors and insane persons which is not envisaged in any other law.

(10) The Islamic Laws are simple to understand and easy in application. The Islamic Procedural Law ensures speedy disposal of cases and quick and free justice.

Perception for Punishment

Crime is a curse and its gravity needs no emphasis. It disturbs the balance of a society and ultimately corrodes it. The secular modern societies, which boast of their resources and theories of crime and punishment, are the living examples of such corrosion. These societies are not fully equipped to curb crime as they are devoid of Allah's guidance and conception of accountability in the life Hereafter and have no moorings in morality. Moreover the man-made laws which control them are fallible and deficient. The only society which has the capability to overcome the menace of crime is the Islamic society as it is based on Divine order and aims at human perfection and peace in this world and felicity in the Hereafter.

It conforms to the dictates of laws and principles of morality as enunciated by Islam and is quite different from the modern societies which reflect a variety of ethical values and throw the door open for all sorts of vices, evils and crimes. Islamic law, which controls the Islamic society and guarantees its preservation, takes a serious view of crime and in order to check it postulates, *inter alia,* an ideal and unique punitive system having fixed as well as variable elements, which are essential for a good legal system. The punishment known as *Hadd,* which is a fixed element in that its quantum has been finally prescribed and can neither be altered nor modified, is the nucleus of this system. It wipes out certain heinous crimes and ensures the preservation of the values that Islam upholds for the dignity of human society and spiritual purification of human soul.

Hadd etymologically means measure, limit or obstruction. Technically it means a punishment the measure of which has been definitely fixed or punishment ordained by Quran and *Sunnah* or the correction appointed and specified by the law on account of the right of Allah or a penalty appointed or specified by law on account of rights of Allah (or public justice). The rights of Allah correspond to the public rights as they involve benefit to the community at large and are referred to Allah because of the magnitude of the risks involved in their violation and of the comprehensive benefits which result from them. In other words, the rights of Allah are to be construed as rights of society because the punishments of *Hadd* are meant to deter from mischief and harm to people and it is a collective obligation of the Muslim community to enforce them. All *Hadd* crimes essentially involve violation of the Text and their punishments are equal to their magnitude. The crimes falling within the pale of *Hadd* are:

(1) *Zina* (whoredom or fornication).

(2) *Sharab* (drinking wine).

(3) *Sarqa* (theft).

(4) *Qate Tariq* or *Haraba* (highway robbery).

(5) *Qazf* (false accusation of adultery).

(6) *Irtidad* (apostasy).

The punishments of *Hadd* have been prescribed for these crimes because they impair human dignity, have far reaching effects on society and violate the public interests or the aim of *Shariah* in regard to man, namely protection of sanctity of family and progeny, protection of reason, protection of property, protection of honour and protection of religion.

Zina includes sexual intercourse between a man and a woman not married to each other and it applies both to adultery (which implies that one or both of the parties are married to a person other than the ones concerned) and to fornication which, in its strict signification, implies that both parties are unmarried." There can be no cavil against the proposition that *Zina* is not only disgraceful in itself but also the root cause of many other evils. It destroys the family structure and brings untold humiliation and sufferings to children born or to be born. It entails blood feuds and loss of reputation and property and causes chaos and disorder in society. Allah has abhorred this major sin and prohibited the Muslims from going near it.

(And come not near unto adultery. Lo! it is an abomination and an evil way).' (And those who cry not unto any other god alongwith Allah, nor take the life which Allah hath forbidden save in (course of) justice, nor commit adultery and whoso doeth this shall pay the penalty).

The punishment of *Zina* ordained by Quran and *Sunnah* is one hundred stripes if committed by unmarried persons and stoning to death if committed by married persons.

(The adulteress and the adulterer, scourge ye each one of them (with) a hundred stripes. And let not pity for the twain withhold you from obedience to Allah, if ye believe in Allah and the Last Day. And let a party of believers witness their punishment). (Obadah-b-Swamet reported that the Messenger of Allah said: Take from me, take from me. Verily Allah chalked out a way for them; (fornication of) a virgin with a virgin – 100 stripes and exile for a year; and one married with another married – 100 stripes and stoning to death).

(Hadrat Umar reported: Verily Allah sent Muhammad with truth and revealed the Book to him out of the verses the Almighty Allah revealed, there was the verse of stoning to death. The Messenger of Allah stoned to death and after him we also stoned to death. And stoning to death in the Book of Allah is a truth against one out of males and females who commits adultery in a married state in case proof is established or there occurs pregnancy or confession).

Though the Quran does not explicitly mention the punishment of stoning to death it does indicate it in a subtle manner which the Holy Prophet understood and enforced. The majority of theologians, the four Imams (Abu Hanifa, Shafii, Malik and Ahmad bin Hambal) and other learned Jurists hold that the order for stoning to death still exists.

The question was raised before the Holy Prophet when it was referred to him. He, as the best interpreter of the Quran said, that, according to the Book, a married adulterer and a married adulteress shall be put to death. Who can be a greater authority in interpreting the Quran than the Prophet himself? This ordinance was carried out by Hadrat Abu Bakr, Hadrat Umar and other Caliphs who came after them. Had the capital sentence in case of married culprits been abrogated, these

Caliphs would not have followed the command of the Prophet (peace be upon him).

Drinking is harmful from both temporal and spiritual points of view. It veils the intellect and obscures the moral sensibilities of the drunkard and for that reason Allah has strictly forbidden the use of all alcoholic beverages.

(They question thee about strong drink and games of chance. Say: In both is great sin, and (some) utility for men; but the sin of them is greater than their usefulness).

(Oh! Ye who believe! Strong drink and games of chance and idols and divining arrows are only an infamy of Satan's handiwork. Leave it aside in order that ye may succeed).

There are many traditions which threaten the drunkards with severe punishment in the Next World. The punishment prescribed for this world is eighty stripes. There is no mention of this punishment in Quran and it is the result of an *Ijma* of the Companions of the Holy Prophet. When Hadrat Umar saw that this crime was on the increase he consulted the Companions on the punishment to be meted out to drunkards. Hadrat Ali bin Abu Talib is reported to have advised: 'We apply the punishment for calumny, namely eighty stripes because if a person becomes intoxicated he knows not what he says and in such a condition he commits calumny'.

Sarqa (theft) is an act of encroachment on the property of someone without any justification and causes unrest in society. Thieves are a terror and with a view to put them under guard a very strict measure has been ordained.

(As for the thief, both male and female, cut off their hands. It is the reward of their own deeds and exemplary punishment from Allah - Allah is Mighty, Wise).

The punishment for the first offence is amputation of hand; for a second that of the left foot up to ankle and for a third a long term of imprisonment until the culprit reforms. Hadrat Ali refused to amputate another hand of a confirmed thief where one hand and foot had already been cut off. To constitute theft it is essential that the thief must be an adult of sound understanding, the property must be in careful custody, the property must be movable, the property must be taken out of the custody of another person in a secret manner and its value must not be less than the prescribed *Nisab* and the thief must have obtained full possession of the stolen property.

Harraba (highway robbery) not only deprives someone of his hard-earned money and property or life but also causes public disorder and as such deserves a harsh punishment.

(The only reward for those who make war upon Allah and His Messenger and strive after corruption in the land will be that they will be killed or crucified, or have their hands and feet on alternate sides cut off, or will be expelled out of the land, such will be their degradation in the world and in the Hereafter, theirs will be an awful doom).

The established punishment is cutting of right hand and left foot if *Harraba* is not accompanied with murder and death if accompanied with murder.

The evil caused by *Qazf* (false accusation of adultery) is similar to that caused by adultery itself. It not only damages the reputation of the slandered but also creates bad blood between the families, renders parentage doubtful and spoils conjugal relations. Allah has, therefore, enjoined severe punishment for this offence.

(Lo! as for those who traduce a virtuous, believing woman (who are) careless, cursed are they in the world and the Hereafter: Theirs will be an awful doom). (And those who accuse honourable women but bring not four witnesses, scourge them (with eighty stripes and never (afterward) accept their testimony. They indeed are evil-doers).

The punishment is eighty stripes. *Irtidad* (Apostasy) means turning from Islam after being a Muslim. It partakes strong condemnation of Allah.

(Whoso disbelieveth in Allah after his belief - save him who is forced thereto and whose heart is still content with faith - but whoso findeth ease in disbelief: on them is wrath from Allah. Theirs will be an awful doom).

(But if they repent and establish worship and pay the poor-due, then are they your brethren in religion. We detail our revelations for a people who have knowledge. And if they break their pledges after their treaty (hath been made with you) and assail your religion, then fight the heads of disbelief. Lo! they have no binding oaths - in order that they may desist).

The sayings and doings of the Holy Prophet (PBUH), the decision and practice of the Caliph Abu Bakr, the consensus of the opinion of the Companions of the Holy Prophet and all the Muslim Jurists prescribe punishment of death for an apostate. The Holy Prophet (PBUH) is reported to have said: (He who substitutes his *Din,* (for another one) put him to death).

The offences punishable with *Hadd* may be established by confession, made voluntarily before the court, or ocular evidence furnished by *Adil* witnesses. The requisite number of eye-witnesses for proof of *Zina* is four. The other offences, namely *Sarqa, Harraba, Qazf, Sharab* and *Irtidad* are proved on the testimony of two witnesses. The witnesses must be sane, adult, male, Muslims who have never been convicted of *Qazf* and about whom the court is satisfied, having regard to the requirements of *Tazkia-al-Shahood,* that they are truthful witnesses and abstain from major sins and are not inclined to indulge in minor sins. The probity of witnesses is indispensable. (Take the evidence of two just men).

All Muslims are *prima facie* just with respect to evidence excepting those who have been punished for slander. If, however, their probity is questioned it is incumbent on the court to initiate an enquiry into their character. The purgation is to be made both privately and openly.

The examination of the credibility of the witnesses is made from the people with whom they have been connected that is to say if they are pupils from trustworthy inhabitants and the master of the school where they have lived, if they are soldiers from the officers and clerks of their battalion and if he is a clerk from his superiors and fellow clerks in his office and if he is a merchant from trustworthy merchants and if he belongs to an incorporated trade from the warden of the trade and the masters in committee and if he belongs to other trades from trustworthy inhabitants of the quarter of village. As regards major sins the Holy Prophet (PBUH) said :

> (The greatest sin is to associate another with God, or to vex your father or mother or to murder your own species or to give false evidence or to tell lies). (The greatest sin before God is that you call any other like unto God who created you or that you murder your child from an idea that it will eat your victuals, or that you commit adultery with your neighbour's wife).

(Abstain ye from seven ruinous destructive things, namely, associating anything with God; magic, killing anyone without reason: taking interest on money; taking the property of the orphan; running away on the day of battle; and taxing an innocent woman with adultery).

The quantum of evidence has been prescribed to ensure that only guilty person is convicted.

There are certain exceptional instances in which *Hadd* is not enforced despite the availability of proof:

(1) When *Zina* or *Sarqa* or *Harraba* or drinking or *Irtidad* is proved only by the confession of the convict but he retracts his confession before the execution of *Hadd.*

(2) When *Zina* or *Sarqa* or *Haraba* or drinking or *Irtidad* is proved by testimony but before the execution of *Hadd* any witness resoles from his testimony so as to reduce the number of witnesses to less than the prescribed.

(3) When the offender and victim of the theft are related to each other as:

(i) spouses;

(ii) ascendants, paternal or maternal;

(iii) descendants, paternal or maternal;

(iv) brothers or sisters or father or mother; or

(v) brothers or sisters or their children.

(4) When a guest has committed theft from the house of his host.

(5) When a servant or employee has committed theft from the *'hirz'* of his master or employer to which he is allowed access.

(6) When the stolen property is wild grass, fish, bird, dog, pig, intoxicant, musical instrument or perishable food stuffs for the preservation of which provision does not exist.

(7) When the offender has a share in the stolen property the value of which, after deduction of his share is less than the *'Nisab'*.

(8) When a creditor steals his debtor's property the value of which, after deduction of the amount due to him, is less than the *'Nisab'*.

(9) When the offender, before his apprehension, has, on account of repentance, returned the stolen property of the victim and surrenders himself to the authority concerned.

(10) When the offences of drinking and theft are committed under *'Ikrah'* or *'Iztirar'*.

(11) When a person has committed *Qazf* against any of his descendants.

(12) When the imputation has been proved to be true.

(13) When the person in respect of whom *Qazf* has been committed and who is a complainant has died during the pendency of the proceedings.

(14) When before the execution of *Hadd* the complainant withdraws his allegation of *Qazf* or states that the accused had made a false confession or that any of the witnesses had deposed falsely and the number of witnesses is thereby reduced to less than two.

(15) When *Zina* is followed by a *Nikah.*

The offences punishable with *Hadd* are non-compoundable and *Hadd* is enforced by the Head of State or his delegates namely Qadis. The Head of State, however, has no rights of pardon and suspension of sentence. If the guilt is proved, the convict must be punished at all costs and there can be no mercy in inflicting it. The punishment cannot be reduced under sentiments of mercy.

> "And let not pity for the twain withhold you from obedience to Allah, if you believe in Allah and the Last Day."

Those who are not familiar with the philosophy behind *Hadd* punishments and their rationale severely criticise these punishments by calling them barbaric and mediaeval. They do not know that Islam leaves no stone unturned to block all the channels leading to crime and the punishments are inflicted as a last resort. The *Hadd* punishments are permissible under very exceptional circumstances when a fool proof case is made out. The standard of evidence for awarding these punishments is very high which suggests that the policy of law is not to remain in search of offenders and fix scaffold in crossings to flog people everyday but to punish only those who despite preventive measures adopted by Islam defy public decency and flaunt their vices openly. These punishments are inflicted under conditions of a stringent nature laid down by law and that is why they are a rare phenomenon. The *Hadd* stands dropped if there crops up even the slightest doubt. The Holy Prophet (PBUH) said, "Remit punishment on account of doubt as long as you have ability." *Ibn-i-Maja.*

"Try to avoid *Hadood* wherever possible. Wherever there is even a mild chance, release him, for releasing by an error on the part of an *Imam* is better than punishing anyone by error."

'The principle of giving benefit of doubt to the accused was taken to such length that the Holy Prophet (PBUH) did not act generally on the confession of an accused unless he was satisfied about the voluntary nature as well as genuineness of the confession. The cases of Maiz and Ghamadiyyah are in point. When Maiz confessed his guilt of *Zina,* the Holy Prophet (PBUH) made an inquiry into his mental state as well as his knowledge about the ingredients of the offence to which he was confessing. Same happened with Ghamadiyyah. Hadrat Ali also did not order the sentence of *Zina* on *Shurahah* without investigating into the voluntary nature or genuineness of her confession."

The punishment of *Hadd* is deterrent and its purpose is humiliation for the convict and lesson for the public. It deters the offender from repetition of the crime and also deters others who are like-minded with him, by his example from the commission of it. Besides, it contains elements of reformation and prevention. Once the punishment of *Hadd* is carried out it so deters the public that no-one can dare commit that crime for years to come. In a way it performs a psychological operation on the minds of those who have criminal tendencies and thus reforms them automatically. Even the modern criminologists have come to the conclusion that the perfect system of criminal justice should not only readjust the criminal but be such as to deter others. It is a matter of common knowledge that *Hadd* punishments have virtually wiped out crime from Saudi Arabia and made it a model for rest of the world. Impressed by the efficacy and results of the punishment of amputation of hand a non-Muslim Scholar Gordon Gaskell remarked, "Foreigners consider this a horrible punishment but even they admit that it has made Saudi Arabia the country with the lowest crime rate in the world".

Imposition of *Hadd* obliterates sins. The Holy Prophet (PBUH) said, "Swear allegiance to me that you will not associate anything with Allah, that you will not commit adultery, that you will not steal, that you will not take any life which it is forbidden by Allah to take but with (legal) justification; and whoever among you fulfils it his reward is with Allah; and he who commits any such thing and is punished for it, that will be an atonement for it. And if anyone commits anything and Allah conceals (his faults) his matter rests with Allah. He may forgive if He likes it and He may punish him if He likes."

The *Hadd* punishments can prove effective in liberating the societies of the world from the curse of crime and its evil consequences.

Principles for Law

I. *Hadd* literally means obstruction, prohibiting from entering and, for that reason, *'Haddad* means a person who prevents from entering, that is, gate keeper. But according to legal terminology the term *'Hadd'* means the prescribed punishment as ordered by Allah through the Holy Prophet (peace be upon him).

II. Guiding principle behind *'Hadd* 'seems to be that evil, perpetrated and crimes committed by a person must be atoned for within his lifetime so that he becomes a better individual and a better member of his society. This principle in turn actively discourages any tendency of leading a life of sin and then becoming a pious individual in the hope of rewards in the life hereafter. Thus *'Hadd'* reinforces the central idea of Islam that the laws of Quran and *Shariah* are the guiding spirit throughout the life of a Muslim. As regards the implementation of *Hadd,* or its plural *Hadood,* in the society in which Prophet Muhammad (peace be upon him) was born, grew up and worked, the Quran says:

> "The only reward of those who make war upon Allah and His Messenger and strive after corruption in the land will be that they will be killed or crucified, or have their hands and feet or alternative side cut off, or will be expelled out of the land. Such will be their degradation in the world, and the hereafter. Theirs' will be an awful doom."

Thus any attempt by any individual to follow or to attempt the law of God and His way in any age and society is definitely in conformity with the Quran and *Sunnah* of the Prophet (PBUH). Conversely, any attempt on the part of the Muslims to subvert the divinely ordained Islamic order is to be condemned. The Quran prescribes a general code of *Hadood:*

> "These are the limits (imposed by) Allah, whoso obeyeth Allah and His Messenger will enter gardens underneath which rivers flow, where such will dwell for ever. That will be the great success.
>
> And who disobeyeth Allah and His Messenger and transgressed His limits, he will make him enter fire, where such will dwell for ever; his will be a shameful doom."

III. The following is the classification of crimes and punishments which fall under the categories of *Hadood* according to Quranic injunctions and the *Sunnah* of Prophet Muhammad (PBUH):

(1) Adultery *(Fitna);*

(2) Theft *(Sarqa);*

(3) Alcoholism *(Shurb-e-Khamr);*

(4) False accusation of adultery *(Qadhaf);* and

(5) Highway robbery *(Qat-e-Tariq).*

The basic role ascribed to *Hadood,* detailed in the Quran is mentioned thus:

> "O Prophet: if believing women come unto thee, taking oath of allegiance unto Thee that they will ascribe nothing as partners unto Allah, and will neither steal nor commit adultery nor kill their children, nor produce any lie that they have devised between their hands and feet, nor disobeyeth Thee in what is right, then accept their allegiance and ask Allah to forgive them, LO! Allah is Forgiving and Merciful."

To ascertain the philosophy behind these laws and their social and moral significance, one has to ponder over the Quranic verses and their practical application during the lifetime of Prophet Muhammad (PBUH) and the period of the early four Caliphs. Taking into consideration the magnitude of these laws and juristic differences, our endeavour to make a brief survey of each of these five laws independently would enlighten the situation as to why *Hadd* or *Hadood* have been fixed for certain offences.

Adultery

The act of adultery is being denounced from time immemorial and different societies in different ages formulated laws and punishments to suppress this act. Christianity and Judaism initially prescribed the same punishment for adultery as did Islam later—stoning to death. But the adherents of the first two religions side stepped the penalty and even started differentiating between adultery and fornication, making the latter less punishable. Islam, however, has retained with vigour the prescribed punishment of the Quran. These punishments are being criticised by others as out-moded and barbaric. The

Quran and the *Sunnah* of the Prophet (PBUH) both take a very serious view of fornication and adultery which damage and militate against the moral order of a society. Islam out rightly condemns adultery in all its forms. However, there is a difference of opinion among scholars about the punishment applicable to married and unmarried persons committing adultery. This controversy is mainly due to the non-availability of any Quranic verse in respect of married offenders.

The penalty for them, *Rajm* – stoning to death, was- codified by the Holy Prophet (PBUH) and implemented by him and the four Caliphs. Muslim and non-Muslim historians are of the unanimous view that just before the advent of Islam, Arab society was corrupt and uncivilized. Even adultery was not considered irreligious or immoral. Prophet Muhammad (PBUH) on assuming his Prophetic mission, was instructed to make people follow the prescribed Quranic social order and thereby free the society from its moral decay. He was to get these people to act in accordance with the earlier *Shariats* and the revelations he received from time to time. The following verses of the chapter of *Al-Maidah* say :

> "And unto thee have we revealed the scripture with the truth, confirming whatever scripture was before it, and a watcher over it. So judge between them by that which Allah hath revealed and follow not their desires away from the truth which hath unto thee.
>
> Oh! Messenger ! make known that which hath been revealed unto thee from thy Lord, for if you do it not then will not have conveyed His Message. Allah will protect thee from mankind. Lo! Allah guideth not the disbelieving folk."

A survey of the first ten years of Prophet Muhammad's (PBUH) life at Mecca shows that all his efforts were directed towards the eradication of polytheistic tendencies and the establishment of the concept of *Tauhid* and *Salat.* All the 90 chapters revealed at Mecca deal with these issues at length. The majority of the cases which relate to legislation and crimes, including adultery, however, belong to the Medinian period. It is evident that during the Meccan period in the absence of any clear legal Quranic injunctions in respect of adultery, Prophet Muhammad (PBUH) preferred to follow the earlier *Shariats* in all their judicial, legal, criminal and social aspects.

In the absence of any Quranic guidance regarding fornication or adultery till the verses of Chapter *Al-Nisa* or *Al-Noor* were revealed, the Prophet (PBUH) had to look into the Jewish code. As immediately after his immigration to Medina, a man and a woman from the Jewish tribes of Khyber committed adultery.

The case was referred to the Prophet of Islam, who according to the Jewish Code, ordered them to be stoned to death. There are three important incidents of adultery reported during the lifetime of Prophet Muhammad (PBUH) in which he ordained the penalty of stoning. They relate to Maiz bin Malik Aslami, Ghamidiyah and a person (not named) reported by Abu Hurrayrah. A study of these cases suggests that the following requirements are essential for the implementation of stoning or any other *Hadd* penalty:

(1) The Quran clearly states that there should be four eye-witnesses. The judge has no right to pass any verdict even though he may have personally seen the act.

(2) Eye-witnesses must be reliable persons.

(3) Four witnesses must attest that they found both man and woman in the exact act of adultery.

(4) All the four witnesses must remain unanimous about the time, place and the persons involved in the act.

(5) Personal commitment in plain and clear words on the part of adulterer or adulteress.

(6) In a case where the crime has been admitted but the

person concerned later refutes the charge out of fear of punishment, he is to be released.

Theft

The punishment prescribed for theft in the Holy Quran is:

> "As for the thief, both male and female, cut off their hands. It is the reward of their own deeds, an exemplary punishment from Allah. Allah is Mighty and Wise."

Following are the sayings of the Holy Prophet (PBUH) in this respect:

> "When an adulterer commits adultery and a thief commits theft they are not *Momins.*"

Once a case of a woman was recommended to Holy Prophet (PBUH) on which he remarked :

> "The preceding nations perished because they implemented the *Hadd* punishment upon poor persons and gave a clear chit to the well-to-do. By God, had Fatima committed a theft, I would have definitely amputated her hand."

Alcoholism

All those things which intoxicate a person stand forbidden by the Quran and the *Sunnah* of the Prophet. However, the Quran does not prescribe any specific punishment for alcoholism. The traditions of the Holy Prophet (PBUH) do not indicate a fixed punishment for alcoholism. Forty lashes, however, stand proved as having been ordered by the First Caliph. Umar, the Second Caliph, due to vast increase in the use of intoxicants raised it to eighty lashes for a free person and forty for slaves. There is also the *Ijma* of the Companions of the Prophet for these punishments. But before the penalty is ordered, two witnesses are essential in the court of a Qadi.

False Accusation of Adultery

The literal meaning of the word *Qadhaf* is to throw; the theological meaning is false accusation of adultery. The Quran makes two categories of this crime. The first relates to the allegation of unchastity, a charge brought about by the husband against the wife and the second relates to a person, other than the husband, who accuses a woman of adultery. The Quran says: "And those who accuse honourable women but bring not four witnesses, scourge them (with) eighty stripes and never (afterwards) accept their testimony. They indeed are evil-doers". The punishment *of Hadd* for a person who is accusing the other party is only applicable when the latter is a *Mohsan* or chaste person coming within the scope of the following:

> "He must be a free person, sane, adult, Muslim and must be pious."

Accusation of adultery is proved by a single commitment of the crime or through the witness of two male persons.

Highway Robbery

Dacoit/robber is one who overpowers the traveller and commits theft. If he did not carry out theft but in the process committed murder, punishment is stoning. If the offender has stolen property amounting to the equivalent of the (fixed price) for theft, that is, ten dirhams, the offender's right hand and left foot are to be cut off. However, if the offender has no right hand or left foot or if he has them but they are paralyzed, the left hand and the right foot are not to be amputated. The offender is then liable to *Tazir.* If the offender has committed robbery as well as murder, his right hand and left foot are to be amputated and he is then to be slained.

Characteristics of Punishment

The implementation of the Quranic laws and the *Sunnah* of the Holy Prophet (PBUH) was the basic aim of the orthodox

Caliphs. There seems no reason to believe that *Hadd* penalties for all the aforementioned crimes were not implemented during the period of the orthodox Caliphs. The Second Caliph Umar took personal interest in suppressing immoral acts. He was the first among the Caliphs to have appointed persons to carry out the *Hadd* punishments. It was again he who established the department of *Hisab* (the department to ensure the implementation of Islamic Laws) and prisons at Mecca and in other districts. Early historical works testify that all the First Four Caliphs applied *Hadd* penalties for adultery, alcoholism, theft and false accusation of adultery. All juristic schools, including the *Shia*-School, are unanimous about the prescribed Quranic penalties.

The social, judicial and philosophical significance of *Hadd* penalties is based on the concept of strict accountability of all those, irrespective of their social status, who outrage the rights, dignity and property of others and thus to purge the society of these heinous social evils, paving the way for the establishment of a society in which all its members; big and small, rich and poor, should breathe with peace and satisfaction. The concept of *Hadd* is also greatly instrumental in the achievement of a social moral order as envisaged in Islam. Above all, the concept of *Hadd* is vitally and unavoidably linked with the establishment of a true Islamic society—a society based on the golden principles of equality and justice.

Bibliography

Adams, C.C. : *Islam and Modernism in Egypt,* Oxford University Press, New York, 1953.

Ahmad, Bherhan : *The Mujaddid's Conception of Tauhid,* Feroz Pub., Lahore, 1940.

Ahmad, Imtiaz : *Divorce and Remarriage among Muslims in India,* Manohar Publishers, New Delhi, 2003.

Ahmad, K. N. : *Muslim Law of Divorce,* Kitab Bhavan, New Delhi, 1988.

Ahmad, Manzuruddin : *Islamic Political System,* Kitab Bhavan, New Delhi, 1991.

Ali, Chiragh : *The Proposed Political Legal and Social Reform under Muslim Rule,* Popular Prakashan, Bombay, 1883.

Badrul, S. : *Muslim Behaviour,* Kitab Bhavan, New Delhi, 1991.

Bahedur, Kalim : *The Jamaat-i-Islami of Pakistan,* Progressive Books, Lahore, 1978.

Baksh, S. K. : *Politics in Islam,* Kitab Bhavan, New Delhi, 2003.

Bawer, Raymond : *The New Man in Soviet Social Psychology,* Oxford, New York, 1990.

Berger, M. : *Islam in Egypt Today : Social and Political Aspects of Popular Religion,* MacMillan, London, 1970.

Bernier, Francois : *Travels in the Mogul Empire*, MacMillan, London, 1916.

Bukhsh, S. K. : *Contribution to the History of Islamic Civilization*, Kitab Bhavan, New Delhi, 2000.

Charles, Howard : *The Constitutionalism*, Great Seal Books, New York, 1947.

Chave, F. : *Islamic Histroriography*, Cambridge University press, New York, 1990.

Davids, Waines : *An Introduction to Islam*, Cambridge University Press, New Delhi, 1995.

Durrani, F.K.K. : *Muhammad (PBUH) the Prophet*, Oxford, New York, 2001.

Enayat, Hamid : *Islam in the Political Process*, Cambridge University Press, Cambridge, 1993.

Engineer, Asghar Ali : *A Rational Approach to Islam*, Gyan Books Pvt. Ltd., New Delhi, 2001.

———: *Islam : Challenge in Twenty-first Century*, Gyan Books Pvt. Ltd., New Delhi, 2004.

Guillaume, A. : *The Traditions of Islam*, Khayats, Beirut, 1966.

Hassan, Ali : *Observations on the Musulmauns of India*, Macmillan & Co., London, 1832.

Helmut, Reifeld : *Islam in South Asia : Adaptation, Accommodation and Conflict*, Social Science Press, New Delhi, 1999.

Houtsma, T. : *Encyclopaedia of Islam*, Macmillan, London, 1934.

Irfan, Habib : *The Agrarian System of Mughal India*, Popular Prakashan, Bombay, 1963.

Jafar, Sharif : *Islam in India*, Oxford, New Delhi, 1972.

James, Burges : *The Muhammadan Architecture of Ahmadabad*, Bernard Quaritch, London,1900.

Jha, V. : *Indian Society: Historical Probings*, Rawat Pub., Delhi, 1974.

Joseph, and Bosworth, C.E. : *The Legacy of Islam,* Oxford University Press, New York, 1979.

Karl, Jaspers : *Man in the Modern Age,* Routledge & Kegan Paul Ltd., London, 1997.

Katharine, Scarfe : *Perception of the Islamic Word,* Cambridge University Press, New Delhi, 1992.

Lewin, Roger : *In the Age of Mankind,* Simithsonian Books, Washington, D.C., 1956.

Lewis, Richards : *Universe,* Harmony Books, New York, 1973.

Martin, Lings : *A Sufi Saint of the Twentieth Century,* Century Pub., London, 1971.

Mirza, Waheed : *The Life and Works of Amir Khusrau,* Kaveri Pub., Calcutta, 1935.

Mortimer, Edward : *Faith and Power, the Politics of Islam,* Oxford, New York, 2002.

Muhammad, Iqbal : *Six Lectures on the Reconstruction of Religious Thought in Islam,* Royal Pub., Lahore, 1930.

Nabith, A. : *The Foundations of the Articles of Faith,* Feroz Pub., Lahore, 1963.

Nasr, Seyyed H. : *An Introduction to Islamic Cosmological Doctrines,* Cambridge, 1964.

Nicholson, R.A. : *Literary History of the Arabs,* Kitab Bhavan, New Delhi, 1994.

Nusservanji, D. : *Zoroastrian Civilization,* Oxford, New York, 1922.

Oage, Charles H. : *The Society,* Macmillan & Co., London, 1959.

Padwick, C.E. : *Muslim Devotions,* MacMillan & Co., London, 1960.

Phillips, O. Hood : *Reform of the Constitution,* MacMillan & Co., London, 1970.

Pierce, R.A.: *Russia in Central Asia, 1867-1917,* University of California, Berkeley, 1960.

Qadir, Abdul, : *Criminal Law of Islam,* Kitab Bhavan, New Delhi, 1999.

Qazi A. Qadir : *The Changing World of Islam,* Royal Pub., Lahore, 1992.

Rizvi, Hasan Askari : *Islami Reassertion : a Socio Political Study,* Progressive Publishers, Lahore, 1981.

Robert, D. : *Exploring our Living Planet,* National Geographic Society, Washington, 1989.

Saukat, S. : *Human Rights in Islam,* Kitab Bhavan, New Delhi, 2001.

Sharma, Arvind : *Women in World Religion,* New York Press, New York, 1990.

Syed, M. H. : *History of Muslims in India,* Anmol Publications, New Delhi, 2003.

——— : *Islamic Terrorism : Myth or Reality,* Gyan Books, New Delhi, 2002.

Tarn, W. W. : *The Greeks in Bactria and India,* Cambridge, London, 1938.

Thomas, Arnold : *The Legacy of Islam,* Oxford University Press, New York, 2000.

Thompson, H.R. : *Sculptures and Inscriptions of Darius the Great on the Rock of Behistan,* Oxford, London, 1907.

Tritton, A.S. : *The Caliphs and their Non-Muslim Subjects,* Oxford, New York, 1930.

Tutsch, Hans E. : *Facets of Arab Nationalism,* Wayne State University Press, Detroit, 1965.

Underhill, E. : *Mysticism : a Study in the Nature and Development of Man's Spiritual Consciousness,* Oxford, New York, 1956.

Usmani, J.M. : *The Authority of Sunnah,* Kitab Bhavan, New Delhi, 1998.

Von, Edmund : *Modern Islam,* University Press, Los Angeles, 1952.

Von, Grunebaum : *Unity and Variety in Muslim World,* Oxford, New York, 2003.

Waheed, Akhtar : *Sufi Approach to the Problem of Alienation,* Wilson & Co., New Delhi, 1975.

Weiner, Myron : *Sons of the Soil : Migration and Ethnic Conflict in India,* University Press, Prineton, 1978.

Williams, Michael : *Outlines of World Military History,* Oxford, New York, 1996.

Wilson, Lambron : *Traditional Modes of Contemplation and Action,* University Press, Tehran, 1977.

Wolfson, H.A. : *Glimpses of Medieval Indian Culture,* Popular Pub., Bombay, 1959.

Yahanan, Friedmann : *Tolerance and Coercion in Islam : Interfaith Relations in the Muslims Traditions,* Cambridge, New York, 1990.

Yazbeck, Haddad : *Islamic Values in the United States,* Oxford, New York, 1997.

Zaehner, R.C. : *Hindu and Muslim Mysticism,* Oxford, London, 1960.

Zahid, Malik : *Subjects of Quran,* Kitab Bhavan, New Delhi, 1998.

Zahurul, Hasan : *Tarikb-i-Sufiya-i-Gujarat,* Jamil Academy, Ahmadabad, 1981.

Zaki, Azam : *The Ideas of Arab Nationalism,* Cornell University Press, New York,1956.

Index

J

L

M

❑❑❑